"Addressing a broad audience with clear pastoral concern, Gerhard Lohfink admits that the questions which he raises in this volume are his own as well. He brings not only a wealth of biblical and theological sources, but also poetry, literature, science, and his own creative speculation to bear on the ultimate question which faces us all: *Is This All There Is?* Confronted with the stark reality of two possibilities—nothingness or radical hope—Lohfink centers his reflections on the Christian conviction that in the resurrection of Jesus, God's final 'new creation' has already begun. Grounded in that hope he invites his readers to consider what it means to live with and in Christ—not only in the future, but here and now. This text is provocative, passionate, and pastoral—a rare combination and a volume well worth pondering."

> —Mary Catherine Hilkert, OP
> Professor of Theology, University of Notre Dame

"Gerhard Lohfink has given us a splendid book: biblically grounded, theologically astute, spiritually concrete and challenging. In a style that is limpid, poetic, and personal, he leads the reader deeper into the mystery of Jesus' life, death, and resurrection and to a renewed sense of the hope that is in all who believe in the risen Christ. Lohfink's work wonderfully rekindles Christian eschatological faith and imagination."

> —Robert Imbelli
> Associate professor emeritus, Boston College, author of *Rekindling the Christic Imagination*

"If you are planning to read this book, prepare for an exhilarating and surprising ride. Lohfink leads us through all the imaginable possibilities of what happens to us when we die and then moves to a most profound description of what our faith teaches us. This is a book that must be read at least twice. Also take time to enjoy Linda Maloney's excellent translation."

> —Irene Nowell, OSB
> Author of *Wisdom: The Good Life*

"Gerhard Lohfink's *Is This All There Is?* is a stunningly original, profound, and spiritually uplifting and challenging book. Three things stand out in it. First, we cannot validly use our notions of space and time when we talk about life after death. There is a purification process but seeing purgatory as a space like ours and reckoning time in the process as we do on earth is profoundly mistaken. Second, eternal life and resurrection is a pure gift from God. We share in the resurrection of Jesus, the firstborn from the dead. Finally, we need to juxtapose God's justice and his mercy. Excellent chapters deal with our caring for the dying and preparing for our own deaths. It is also a very well-written book."

> —John A. Coleman
> Casassa Professor Emeritus at Loyola Marymount University
> Associate Pastor at Saint Ignatius Parish, San Francisco

"This is exactly what one expects from Lohfink, the distinguished biblical scholar and respected theologian: a book that is hugely informed, consistently provocative, conscientiously pastoral, and—in the best sense of the word—imaginative."

—Dale C. Allison Jr.
Princeton Theological Seminary, author of *Night Comes: Death, Imagination, and the Last Things*

"Gerhard Lohfink's *Is This All There Is?* is an extraordinarily clear, well-argued, and thoroughly engaging book. Beginning with a discussion of basic human questions about the meaning of life and death, Lohfink explores Christian beliefs in dialogue with other religious and nonreligious perspectives. Undergraduates will find this book accessible and thought-provoking, while the nuance of Lohfink's analysis will challenge theological experts to reconsider their views. I know of no better overview of Christian eschatology and would encourage its use at all levels."

—Mary Doak
Associate Professor of Theology and Religious Studies
University of San Diego

"Lohfink walks through a theology of the 'last things,' examining ideas of heaven, judgment, mercy, purgatory, and hell in a way that balances speaking about what is ultimately inconceivable while at the same time grounding his ideas in the everyday encounter with God that happens even before death. He addresses popular misconceptions of the last things that have concretized and mythologized our understanding of life after death in a way that has alienated the contemporary critical thinker. In doing so, Lohfink has offered the reader a sophisticated theology that has depth and maturity and can stand up to the challenges of our time, while at the same time maintaining a style of writing that makes these more abstract concepts accessible to all. One does not have to be a theologian to read this book, but this book will offer the reader some of the best ideas of contemporary theology."

—Heidi Ann Russell
Author of *Quantum Shift: Theological and Pastoral Implications of Contemporary Developments in Science*

"It's dangerous to plunge into mystery, be that mystery one of life or death. Fr. Lohfink has no fear here and, with erudition and clarity of style, provides us with new and hopeful vistas on this great mystery. We are indebted to him for a challenging and engaging work."

—Robert F. Morneau
Auxiliary Bishop Emeritus of Green Bay

Gerhard Lohfink

Is This All There Is?

On Resurrection
and Eternal Life

Translated by

Linda M. Maloney

**LITURGICAL PRESS
ACADEMIC**

Collegeville, Minnesota
www.litpress.org

Originally published as *Am Ende das Nichts? Über Auferstehung und Ewiges Leben* by Verlag Herder © 2017

Biblical passages are translated from the author's originals, with modern English translations, primarily the NRSV, as reference text.

1   2   3   4   5   6   7   8   9

Library of Congress Control Number: 2017029939

ISBN 978-0-8146-8451-1   978-0-8146-8476-4 (ebook)

For Gerlinde Back

Contents

Preface

"Is this all there is?" The question reflects far more than the title of a hit song from the 1960s. It even contains more than the question many people ask when they enter the midlife crisis. It is not simply about the destiny of individual lives, or about dealing with life here and now. It is a question that means to lead us to the ultimate question and at the same time to a hard alternative we cannot avoid: in the end is there just nothing, or is there a resurrection of the dead? It would be a good thing if that alternative would shape reflection on life after death in our day. Alas, that is not the case. A sober "either-or" is rare. Instead, many of our contemporaries entertain a range of gentle and consoling intermediate solutions such as "dissolution in Nature," "survival in our descendants," or "continual reincarnation." Often the individual's whole interpretation of the world consists merely in a repression of her or his own death.

This book will examine all the intermediate and apparent solutions, one at a time. It will attempt to show that they are not real possibilities. In the end there remains only a genuine "either-or": either resurrection or inexorable nothingness. In this case "nothingness" means not only that the great questions of human existence remain eternally unanswered but that the countless victims of rape, deadly torture, and "disappearance" throughout history will never recover their life and dignity.

The book addresses a great many other questions as well: for example, why does the Old Testament, through its earlier stages, reflect no hope of resurrection? Is ancient Israel's solid and overpoweringly worldly belief ultimately something that remains fundamental even for Christians who hope for resurrection?

Still more: Is Jesus' resurrection only an affirmation of Christians' resurrection hope, or is it the elementary starting point without which there is not only no resurrection but resurrection itself cannot be adequately conceived?

Above all: When does resurrection begin? Ten thousand years from now? sometime in the vague future? at the end of the world? Aren't those who think that way adopting a naïve view of time, one that modern physics already sees as deficient and that is nevertheless applied to the world beyond death? But if all earthly time gives way in death, does that not mean that Jesus' resurrection and, with it, the resurrection of all the dead is then immediately present to us?

And so: What is it, really, that is resurrected? an abstract human being? Or is it the whole history of this particular human being, with its defeats and its victories, its sufferings and its ecstasies—everything this person has thought and willed, longed for and loved?

Still more: What about the universe, matter, animals, the pre-human ancestors in transition to humanity, the countless unborn lives that never had a chance to enter the world? Is there a resurrection for them?

Finally: Is there nothing in heaven besides God? or is everything we have ever longed for and everything we have ever loved there, too—but *with God* and *in God*, so that God is "all in all"?

It is because of such questions that I wrote this book. They are my own questions. Obviously I have not looked for the answers in my private and very deficient wisdom. I have sought them in the Old and New Testaments, in the tradition of Christian faith, and in what the great theologians of past and present have thought. But I have also sought them in reason, one of the supreme gifts God has given to human beings.

Because everything in this book is about my own questions, I have constantly struggled to find the right words. How can we speak responsibly today about death and resurrection, judgment and purgatory, hell and eternal life, and ultimately about the perfection of creation? What kind of language can the people of today understand? What words would come across as neither sanctimonious nor sappy?

There is *one* thing I have feared and tried to avoid as I was writing this book: boring the readers. Hence, as far as was possible, I have relegated arguments over theological opinions to the notes. Those confrontations, sometimes rather lengthy, can easily be found there. But those who don't want to read them do not have to.*

Contemplating and then writing this book have made me newly aware of how liberating Christian faith in the resurrection of the dead really is. Those who root themselves in that faith can live without fear in the biblical "now," because every hour of their lives has both weight and hope. They can invest their strength in building up a just society, because the world to be resurrected in the final form intended for it by God is precisely the world for which we are fighting here, in this history.

But I dedicate this book to Gerlinde Back, in respect and gratitude, because she put the whole project in motion.

Munich, April 2017   *Gerhard Lohfink*

---

* To make this book more reader-friendly, the editors and translator have placed notes containing sources and extended discussion of theological questions at the end of the book. Those notes that are purely explanatory and aids to reading are retained at the foot of the page.

PART ONE

What People Think

1

The Question of Questions

What happens after death? It seems that as our animal ancestors gradually became *homo sapiens* over enormously long periods of time they may not have been able to distinguish between the life of the living and the deadness of the dead. There are indications that in the early stages of humanity there was no clear awareness of the finality of death.* But at some point that finality became clearly evident. And with that the question of what happens to people after death entered the world. Its elementary character is obvious from the dizzying numbers of rituals for the dead. The oldest graves we know are from the Paleolithic period, the Old Stone Age. The bones found in these graves testify that the dead were buried with care. Some are laid out as if sleeping, while others are curled up like embryos. Did people think they would be reborn? Often they were equipped as if for a long journey: they were given weapons, stone tools, pieces of meat to eat on the way.

---

*The fact that highly developed animals can mourn is not an objection. It has often been noted that mother chimpanzees have carried the corpses of their dead infants with them for days on end. It has even been observed that elephants have returned day after day to the body of a dead companion. But none of that necessarily indicates an awareness of what death is.

The practice of dusting the bodies with red ochre for burial is also very ancient. It seems that red-hued ochre was considered a ritual substitute for blood and thus a powerful symbol of the continuing life of the dead person.* Application of red earth was amazingly widespread: corresponding burials have been discovered in Europe, Africa, and the Americas. Often the dead were also laid out facing east, toward the rising sun, or else they were mummified to preserve the body and thus ensure its survival in the world beyond.

People must have begun very soon to celebrate meals at the graves of the dead—most certainly not merely as a consolation for survivors. Rather, it was about ensuring an unbreakable community with those who had died. A festal meal was a coming-together that created enduring connection and gave life.

But the scope of securing the life beyond extended much further: in many cultures there were cultic sacrifices for the dead. Often the deceased were presented with pure water as a drink-offering, to shield them from the bad water of the underworld. Also widespread were magical formulae for the purpose of preparing a path for the dead on their dangerous journey to the land beyond death. In ancient Egypt's *Book of the Dead*, a kind of guidebook to that world, those still living were given formulae with which to meet judgment after death.[1] With their assistance the deceased could tell the forty-two judges of the dead what evil deeds they had *not* committed.[2] Then the deceased were to recite the following formulae (among others in a long list of declarations of innocence):

> I have not despised God.
> I have not caused misery; nor have I worked affliction [*of the poor*].
> I have caused none to feel pain [*through magic*].
> I have made [no man] to weep.
> I have not committed murder;
> nor have I ever bidden any man to slay on my behalf.
> I have not wronged the people.
> I have not carried away the offerings made unto the blessed dead.

*The use of ochre can also be regarded as practical: it has an antibacterial and preservative effect. That, of course, as in the case of mummification, by no means excludes a symbolic meaning.

I have not committed fornication; I have not defiled the wife of any man.[3]

The whole is conceived as a magical event. If the dead person is able to utter these and the other declarations of innocence correctly, the judging gods will allow that person to pass, and to enter the realm of eternal life. But it is obvious that belief in such testing after death also changed life before death. Those still living who learned and internalized the formulae knew quite clearly that it would not be possible to lie to the divine judges after death.

But it was not only through this kind of device that people dealt with death. They also struggled with it through philosophy. The Greek philosopher Plato (428/27–348/47 BCE) tells in one of his most profound writings, the dialogue *Phaedo*, of conversations Socrates held with his friends on the day when he was to be executed in the evening. The subject was the continued life of the soul.

The life of the just, the wise, the philosophical person, says Plato through the mouth of Socrates, is a gradual dying, for those who are truly wise strive throughout their lives for insight and prudence. They seek true being, true reality. Therefore their lives are wholly focused on the soul. They close themselves off from the constant demands of the body, and in this way they cause their inmost being to distance itself from the body even in this life. For there cannot be pure knowledge as long as the soul labors under the heavy burden of the body. Pure knowledge presupposes release from the body.

The mortification, the dying practiced in life, is completed at death, when the soul separates from the body. What dies in death is the mortal part of the person, but what is deathless passes through death whole and undisturbed. In death, Plato says, the souls of the wise and just enter into the realm of what always Is, the eternal, indisturbable, and unchangeable. Then, separated from the unreason and fetters of the body, the soul obtains a share in eternal Being, together with the many who have also sought true knowledge: they participate in the perfect world of truth and beauty.

The greatness of the *Phaedo* lies in the fact that all this is not simply decreed as indisputable truth. As in most of Plato's dialogues, Socrates struggles in stages toward knowledge, together with his friends.

At the end of the long day, shortly before he dies by drinking the cup
of hemlock, Socrates says:

> A [person] of sense ought not to say, nor will I be very confident,
> that the description which I have given of the soul and her man-
> sions is exactly true. But I do say that, inasmuch as the soul is
> shown to be immortal, [one] may venture to think, not improp-
> erly or unworthily, that something of the kind is true. The venture
> is a glorious one.[4]

Socrates then goes calmly, almost joyfully to the death the Athenian
judges have decreed for him. He drinks the hemlock in the presence
of his friends—at least that is how Plato depicts it. The *Phaedo* has
had an extraordinary influence in Western history. Its ideas have been
repeatedly rejected or adopted, ridiculed or admired.

The question of what comes after death has not died, even today.
One need only look closely at the obituaries in any newspaper to find
a swarm of Christian and non-Christian, philosophical and aesthetic
affirmations of the meaning of death. The question of what comes
after death seeps through every society, even the most enlightened.
It erupts over and over again, even when it is suppressed and various
rituals are invented to veil and repress the reality of death. This question is indestructible.

But does it make any sense? Can there be any answer to such a
question? Is Plato too self-assured here? In this situation are we not
in a state like that of the Jewish joke? Here two Jews, one of them
blind from birth, are sitting together:

> "Do you want a glass of milk?" asks the one who can see.
> "Well, describe milk for me," says the blind one.
> "Milk is a white liquid."
> "Great. And what is white?"
> "Well . . . for example, a swan is white."
> "Aha. And what is a swan?"
> "A swan? It's a bird with a long, curved neck."
> "Good. But what is 'curved'?"
> "Curved? Well, I'll bend my arm, and you can feel it. Then you
>   will know what 'curved' means."
> The blind person carefully feels the other's up-curved arm, and says:
>   "Terrific! Now I know what milk is!"

The joke is absurd, yet it is as subtle as many Jewish jokes. Why does the blind person ask the question in the first place? Why not just drink? Then she or he would know quite a bit about milk just by tasting it. Instead we have these intelligent but slightly crazy attempts to explain milk!

And don't we do something similar? We want to explain human life, to know exactly what it is, and while we are doing that we avoid life itself, talk about a life *after* life, think we have to explain life through something beyond it. And in doing so we make the craziest detours instead of simply living. Why don't we just drink the milk of our lives?

Wouldn't it be better to expend all our energies on this life into which we were thrown? Shouldn't we do everything we can to lead our lives as appropriately as possible and keep quiet about everything else? Wouldn't it be better to accept the crooked lines of life, its complexities and riddles, in silence—angry about many things, but still with a great deal of trust—and leave everything beyond this life a mystery about which we can gain no knowledge?

A good many years ago now I spoke with an older priest whom I deeply admired. He was respected and revered in his congregation. Every Sunday he explained the Gospel to them, mindfully, and with empathy. No one could accuse him of being thoughtless or flippant. So I was shocked when, in the course of a long conversation, this man said to me:

> We are much too quick to speak about life after death, the hereafter, the resurrection. All that trips too lightly off our tongues. God knows, in the course of my work I have met a lot of people, and especially a lot of old and sick people. Those people's problem was not what comes after death. Their sole concern was: "What will become of my children? Did I do enough for them? What will happen to my family? How will my husband/my wife manage when I am not there? Doesn't my illness make me a burden to others?" Those were their questions. I have met a lot of people who never spoke of the hereafter but had learned to accept their lives and ultimately came to their end quietly and calmly. Is that not the real Christianity? Can anyone wish for more? Should we trouble such people with talk about the hereafter?

As I said, that shocked me at first, precisely because it was spoken by a pastor who, I knew, had never rejected any part of the church's teaching. He certainly spoke of Christian death in his sermons when the situation or the liturgical texts required it; he spoke of the judgment and the resurrection of the dead. I was disturbed that in private he could speak so very differently. I couldn't get it out of my head.

Still, there was something prophetic about what this man told me then. What he said—with foresight, one might say—has since happened. Today many whom the church entrusts with the task of preaching scarcely venture to speak of the "last things." When does any preacher talk about the right way to die, the return of Christ, judgment on our deeds, eternal life and the consummation of the world? Of course, those old ideas have to be translated—but what preacher dares to do so?

It should be clear by now that the pastor's thinking had caused me to reflect, and yet I could not agree with it. Certainly it is true that there are countless people who do not make big speeches about life, scarcely ask about the hereafter, but say "yes" to their lives and are unquestioningly present for others. That is true. But that silent humanity cannot be the ultimate. As honorable and stoic as it is for people to accept in silence what is unfathomable to them, still the human being is by nature one who questions, indeed, one who asks about the *whole* and never stops questioning. The fact that humans are questioning beings is what distinguishes them from the lower animals.

Truly, the questions of "why" and "after" keep erupting over and over again. In a certain phase of their lives, children never seem to stop asking "why?" It is not good for their insistence to be swiftly and thoroughly quashed by grown-ups. They also ask, in the same way, about "after."

Not long ago a mother and her little son were walking along the sidewalk in front of me. The mother said, at the very moment when they caught my attention, "It will soon be winter."

"And then?" the child asked.
"Then it will snow."
"And then?"
"Then we will go sledding."
"And then?"

"Then it will be spring."

"And then?"

"Then you will go to school."

"And then?"

"Then you will learn a trade or a profession . . ."

I don't know whether the child kept on asking. We drifted apart. Of course, it was a game for him, a "ping pong" with words that was almost a ritual. But was it *only* a game? Wasn't there an elementary question behind the game—the question of questions?

2

Between Skepticism
and Belief in the Soul

Anyone who reads Greek or Roman epitaphs and tomb inscriptions
will see right away how the question about "and then?" preoccupied
ancient people. It is true that not all the inscriptions indicate that:
certainly not. Many are silent about the question of the hereafter.
They simply say who is buried here. Thus, for example, on a Roman
tomb in the south of France we read:

> Fabius Zoilus had [this tomb] made for himself and his dearly
> beloved wife Consuadullia Primilla during his lifetime, so that
> we might have it.

The Latin text is much shorter,[1] and it is as formulaic as many of our
gravestone inscriptions today. The tomb does not give the slightest
hint about the worldview of this Fabius and his Consuadullia.

Yet there are a great many ancient grave steles and stone coffins that
are more eloquent. It is true that they do not always speak directly

---

[1] Hieronymus Geist, with Gerhard Pfohl, *Römische Grabinschriften* (Berlin: de
Gruyter, 2014), no. 575. Original text: *Fabius Zoilus sibi et Consuadulliae Primillae,
maritae karissimae. Vivus ut haberemus feci.*

about the ideas of those who commissioned them regarding the world and the hereafter. Even in antiquity it was the case that the masons who carved gravestones and sarcophagi offered their customers standard texts to choose from. But the customers *could* choose, depending on their own images of the world, and those worldviews could be very different. Many of the ancient tombstones breathe nothing but melancholy and resignation, and so indirectly reveal that for those who commissioned them there was no "after." One example is a Roman tomb text for a young girl:

> Let all who pass this way weep at my sad fate and remain a while by my poor ashes. Weep for me, unfortunate maiden, for whose sake my stricken parents day and night bear deepest pain. It was their ill fate that they begot me; they will never see me married. No wine-exalted singer has struck up a wedding song outside my chamber.[2]

Other such texts, in contrast, reflect profound confidence, such as this one for a dead man named Menelaos:

> My name is Menelaos. But only my body remains here,
> whereas my soul is in the Ether immortal.[3]

Specific ideas nourished by ancient cosmology and physics underlie such epitaphs. Many ancient scientists pictured the "ether"* as the highest, brightest dimension of the cosmos. It was equated with heavenly fire and said to be the home of the gods. Insofar as a person of that time was not a skeptic, she or he then often thought this way: the human body is material and therefore heavy and resistant. The human soul, on the other hand, is weightless. Hence at death it would rise to heaven, as hot air rises above a fire. The countless stars that twinkle in the firmament are nothing other than the souls of the dead. This idea is evident in many tomb inscriptions, such as:

> My name was Philostorgos, raised, as a support** for old age, by
> [my mother] Nike;

* Greek *aithēr*, "upper air," from *aithein*, "burn, shine."
** Lit. "anchor."

> I lived [barely] twenty years. . . . I . . . was suddenly abducted
> . . . [my lifetime, determined] by the goddesses of threads,
> fulfilled.
> Mother, do not cry over me, what is the use?
> Now that I have become a star in the night sky, among the gods,
> show reverence to me![4]

We can imagine how such ideas arose. Our minds are lightning-fast and our thoughts run everywhere. Our spirits conquer worlds, while our bodies move much more slowly. Often they are even a hindrance, especially as we get older. We would still like to travel, but our bodies won't. Ultimately they become prisons.

That idea was formulated quite explicitly in antiquity, especially by followers of the philosopher Pythagoras. *Sōma—sēma*, said the Greeks: "body—tomb." In this world of ideas the soul is what really makes the human; the body is only an obstacle. In death the soul is liberated as if from a tomb, a prison. As we have seen, Plato also presents such ideas in his *Phaedo*. Hence the following Roman inscription from the third century CE sounds very Platonic:

> This tomb hides the body of unmarried Kalokairos, but his im-
> mortal soul has left the body of the young man. She, his soul,
> has left far behind the cares of a bitter life and hurries on the
> divine road so that she might arrive purified.[5]

The only clue that this inscription was for a Christian is the anchor carved beneath the epigram. There is nothing in the language itself that would distinguish it from other, non-Christian tomb texts. There are many similar examples. The pagan formulations of the continued life of the immortal soul were adopted for Christian tomb inscriptions without alteration; only a particular set of symbols shows that the graves are those of Christians: a dove, a fish, an anchor, or the Chi-Rho monogram.

Nevertheless, there are differences, even if they cannot always be perceived in the texts, for ancient ideas about the soul very often make it something divine, and—this is the essential point—divine *by nature*. In death, which liberates from all chains, this divine within the human finally comes into its own. The soul rises to the firmament and is received once more into the sphere of the eternal, from which it came and where it belongs. Thus the continued life of the soul represents the continued existence of what is eternally divine in human nature.

The attractiveness of that idea can be seen in the fact that aspects of it entered into Christianity and burrowed into many corners and crannies, despite the fact that it is incompatible with the Christian idea of creation and redemption.* One day I came across the following verses in a prayerbook belonging to an elderly religious sister; they sound very pious, but they are basically pagan:

> To earth I came without a load,
> nothing outward brought with me
> except only my soul.
>
> Nothing will I take with me
> beyond into the lightsome day
> except again my soul.
>
> What, then, to me is earthly life
> when in but lightsome garments clad
> and shedding every earthly fault
> my own and only soul shall fly
> to God's paternal hand.[6]

Certainly the verses were meant to be Christian, and they can be interpreted that way, but on closer inspection they reflect nothing but the ancient ideas: the soul is the eternal aspect of the human. The body is only something we make do with. The soul guides the body as a steerer guides a ship, but at some point the steerer leaves the ship, when it has reached its destination.

Of course, we should not suppose that everyone in antiquity thought that way. For a long time the Greeks were convinced that human life ends as a shadowy existence in the darkness of the underworld, and in later periods belief in the soul was by no means the only philosophy. There was also a powerful strand of materialism for which the body was the one and only human reality. That materialism was usually associated with a profound skepticism, and especially the conviction that everything ends with death. At death the

---

*This took place especially in Gnosticism, one of the most dangerous heresies of early Christianity.

human person falls back into absolute nothingness. A dead person has no "I" any longer, no memory, no awareness, no future.

We find many ancient tomb inscriptions reflecting that idea as well. Often they exhibit pure hopelessness, and they frequently make use of an almost existentialist language. Thus one from ancient Rome reads:

> We are nothing and we were but mortals.
> You who read this, consider:
> We fall in the shortest space of time
> from nothing back to nothing.[7]

Similarly, the following inscription says laconically:

> I was not, I was,
> I am not, I do not care.[8]

A tombstone in Aquileia reads:

> Do you, O comrade, who read this, enjoy your life; for after death
> there is neither pain nor laughter, nor joy of any kind.[9]

Here, then—as is often the case with ancient graves—advice is given to those still living but who will follow the same path. The inscription for a certain Tiberius Claudius Secundus in Rome is similar. The translation attempts to reflect the classical rhythms of the original inscription:

> Baths, the love goddess, and wine—
> they do spoil our bodies, it's true.
> But that's what life is about:
> Baths, the love goddess, and wine.*

There are many other ancient tomb inscriptions that speak just that way. Those in transit are urged to enjoy as many good things as possible, to eat and drink and enjoy the pleasures of love, because when death comes, as is often said, "darkness will surround you and eternal oblivion." Some tombs even deliver little sermons to passersby urging them not to neglect any of life's pleasures. However, in the other

---

* In the Baths of Caracalla in Rome. Translation LMM. Original text: *Balnea, vina, Venus corrumpunt corpora nostra, / sed vitam faciunt balnea, vina, Venus.*

direction there are speeches addressed to the one in the tomb. The tomb inscription can say to the dead person, with all the sarcasm of which antiquity was so capable:

> What good was it for you to have lived a disciplined life for so many years?[10]

In reality the sarcasm was not directed so much at the dead person. It, too, was for those passing by the monument. So belief in the soul was not universal in antiquity. As far as death and the afterlife were concerned there were equal amounts of skepticism, sarcasm, doubt, and bitterness. When figures are carved on the stones—often those of mourning women—their faces quite often show deep despondency and sorrow.

In our times the skeptical voices of antiquity are being heard again. The young Bertolt Brecht (1898–1956), for example, offers a rhyming sermon entitled "Lucifer's Evening Song"[11] that asserts there is only *one* day of life. Then comes eternal night, and everything is over. So one must enjoy this one and only day without any fear, because that is all that humans get. There is nothing "waiting for us." Those who say that after night comes a new morning are nothing but false promisers, seducers, and betrayers:

1

Do not let them fool you!
There is no way back home.
Day's on the point of going
Already the night wind's blowing.
No dawn will ever come.

2

Do not let them gyp you!
Life is not very big.
Drink it! And go on drinking
And when at last you're sinking
You'll want another swig.

3

Don't let them get your hopes up!
Today is all there is.

Let pious people suffer!
Life's all earth has to offer.
There's no life after this.

4

Don't let them lure you into
Exhaustion and duress!
Why all the trepidation?
You die like all creation.
And after: nothingness.[12]

Of course, this sermon with its emphatic rhythms is aimed primarily at Christians. In Brecht's eyes they considered themselves the "saved" because they believed in salvation from the world. It is the old accusation that has never been silenced since Karl Marx and Friedrich Nietzsche: that Christians despise the world and console the poor with pie in the sky; instead of loving this world they hope for another. The charge hits home as far as some false undertones in Christianity are concerned, but it does not touch the fundamental note of Christian faith. The biblical message itself says something completely different, as we will see.

Marie Luise Kaschnitz (1901–1974) was much less dogmatic than Bertolt Brecht. One of her poems on resurrection, entitled "Nicht mutig" ["Not brave"] reads:

The brave know
They will not rise again
That no flesh will grow around them
On Judgment Morning
That they won't remember anything
That they won't see anyone ever again
That nothing of theirs is waiting
No salvation
No torture
I
Am not brave.[13]

The poem articulates two philosophies of life: First, that of those for whom death is the end of everything. It seems sober and realistic to think that way. Who can really imagine that flesh will grow again on our bones or that there is a hell in which people are tortured? That philosophy even seems to be based on "knowledge": "The brave know." But why are those who know this "the brave"?

The contrary philosophy is so unsure of itself that it emerges only indirectly, through a questioning of the position of the brave. It appears only at the end, in a single sentence: "I—am not brave." Could it be that there is a resurrection after all?

If we look more closely, of course, we can see that "I—am not brave" implies a hidden critique of the "brave." Apparently the poem is not so respectful of the "brave" as it seems at first glance.

We might state the underlying thought of the poem in this way: the skeptics who are so confident that they will not rise cannot be sure of themselves either. They describe a position that portrays resurrection in a rather crude and superficial way (flesh on bones, fires of hell) in order to reject it. But even for that they need to be "brave," and if bravery is needed in any situation, then the outcome is still open and uncertain. Perhaps the "brave" are mightily deceiving themselves.

Does the poem perhaps even contain a breath of mockery at the "brave," who so boldly open their mouths and fill the world with the sound of their "knowledge" and the universal perspective they pretend to possess? Kaschnitz's poem will not open its mouth. It does not even dare to express its own idea of resurrection. It does not come forth preaching and cocky like Bertolt Brecht's verses. The poem's sole argument is at the end: "I—am not brave."

Kurt Marti (b. 1921) was far more self-assured in a much-quoted poem in which he preached like Brecht, but in the opposite direction:

> it might readily suit many lords of this world
> if everything were settled at death
> if the dominion of the lords
> and the servitude of the slaves
> were confirmed forever
>
> it might readily suit many lords of this world
> if in eternity they remained lords
> in expensive private tombs

and their slaves remained slaves
in rows of common graves

but a resurrection is coming
quite different from what we thought
a resurrection is coming which is
god's rising up against the lords
and against the lord of lords—death.[14]

That is a funeral oration pregnant with class conflict. It argues that if there were no resurrection the world's exploiters and slaveholders would always be in the right and triumph even in death. But they will not triumph, because God has long been preparing a revolution that will cast all the mighty of this world, and ultimately even death, from their thrones.

The sermon-text by Bertolt Brecht, the hesitatingly confessional (and perhaps even gently mocking refutational) text by Marie Luise Kaschnitz, and then the provocative one from Kurt Marti show that the dissonant polyphony of voices from antiquity is still with us. The question of questions remains, and the answer still swings between radical skepticism and hope for the wholly "other" that will finally answer all questions.

3

Survival in Our Descendants?

The Greek and Roman tomb inscriptions show again and again that people in antiquity liked to think up striking texts in memory of their dead and put them into words. Often they were even rendered in verse. And they were almost always intended to convey a message to those passing by the tomb.

It is the same today. The texts on our gravestones deserve to be collected and analyzed by folklorists (more properly: cultural anthropologists), because we have not only inscriptions that simply give the name and the birth and death dates, their spartanness symbolizing that this is the grave of a particular person with her or his unique, distinctive, and irreplaceable history. There are also countless gravestones with shorter or longer additions that shine a bright light on the worldview of our predecessors and our contemporaries as well. Let me choose a random example. A recent grave in a cemetery in the north of Germany contains the saying:

> Released from Mother Earth
> we slumber, content,
> toward the great enigma.

There is a vast difference between that and a gravestone in Detwang, near Rothenburg ob der Tauber in the south. I wrote it down many years ago when I was traveling through the Tauber valley:

> Anno 1651, Sunday, 27 April
> in the night, between 12 and 1 o'clock
> slept away in her Redeemer, Jesus Christ,
> softly and blest,
> at the white mill
> the whilom, virtuous Maria Bülgin
> a Waltmännin born,
> her life 22 years, 2 months, 2 days,
> her soul in the grace of God.
> Amen

We could collect many such. It was not only the Greeks and Romans who were drawn to communicate their view of death to passersby. For us, too, death provokes testimony by those left behind. But today the truly revealing texts are no longer written on gravestones but on virtual graves in an internet cemetery or in obituaries sent as letters or published in the newspaper. Those are a positive treasure trove for anyone who wants to know what people today think about death or life after death.

Obituaries contain every imaginable position, from Christian testimonies of faith to poetically veiled nihilism. The words of the Bible or those of poets and authors are frequently quoted. Thus a major newspaper published this text as part of an obituary:

> Dear Mama, you had my back in everything I did in life. Dear Papa, you modeled what it means to work with passion and dedication. I owe you everything. You are in me, and you live on in me.

What is interesting here is "you are in me, and you live on in me." Behind that statement lies the idea that those who have died live on in their descendants. Death is the end for them personally, but the good they have brought into the world is not lost; it continues through their children and grandchildren to distant generations. So it endures, and so the dead themselves remain in the world.

This idea is amazingly widespread, sometimes even in tangible form. In New Guinea it can still happen that family members eat the ashes of their dead. The ritual consumption of the ashes is supposed to ensure that the dead do not die entirely, but remain present in their families or in the clan. These and similar rituals are very ancient; probably they go back to the early ages of humanity.

The idea of survival in one's descendants also appears in the Old Testament. In early Israel every individual was deeply embedded in the extended family as well as the clan structure and its history.[1] The individual's self-concept was nearly identical with that of her or his familial group. Everything one had been went on living, so it was believed, in one's progeny. One's own name lived on in children and children's children. Therefore a family must not die out, a name must not be extinguished, the memory of the ancestors must not disappear. One of the most dreadful curses that could be uttered against anyone was to wish that his or her family would vanish and all memory of it be swept from the land. Psalm 109, whose central portion describes how the one praying the psalm curses opponents, reads:

> May his posterity be cut off;
> in the very next generation may their name be blotted out.
>   (Ps 109:13)[2]

The desire here is that an entire family and—this is crucial—even the memory of them will be destroyed by a death-dealing curse. Only from this perspective can we understand what a sorrowful fate it was in Israel to be childless. Not having children was not only a problem of having no one to care for a couple in old age or to secure the rights of inheritance. Not having children decimated one's whole life. It was an element of death in the midst of life. In contrast, having many children reduced the affliction of death. It was seen as a blessing to have a lot of children; it gave one a share in the blessing bestowed on all Israel—from generation to generation.

It would seem that this interwovenness in the sequence of generations is still a consolation for many people in the twenty-first century. They see themselves in their children and are convinced that in those children they will be able to hand on their achievements to the world. Correspondingly, children also believe that their parents live in them.

What was it the obituary said? "You are in me, and you live on in me."

There is certainly a good deal of truth in that. Much of our ancestors does live on in us. We owe so much to our parents, grandparents, and great-grandparents. But we should consider that in the Old Testament the idea of being embedded in the sequence of generations was firmly tied to the belief that in coming generations God's promises would continue to be fulfilled again and again. If that faith in the promise should fail, the hope to live on in one's descendants loses its foundation.

But still more: the devout Israelite not only believed that God would fulfill the divine promises. Such a one was also convinced that every generation, the present one and those to come, was already under God's blessing—so long as Israel continually returned to its God and turned away from the gods of the world.

If such a faith, which had to be handed on from generation to generation, were to disappear, the hope of living on in one's descendants would look very different. In that case the ancient biblical idea would suddenly become tragic or even ridiculous. We frequently read a sentence in obituaries today that is attributed now to Lucius Annaeus Seneca, now to Immanuel Kant, even to Ernest Hemingway:

> [The one] who lives in the memory of the beloved
> is not dead, but only far away;
> dead is [the one] who is forgotten.[3]

This saying is extremely popular. It is constantly used to adorn obituaries and give them some meaning. Incidentally, the fact that we read the same sayings over and over again in obituaries is connected, of course, with the fact that the various mortuaries, as well as the internet, offer sample texts for use by the survivors. The following is also part of the ironclad trove of current texts for the use of those in mourning:

> You are not dead, you have only gone away.
> You live in us and visit us in our dreams.[4]

But is that true? In death do we only move to another place? And can human memory conquer death? Almost the same idea, though stated more sublimely, underlies the following motto that also appears at the head of many modern obituaries:

> You are no longer where you were,
> but wherever we are, you are there.[5]

So the dead person lives on, though no longer visibly present. She or he no longer exists as a real person but lives in memory, in the hearts of her or his descendants. Hence also this mourning verse:

> If you seek me,
> then seek me in your hearts.
> If I have found a home there,
> I will live on in you.[6]

The dead are really dead, but they live virtually: in the hearts of their relatives and friends and, just as often invoked, in their successes, their works, their deeds, in what they have done in the world. The obituary of a famous individual in Europe's cultural life who died in 2014 was introduced with the following:

> Every life continues somewhere,
> my father and mother in me,
> and I in everything I have brought to be.
> That is what resurrection means to me.
> Paradises do not interest me.[7]

That was a clear acknowledgment by the dead person of his view of life and the world. What should we think of such a worldview? Certainly it is true that everything good, true, and beautiful that a person has brought about enters into history. Every accomplishment becomes part of the course of the world, changes some things or even many. How long it remains a part of history is another question. What one has built up can become a ruin in the next generation. And even ruins can be destroyed and simply disappear. The good one has done can crumble. Evil can take its place and destroy it. Untruth and manipulation can triumph over the truth. The beautiful can be destroyed or made ugly.

And human memory, so often invoked, in which we supposedly live on? An equally popular sentiment, placed at the beginning of many obituaries, reads:

> After the tears and deep mourning, memory remains. Memory
> is immortal and gives us consolation and strength.

Or, still more briefly and pithily:

> Life is short but memory is forever.

Or more poetically:

> Memories are like the stars in the heavens.
> Yours will shine forever.

Or, with a touch of "primitive" romanticism:

> One day we will sing of you
> by the fires of our clans.
> Poems will be woven from your life
> and the stories will never die.

That is as smooth as an elegant cocktail, but still it is pure illusion. I
am constantly amazed at how feeble today's obituaries can be. "The
stars of memory will always shine on you"? Did the author of the
obituary really believe that? "The stories will never die"? Really?
Even stories die, especially when they are private stories that are of
interest to no one else. And the power of human memory is by no
means "immortal" and "forever." Even our memories of our own life
stories are fragile, have many gaps, and are full of self-deceptions.
Our grandchildren will still know something about us. But beyond
that we inevitably begin to be forgotten.

Test yourself: you probably know quite a bit about your parents,
though not everything. You know considerably less about your
grandparents, but still relatively a lot. You know almost nothing about
your great-grandparents, and beyond that, nothing at all—unless, of
course, you do genealogical research. But even then all you find are
external facts. Of the reality of those lives we know nothing.

The popular author Lee Child describes this accurately in his book,
The Enemy. The mother of Jack Reacher, the main character in the
book, has died of cancer. After her death the following conversation
takes place between Jack and his brother Joe:

> "Life," Joe said. "What a completely weird thing it is. A person
> lives sixty years, does all kinds of things, knows all kinds of

things, feels all kinds of things, and then it's over. Like it never
happened at all."
  "We'll always remember her."
  "No, we'll remember parts of her. The parts she chose to share.
The tip of the iceberg. The rest, only she knew about. Therefore
the rest already doesn't exist. As of now."[8]

That says everything there is to say about memory. One doesn't really
know even one's own mother. And the little we do remember vanishes like smoke. But all the same, our unfailing remembrance by our
descendants is untiringly invoked. Denis Diderot (1713–1784), the
editor of a famed encyclopedia of the European Enlightenment, permitted himself to say:

> We are instruments endowed with feeling and memory. . . .
> There is only one substance in the universe, in man and in the
> animals.[9]

For Diderot, Nature requires no personal God any more than the
human requires immortality other than survival in posthumous fame.
  Evidently Diderot was all too fascinated by the player piano, then
recently invented. Unfortunately, this great mind of the Enlightenment overlooked the fact that pianos do not play by themselves, not
even player pianos! But Diderot's other presupposition also has feet
of clay. "Posthumous fame" is badly distributed demographically.
Only a tiny percentage of the countless people who have lived in this
world have found their way into a reference work!
  And what kind of miserable immortality is that, to live on in an
encyclopedia! Who finds consolation in being buried sometime,
somewhere, in the immeasurable flood of information provided by
the World Wide Web? In some form of cloud computing, perhaps?
"Survival in posthumous fame" is a drafty and absolutely unsatis-
fying hope. A wisdom teacher in ancient Israel named Qoheleth was
much more honest and realistic when he wrote:

> There is no enduring remembrance of the wise or of fools, see-
> ing that in the days to come all will have been long forgotten.
> (Eccl 2:16)

Woody Allen (b. 1935) demystified the sweet self-deception that we will live on in our admirers and descendants in an interview:

> I don't want to achieve immortality through my work; I want to achieve immortality through not dying. I don't want to live on in the hearts of my countrymen; I want to live on in my apartment.[10]

4

Continual Reincarnation?

In the previous chapter we spoke about our yearning to live on in our own descendants. It may be that gradually and over a long time that yearning produced the notion of the transmigration of souls. At any rate, scholars in religious studies have pursued the question of how the teaching about transmigration of souls, or reincarnation, came to be.* At least *one* of the many theories says that it began with the idea that a father's life-force passed into his son, and correspondingly the vitality of the mother into the daughter.

"Life-force" in many cultures is the same as "soul." Thus the idea was that the father's soul enters into the son and transfers to him the prowess, courage, experience, and all the capabilities of the father. Religious studies scholars tell us that this widespread notion gradually expanded into a general doctrine of the indwelling of the soul in ever-new bodies—on and on—through many generations.

Of course, there are other quite different explanations for the origins of belief in reincarnation; for example: everyone wants to become one's best self, overcome one's past, erase mistakes, change guilt into innocence; in short: to become a new person. But life is limited. A

---

*Reincarnation literally means re-enfleshment.

single life is not sufficient for the protracted process of transformation, and so, necessarily, a fulfilled life requires the possibility for new and ever-new entry into new bodies so that, in the end, the individual, cleansed and purified, may attain the goal of true humanity.

We ourselves may be indifferent to the ways in which the idea of a long series of reincarnations came about, or all the things that contributed to its success. It is much more important to know that the idea has spread throughout the world, was already known among many ancient peoples, and is finding new adherents everywhere today, even among Christians. Already in antiquity it advanced from India, the classic land of the doctrine of transmigration of souls, to Europe, where the Greek philosophers Pythagoras, Empedocles, and Plato advocated it. Beginning in the eighteenth and nineteenth centuries a new wave of belief in reincarnation swept from India into the West. According to a survey conducted between 1990 and 1993, 26% of those polled in West Germany believed in their own reincarnation, 29% in Austria, and 36% in Switzerland. In 2015, researchers found that 25% of Americans—including a quarter of all Christians— likewise believe in reincarnation.[1]

In Hinduism (though not only there) the doctrine of reincarnation is closely tied to the idea of *karma*. The ancient Indian word *karma* (Sanskrit: *karman*) describes a kind of retributive causality: every human action has consequences for the person's future fate. Everything a person does returns on him or her like an echo. If one acts well, one's future life is shaped positively. If one acts badly, it is negatively shaped. Every attitude or behavior is reflected as health or illness, good or bad fortune, well-being or suffering—and all that in this life. We could also say that every "action" leads to an "effect" or that every act returns on the agent.

The potential that, according to Hindu teaching, arises out of good or bad deeds extends even beyond death. *Karma* requires ongoing life. Therefore, after death and an intermediate stage that follows death, the soul takes on a new body. Indeed, depending on how one has lived, that body may belong to a lower or higher form of existence. The one who has lived rightly achieves a qualitatively better level of being in the next rebirth. One can become a spirit or even a god. But the one who has lived badly will be found, depending on the weight of her or his misdeeds, on a worse level, becoming a demon or a beast—or, possibly, a human being again, but (once more depending on the quality of the prior existence) a poor or rich, sick or well, unfortunate or fortunate person.

As we have seen, the classic land of origin of the idea of reincarnation is India, but it is manifest there in many facets. There has never been a unified theory of rebirth in India and the lands subject to its influence. In that sense every generalizing statement has its weaknesses. The various traditions, schools, writings, and authors differ, often quite significantly. But *one* central idea seems to be maintained everywhere: that of self-redemption. That is closely tied to the *karma* system:[2] every person must work through the distortions in his or her soul until at last she or he escapes the circle of reincarnations and is absorbed into the world soul. As long as one is unable to divest oneself of one's impurities and desires, one remains on the inexorably turning wheel of new reincarnations.

In Buddhism this whole idea is associated with a definitive doctrine of renunciation: all "desire" entangles one more and more firmly within the world and brings one into deeper and deeper misery. The cause of all suffering in the world is that human beings constantly "desire," and that desiring never ceases. Redemption consists precisely in becoming free from all desires, and so from suffering. It is therefore inextricably linked with detachment from the world. *Nirvana* is ultimate freedom from all passions, all desires, all willing, everything that is world, and thereby from the maelstrom of rebirths.

The issue, then—at least in the strictest forms of Buddhism—is detachment from oneself. Still more: it is a matter of liberation from the illusion that there is such a thing as an "I" or a "self." "Becoming-not-I" is true salvation.[3] Everything unredeemed must return continually to the stream of reincarnations.

It must be said that the Buddha (Siddhartha Gautama, ca. 500 BCE) did speak of rebirth but was apparently not interested in pursuing the idea or even communicating it as a "teaching," because in the Buddha's opinion no reflection on a system of rebirths could ever lead to a liberation from suffering. It was different later, in Theravada and most certainly in Mahayana Buddhism, where the doctrine of rebirth definitely plays a role.

Buddhism in its original form is practical atheism.[4] Note: *"practical atheism,"* because strict Buddhism rejects any statement about God. The truly enlightened pursues no insights about whether God is or is not. Even wanting to know such a thing would be seeking false knowledge; it would be "wanting" and "desiring."

Therefore the Buddhist lives as if there were no God but only the eternal, impersonal world-law of *karma* according to which every act receives repayment. That law forces the eternal circle of rebirths, and everything depends on breaking out of the circle of ever-new desiring. That is true knowledge. That is real insight. The one who achieves this knowledge is "awakened."

The result, however, is that even in Buddhism human beings are compelled to self-redemption. They must make themselves free of all desires. They must save themselves. The person (insofar as there really is any such thing as an "I") must become free of that "I," of what the European tradition calls the "person."

At least in Hinduism this compulsion has become one of the most dangerous aspects of the doctrine of transmigration of souls. Why? Because human beings must *themselves* improve their life-force. May I truly help a poor person, a sick person, someone socially isolated? If I do, I interfere with that person's *karma*, and so I am not helping. The individual herself or himself must suffer and endure in order to improve her or his *karma* situation. That can lead to a social fatalism, an indifferent acceptance of unbearable social conditions, and ultimately to a kind of caste system that builds insurmountable barriers between different social classes.

This is precisely what is inhuman about the notion of rebirth, originating in the East and then introduced into Europe and beyond, because in reality the human person is not an island but is created for community. Humans constantly need the concern, the good will, even the mercy of others. They depend on others' intervention and help on their behalf. They live because others act as their representatives.

It is true that in the infinite variety of Indian religious forms, especially in newer Hinduism, there is also something that Christians would call "grace." But in and of itself the circle of ever-new rebirths shows how little real influence the principle of grace enjoys. To outsiders the whole seems more like an implacable mechanism of retribution.

Add to this still another point: the idea of reincarnation devalues history. The life given to every human being has dignity and weight precisely because it is limited. Every human life is something unique. Because it is unrepeatable, it is precious. Nothing can be delayed, nothing can be delegated to future embodiments. Human beings cannot console themselves with "soon!" or "later!" or "perhaps in the next life!" No: one must decide *now* and act *today*.

This transforms time. It is no longer an eternal loop. It becomes linear; time runs irreversibly toward a goal. It is possible to miss that goal, and so I must keep my eye fixed on it. One can sleep through one's life, and therefore one has to keep awake. The Old Testament "today" and Jesus' "the time is now" brought to many peoples that were caught up in the idea of an a-historical loop an incredibly sharpened awareness of "history" and of *kairos*, that is, the right moment, the historical hour that must not be missed.

Many Western esotericists and admirers of Eastern religions who dream of reincarnation are not at all clear about the basic structure of the doctrine and its consequences. They don't want to know about the need that is associated with the genuine Eastern idea of the circle of rebirth, or about the longing to break out of it. They certainly don't want to hear about renunciation and self-denial. They prefer to combine the original doctrine of the circle of rebirths with the worldview of evolutionary theory: in an unbroken chain of "trial and error" the individual or the "human" race in general is gradually improving. Against that horizon, then, believers in reincarnation arrive at the construct of a steadily ascending "self" that, from rebirth to rebirth, acquires more and more life-force and quality of life.

The esotericist and anthroposophist Rudolf Steiner (1861–1925) offered an especially striking form of this combination of transmigration of souls and evolutionary theory. For him, too, the notion of *karma* played a decisive role. Whatever the "I" did wrongly or fell short of in its previous incarnation will be made good in the next incarnation, in accordance with *karma* as the "ledger of life." All suffering, every blow of fate is a "karmic equalizer" and reparation for wrongful deeds in the previous incarnation. The result is a spiritual-moral ascent from reincarnation to reincarnation.

It is also part of this constant ascent of the spiritual "I" that it is reembodied in alternating genders: thus, for example, in *one* incarnation it is male and in a subsequent incarnation it is female. Thus the "I" is gradually perfected and made whole—with male and female qualities.

It can be that centuries intervene between individual reembodiments. In any case, for Rudolf Steiner there is no going backward, for example, into an existence as a lower animal; there is only constant advance. This separates his doctrine of rebirth from all its Eastern models. The long periods of alternating incarnations lead to a deeper and deeper ensoulment of the human—until the Divine emerges fully in every individual.

Precisely this makes it clear that, while Steiner adopted many features of Buddhism, he ultimately held fast to the Western concept of the person. In original Buddhism there is, in fact, no "self" at all. Anyone who wants to be an "I" or a "self" has already fallen victim to greed and illusion.

In the West today it is more and more common to see a superficial mixture of Eastern worldview, Western psychotherapy, and Christian tradition being brewed together; it sells like hotcakes and has as little to do with genuine Buddhism as the medieval crusades had to do with Jesus. Thus, for example, centers for "consciousness" or "spiritual healing" advertise journeys of the soul that supposedly take us back into earlier incarnations—for example, with texts like this:

> The soul's journey will take you back to a time before the beginning of the life you are living now. Then the soul will be able to view its previous lives, learn from them, and prepare itself for the next life. During the soul-journey you will visit some of the "stations" of your earlier incarnations and learn what kinds of knowledge your soul acquired in them. Your soul itself will decide, with the support of your spiritual leader, which "stations" to visit.
>
> In normal reincarnation therapy we usually work with traumatic experiences in order afterward to alleviate pain, fear, suffering, and other unpleasant feelings. Often this causes tears, but the soul-journey is the opposite of sorrow. In it we experience only love, gentleness, understanding, and a great, great deal of

wisdom. Here, too, there are tears: those of emotion, gratitude, and joy. The soul-journey is an experience that will remain with you throughout your life—and many subsequent lives as well.

Another text reads:

> During your soul-journey you will find yourself in a condition of deep relaxation. I, as your spiritual guide, will accompany you on this journey into the spiritual world, in which all we souls are truly at home. The spiritual world in which the soul lives eternally is shaped by love, respect, empowerment, knowledge, and healing. The soul-journey takes you into the time before your present life, what we may call a time between lives. There the soul can view its past life, learn more, and prepare itself for its life of the moment. It proceeds through a number of "stations." During the soul-journey you will visit some of these "places" and discover what knowledge your soul gained there. Your soul itself, with the support of your spiritual leader, will decide which "stations" are visited. The choice is shaped by harnessing the information you need for this present life. For some people, processes of soul-healing dominate; some are strengthened and receive greater energy; some obtain gifts that they carry with them into their waking lives. Every soul-journey encounters the all-encompassing love that is present there, as well as a loving guidance by spiritual beings.

Ads of this kind—the internet is full of them—are already reactions. They are sensitive and cleverly designed responses to the thoughts that are circulating in many people's heads, and at the same time they reveal what is so seductive about the new religious mixtures. A "therapy" of the kind they offer promises control over one's life, but it avoids genuine conversion, real change. It promises a higher existence from one incarnation to another. History and society are completely out of the picture; this is only about the individual and his or her individual happiness.

We can also see clearly from the promotional texts I have quoted how diligently the promoters of rebirth work to overcome one of the basic problems of all projections of a transmigration of souls, namely, that no one knows anything about her or his previous incarnations. If I really was already embodied somewhere else, in some other way,

I simply can't remember that previous life, and "tears of emotion, gratitude, and joy" are no help at all. Tears may flow for all kinds of reasons in the course of any kind of therapy.

No, I know nothing of previous embodiments, absolutely nothing—and yet that seems odd if I suppose that a "self" has maintained itself throughout, simply traveling a path of testing from rebirth to rebirth and perfecting itself more and more.

But this lack of memory of previous incarnations is not even the main objection to the phantom of "Western" transmigration of souls. I have already indicated that objection more than once: doctrines of reincarnation such as those represented by the two promotional texts empty history of its meaning. They do so by relativizing it. For if life is a long chain of incarnations I can always make a new decision, revise every previous decision; I never have to decide once and for all because I still have an infinite number of evolutionary opportunities for self-optimization ahead of me.

That, of course, responds to today's fear of commitment and postmodern "whateverism." No one wants to commit; it's better to keep all options open. It's best to try everything but not be obligated to anything or tie yourself down. But the constant misery that results shows that a lack of direction is out of sync with the mystery of the human.

It belongs to the nature of humanity that we are incapable of saying yes and no at the same time, that we commit ourselves, that we tie ourselves in fidelity to the truth we recognize or to a person we love. Theologian Gisbert Greshake said it this way:

> In fact, the human person is that being the sole power of whose freedom is to create finality in time and that therefore is also able to commit to fidelity.* That is precisely the greatness and dignity of the human, to be capable of such finality within the flow of time and to be able to hold fast to freely chosen ways of life, commitments, and responsibilities beyond the present moment.[5]

---

*Clearly there can also be fidelity among the lower animals, but such fidelity does not rest on free choice.—GL

Certainly it is true that every religion and every worldview contains elements of truth, and that is the case with reincarnation also. Obviously it senses something real: for one thing, the justified longing for purification; for another, the insight that human existence is not simply extinguished in death. Finally—especially in Buddhism—there is the elementary drive to escape the circle of ever-new and constantly self-reproducing suffering. But these justified hopes do not require the construction of reincarnations. All of them are fulfilled in much better ways, in ways that are much more in line with human dignity, in Christian faith.

Let me make this clear with respect to just one point here: behind the idea of reincarnation lies—along with many other things—the deep human longing for justice. Why are there rich and poor people within the same society? Why are there rulers and the ruled? Why are there the intelligent and the unintelligent, the wise and the foolish, the sick and the well?

If every form of existence is the consequence of our own behavior, shouldn't we see the poor, the sick, and in fact all those who suffer as people who are being punished for having lived badly in their previous existence? Then the world would contain a system of compensatory justice that constantly corrects and levels everything.

At first glance such a system of retribution could seem plausible, but in reality it is profoundly inhumane. It overlooks the fact that poverty, illness, and need, as well as all forms of social exclusion, can result from causes that have nothing at all to do with personal guilt. Poverty can be caused by natural catastrophes or long-existing structures of injustice, or simply by the brutal violence of powerful contemporaries.

That is why every society has to ask itself what it can do to combat poverty in its midst. To see poverty as *karma*, that is, as the consequence of a previous incarnation badly lived, not only cripples effective help but denies the poor their dignity. Justice does not happen in the world through a system of *karma*-engendered rebirths but from our working toward a just society.

Jewish-Christian faith certainly knows that people can never create complete justice; only God can do that. That is why the Bible speaks constantly of the one God who creates justice for the poor and the persecuted, and who in the end will untangle all this world's injustice and distinguish the good from the evil. It is not an impersonal *karma* that rules the world but the God of the Bible, who is both the just judge and the font of all mercy.

5

Dissolution into the Universe?

Previously I quoted a text from Denis Diderot that echoed an idea that is found among all peoples and has always been oddly attractive—namely, that the human being is one with all Being: with the stars, the stones, the plants, the animals, the whole cosmos. Diderot speaks of the universe as a "single great individual." The individual is the indivisible, the unity, the whole that cannot be separated into smaller units.

If we say that the universe is a single individual, that of course has consequences for humanity: it deprives individual human persons of the dignity of being something singular and unique. Each is then only a tiny speck in a gigantic machine or—as Diderot would say—in the autonomous instrument of the universe.

The universe as a gigantic, self-driving machine? The Age of Enlightenment was very familiar with the image, but fundamentally it was much fonder of another, namely, "Mother Nature" as the great universal unity from which everything emerges and that draws everything back into itself. Death is then a return to the womb of Nature. That was never expressed more eloquently than in the era of so-called "Storm and Stress" and the Goethe period that followed. In 1782 the *Tiefurter Journal* published an anonymous set of "Aphorisms on

Nature," later revealingly attributed to the young Johann Wolfgang von Goethe:[1]

> NATURE! We are surrounded and embraced by her: powerless to separate ourselves from her, and powerless to penetrate beyond her. Without asking, or warning, she snatches us up into her circling dance, and whirls us on until we are tired, and drop from her arms.
>
> She is ever shaping new forms: what is, has never yet been; what has been, comes not again. Everything is new, and yet nought but the old.
>
> We live in her midst and know her not. She is incessantly speaking to us, but betrays not her secret. We constantly act upon her, and yet have no power over her.
>
> The one thing she seems to aim at is Individuality; yet she cares nothing for individuals. She is always building up and destroying; but her workshop is inaccessible.
>
> . . .
>
> She tosses her creatures out of nothingness, and tells them not whence they came, nor whither they go. It is their business to run, she knows the road.
>
> . . .
>
> The spectacle of Nature is always new, for she is always renewing the spectators. Life is her most exquisite invention; and death is her expert contrivance to get plenty of life.
>
> . . .
>
> She is all things. She rewards herself and punishes herself; is her own joy and her own misery. She is rough and tender, lovely and hateful, powerless and omnipotent. She is an eternal present. Past and future are unknown to her. The present is her eternity. She is beneficent. I praise her and all her works. She is silent and wise.
>
> . . .
>
> She has brought me here and will also lead me away. I trust her. She may scold me, but she will not hate her work. It was not I who spoke of her. No! What is false and what is true, she has spoken it all. The fault, the merit, is all hers.

Clearly enough, Nature here takes the place of God and is celebrated in what amounts to a hymn. She is the great Creator, she is holy and divine, she is the ultimate meaning and at the same time the deepest mystery. The author of the ode speaks of her almost as his ancestors spoke of the God of the Bible.

The "Aphorisms on Nature"[2] may serve as illustration of a world-sentiment that is more widespread than we suppose. It has a great deal in common with the way ancient peoples saw the world, and during the epoch of the Enlightenment it made its way again into European thought. The young Goethe and many of his contemporaries were inspired by it, and its influence continued.

In 1819 the German philosopher Arthur Schopenhauer published a book entitled *The World as Will and Idea.*[3] Like the later work of Friedrich Nietzsche, Schopenhauer's book exercised an unbelievable fascination. The forty-first chapter of the third edition (1859) was entitled "On Death and Its Relation to the Indestructibility of Our True Nature." Here Schopenhauer takes Nature as the gauge for the question of immortality: plants grow, die, and dissolve. From the organic matter left by dying plants and animals, new plants and animals arise. An endless circle of life! Nature takes no interest in the life of the individual; she is completely indifferent to single beings. She constantly destroys the life she has produced. For Nature, all that matters is the survival of the species.

Why should human beings be different? Schopenhauer asks. We should regard them as part of Nature, like all other beings. In death the "universal mother Nature" receives humans back into her arms. They are only immortal in that the matter out of which she made them and the powers that worked within them will reappear again and again in new people—not as the person whom the individual was, but as the "human" being that enters into the circling of Nature in constantly recurring manifestations.

The true "human" is therefore by no means the single being, the individual, the person. The individual is a "mistake," a "deviation," a "basic error," something that would better not have existed, for the existence of the individual is always only misery and suffering in existence. The meaning of death is our deliverance from the burden of our "I," from exposure to our individuality. Hence death is the final step into true freedom. It is the "return to the womb of nature" from which the individual emerged for a short time, "enticed by the hope of more favourable conditions of existence." Death restores the true, original being of the human that belongs entirely to Nature, to the universe.

> The peace and quietness upon the countenance of most dead persons seems to have its origin in this . . .

according to Schopenhauer. Further:

> If one knocked on graves, and asked the dead whether they wished to rise again, they would shake their heads.[4]

Hence one who has truly grasped what death and life are will die gladly and joyfully, desiring no "continuance of his person." Such a one knows that the living being does not suffer absolute destruction in death but endures in the whole of Nature.

So much for Arthur Schopenhauer and his Nature mysticism—in its shorthand version. What happened? What is going on here in terms of intellectual history? Essentially, it is a gigantic upheaval. Greek philosophy and Roman jurisprudence in antiquity had created the bases for today's concept of the "person" or "personality." Christian theology pursued the idea more deeply and, in trinitarian theology, applied it even to God. Medieval theologians developed their philosophy of personhood within their tractates on the triune God. For them the human "person" involved a unique "I"; an irreplaceable, non-exchangeable individuality; a singular self, never existing before and thus never repeatable, indivisible and free. And, despite this irreplaceable individuality, the person also involved an orientation to others, to those "alongside" and "with" the individual, an inextinguishable orientation even to God. The fact that every human being is a person created by God, called by name and loved by God, gives the person her or his most profound worth. Many centuries lived in this Christian concept of the person and were sustained and upheld by it.

But in the eighteenth and nineteenth centuries Christianity became superfluous to many in Europe. As a result the Christian concept of the person also dissolved for them—and, consequently, so did belief in an encounter with God in death. Arthur Schopenhauer formulated all that in seductive fashion, at the same time whisking it together with a good dose of Western world-weariness and resignation. But he only expressed in the most radical terms what many longed for, knowingly or unknowingly: death as a dissolution into the cosmos or the world-soul; death as a return to the unity of all being; even an identity with all human beings who ever lived or would live. Eastern religious systems that had fascinated many European intellectuals from the eighteenth century onward played an important role in this development. Buddhism in particular was celebrated in the West as a successful combination of rationality and spirituality.

Thomas Mann (1875–1955) masterfully depicted this sense of the world, newly emerging in Europe as defeatism and pessimism, in his great novel on the fall of the house of "Buddenbrook."[5] Senator Thomas Buddenbrook of Lübeck finds himself, at the age of fifty, in a deep existential crisis. He has grown weary. He no longer knows whether his life makes any sense. He has long ceased to believe in the Christian resurrection, and he is immeasurably disappointed in his bumbling son Hanno, who is a failure in business.

One day a book buried in the shelves of his library falls into his hands. Thomas Mann does not name the book or its author, but of course it is Schopenhauer's *The World as Will and Idea*. The senator reads it like a drunkard; for days it throws him into a blissful turmoil. Here he suddenly finds what he sees as a plausible hope for continued existence. Until that hour he had supposed

> that he had lived in his ancestors and would continue to live in his descendants. The idea had fitted well with his sense of family, his patrician self-confidence, and his reverence for history; and it had also supported his ambitions and strengthened him as he went about the tasks of life. But now, as he gazed into the piercing eye of approaching death, it was apparent that such a view fell away to nothing. . . . And Thomas Buddenbrook turned away in hopeless disappointment from his only son, in whom he had hoped to live on, strong and rejuvenated, and began in haste and fear to seek for truth which had to exist somewhere for him.

He finds this "truth" in the nearly ecstatic hours of his reading of Schopenhauer:

"I'm going to live!" Thomas Buddenbrook said half aloud and felt his chest jolted by sobs somewhere deep inside. "That's it—I'm going to live. It is going to live." . . .

What was death? The answer to the question came to him now, but not in poor, pretentious words—instead, he felt it, possessed it somewhere within him. Death was a blessing, so great, so deep that we can fathom it only at those moments, like this one now, when we are reprieved from it. It was the return home from long, unspeakably painful wanderings, the correction of a great error, the loosening of tormenting chains, the removal of barriers—it set a horrible accident to rights again.

An end, a dissolution? Empty words, and whoever was terrified by them was a pitiable wretch. What would end, what would dissolve? His body, his personality and individuality—this cumbersome, intractable, defective, and contemptible barrier to becoming something different and better.

Was not every human being a mistake, a blunder? Did we not, at the very moment of birth, stumble into agonizing captivity? A prison, a prison with bars and chains everywhere! And, staring out hopelessly from between the bars of his individuality, a man sees only the surrounding walls of external circumstance, until death comes and calls him home to freedom.

. . .

And I hoped to live on in my son? In another personality, even weaker, more fearful, more wavering than my own? What childish, misguided nonsense! What good does a son do me? I don't need a son. And where will I be once I am dead? It's so dazzlingly clear, so overwhelmingly simple. I will be a part of all those who say, who have ever said, or will say "I": and, most especially, a part of those who say it more forcibly, joyfully, powerfully.

Naturally, that is not consistent. The senator so drunk on the idea of universal Nature did not quite understand Schopenhauer. Joyfully and powerfully saying "I" is again, after all, that damned greed for individuality, the self, one's own person. The truly wise person, in Schopenhauer's sense, refuses the will to live; such a one abandons all willing and enters into the "condition of free renunciation, resignation, true serenity, and complete lack of will." And it is in just that way that she or he, dying to self, streams into the nothingness that is free of all desire.

Of course, Buddhism itself is burdened by Senator Thomas Buddenbrook's inconsistency. According to Buddhism, after all, humans are subjected to rebirth because they have not yet abandoned their desires and still thirst for being—but in reality the human being possesses no continuing "I," but rather, from incarnation to incarnation, a new energy potential is transmitted, a complex of psychic energies and ongoing neuronal processes.

Here Buddhism is self-contradictory, for either these floating energies still guarantee the selfhood of the person, in which case the "I" continues to exist, or there never was an "I" in the first place, in which case it is impossible to speak of the salvation of the human person from her or his "I," and one cannot even speak of becoming free of the illusion of the "I."

A particular sector of currently popular esotericism tries to adopt the philosophy of Buddhism, but in doing so it is as inconsistent as Thomas Buddenbrook—who, incidentally, can no longer believe Schopenhauer's pseudo-mysticism two weeks later. The new esotericists prefer to leave out radical asceticism and the denial of the will to live but instead paint death in brilliant colors. For them, too, death means becoming free of all burdens, being liberated from the fetters of individuality, and finally brings true freedom, which means becoming one with all Being and melting into the motions and powers of the cosmos.

Here again it is worthwhile to glance at the variety of today's obituaries. They speak not only of Christian hope, not only of living on in one's descendants, but also of the alluring idea of the self's dissolution into universal Nature. Take, for example, the following tribute heading an obituary that occupied more than half a page in the newspaper:

> I am only a wavelet in the ocean.
> The wave comes and goes.
> The ocean remains; it is forever.

The obituary then ends with:

> Burial at sea took place on the Mediterranean among those closest to the deceased, on 11 August 2009.

In another instance the death notice was headed by an ironic text from the Austrian poet Ernst Jandl (1925–2000):

> we're the people who walk the fields
> soon we'll be people under the fields
> and will all become field and oak
> yes, we'll be proper country folk.[6]

Above the obituary is not a cross but a broad-branching tree, which is only consistent. Christians have for centuries buried their dead as a sign of their faith in the resurrection. When that faith vanishes in mist and is replaced by a definite (or rather vague) faith in a return to the eternal universe it is much more appropriate to scatter one's ashes in the wind or the sea, or to bury them anonymously in the forest, at the roots of an ancient tree—ideally in a biodegradable urn. The family and friends can then console themselves with the thought that the organic remains of the dead person will one day reach out to the sun in the whispering leaves of the tree.

In fact, burial forms are changing nowadays with lightning speed. More and more people are ready to imagine having their future place of rest outside an old-fashioned cemetery: as compressed ashes in a "remembrance diamond," or strewn over the sea, or swept from the top of a mountain by the wind, or in "forest cemeteries" and "forests of repose," buried beneath a tree in the lap of Nature—or quite simply sprinkled over a meadow reserved for the purpose.[7] Thus it is no accident that a sentence attributed to the Roman emperor Marcus Aurelius is gaining favor as a memorial:

> You came into being as part of a whole,
> You will vanish again into what engendered you.

Whoever wrote those lines, they are certainly pantheistic in intent. The human being returns to the womb of a Nature that is all-encompassing, immeasurable, eternal, and divine. Those who quote the saying today would scarcely understand it so clearly any longer—for them the whole thing is probably pretty much diluted—but there remains a certain percentage of pantheism, with vague projections of a "great ensouled connectedness" in which the human as person is dissolved.

Obviously this dissolution-mysticism is also supported by what we now know about biology and physics. We are informed that about thirty million cells die in our bodies every minute and are replaced by thirty million others. From a biological point of view we are completely replaced every couple of years. But at death this constant exchange within our organism ceases. What happens then? Lorenz Marti, a radio journalist and son of the theologian Kurt Marti, has written a book that tries to link natural science, esotericism, and mysticism. He writes:

> At some point, hopefully not too soon, the atoms of your body will finally separate and move on. For you, alas, that is the end. But not so for the atoms. They will enter into new associations, revealing themselves perhaps in the brilliant yellow of a dandelion, in the wetness of a drop of rain, or in the throat of a giraffe. And certainly in the hearts of some people as well.[8]

In the next chapter of his book Marti then speaks of the constant exchange of energy between humans and their world, and he asks:

> But what happens to your energy when you are no longer there? It reveals itself in new forms: in trees, clouds, and stones. In strawberries, rhinos, and people. Maybe even in a blazing meteor. This certainty may reconcile us to the finitude of our existence. Something continues on.

Then he quotes the Vietnamese Zen master Thich Nhat Hanh (b. 1926), who constantly reminds himself:

> Every day I look deeply at everything around me: the trees, the hills, my friends. I see myself in them all and I know I shall not die. I will continue in many other forms.[9]

I have to admit that I am not the least bit consoled about the finitude of my existence because my physical energy may live on in strawberries or rhinos. Nor am I satisfied that "something" goes on or that I will continue "in many other forms." I want, through God's creative grace, to live on in my own person—or not at all.

When I look at this whole mysticism of dissolution, which (supposedly) is happy that we can flow into trees, mountains, and meteors, I ask myself: Didn't human biological and cultural evolution develop in precisely the contrary direction?—namely, to a more and more powerful awareness of the self, freedom from mere instincts and compulsions, emancipation from the dominance of the collective, becoming persons, a more and more intense understanding of the irreplaceable nature of every individual?

We can see all of that in the development of a small child: First it must learn to distinguish between itself and others. It learns to recognize other people and in the process to recognize itself. It learns to sit, stand, speak. It learns how to use ideas. One day it says "I" for the first time. Gradually it becomes capable of real encounter, of going outside itself, of perceiving others, of sympathy, of loving.

Human beings as a whole are like that child. Their whole development moves not toward the task of total individuality but toward the deepest knowledge there is: perceiving others as persons, with their difference, their freedom, their whole capability for resistance and their histories, foreign to the observer—and it is precisely through all this that each of us becomes an "I." Martin Buber rightly emphasized that our "I" only becomes a real "I" in the encounter with the "thou."[10]

Human beings are designed for encounter; that orientation developed over millions of years. They neither remained lonely starfish bobbing in the waves, fertilized by sperm swimming in the water, nor did they become herd animals, bleating along behind the tails of their leaders. Human beings stand and walk upright and have unique, individual faces, and every one of us longs to look into the beloved face of another human being. What is the purpose of all that, if after death the human being vanishes into an anonymous universe and the end of a life is not arrival, but dissolution—not knowing and being known, but the dissolving of everything that person was; no blissful seeing face-to-face, but losing oneself in a faceless cosmos?

Jean Paul, the great and nearly forgotten German poet (1763–1825), described this empty cosmos in a dreadful dream-image entitled "Speech of the Dead Christ from the Universe That There Is No God." In this fictive vision Jean Paul sees the night sky open up and present a view of an immeasurable universe. He sees how the outermost and innermost parts of the world are laid bare, how the graves open and the dead totter toward the resurrection.

Then the dead Christ appears in the heavens, a sublimely noble figure. When he appears, the countless dead of the earth, filled with a horrible suspicion, shout to him: "Christ, tell us, is there no God?" He has to answer: "There is none!" and then Christ tells the dead in their graves what happened to him at the moment of his death:

> "I traversed the worlds, I ascended into the suns, and soared with the Milky Ways through the wastes of heaven; but there is no God. I descended to the last reaches of the shadows of Being, and I looked into the chasm and cried: 'Father, where art thou?' But I heard only the eternal storm ruled by none . . ."[11]

Then comes the most horrifying passage in the text. Christ tells how he sought the face of the Father through infinite space. He did not find it. Only the endless cosmos stared at him

> . . . from an empty bottomless socket; and Eternity lay on Chaos and gnawed it and ruminated itself.[12]

Literarily speaking, the "Speech of the Dead Christ from the Universe That There Is No God" is one of the greatest texts of German literature—and probably one of the most sinister—even though the narrator finally awakes and recognizes that he was only having a bad dream. The text mercilessly unmasks all the mystifications that suppose a "Mother Nature" that will surround us in death and into which we can peacefully dissolve. If there is no God, if there is no encounter with the one toward whom we have always been moving, if there is no "face-to-face," then we die into an icy, faceless nothingness.

6

The Longing for Extinction

"Icy nothingness" is, of course, only an image. The Greek philosopher Epicurus (ca. 341–271 BCE) stressed that we should not fear death because the time *before* death is not yet death, and death *itself* is the entry into pure nothingness; that is, all feeling ceases: "when we are, death is not come, and, when death is come, we are not."[1] Hence no one need fear death.

In fact, we encounter many people today who have no interest in their deaths. They are so busy living that death means nothing to them. Certainly, they know that they will someday die. Someday. But not yet.[2] And they no longer ask about "after." The subject of death is not part of their lives.

Of course, the media show us thousands of deaths, and not only in the news. The entertainment industry thrives on bodies: burned, emaciated, mutilated, dismembered. For example, the motifs of crime novels inevitably include a post-mortem, as detailed as possible and full of information. In the same way, in the last twenty years or so a new figure has been added to the inventory of those peopling this kind of popular literature: the forensic anthropologist, who calculates the time of the victim's death from the stage of development of the

maggots of blowflies in the corpse. Simon Beckett begins his novel
The Chemistry of Death as follows:

> A human body starts to decompose four minutes after death.
> Once the encapsulation of life, it now undergoes its final meta-
> morphoses. It begins to digest itself. Cells dissolve from the in-
> side out. Tissue turns to liquid, then to gas. No longer animate,
> the body becomes an immovable feast for other organisms. Bac-
> teria first, then insects.[3]

Popular novels offer reams of texts of this sort, and the clinically
white halls of judicial medicine have long been the most important
location for television crime shows. Autopsies are obligatory. We
could also mention countless computer games based on swift and
effective killing. So death is certainly present in our society, but for
those who consume it daily it is not an existential theme. If the con-
sumers of corpses and death are confronted one day with actual death
in their own families they fall into profound consternation and silent
helplessness. Luckily, there is a funeral home nearby that will take
care of everything.

And yet that is true of only a part of society. In philosophy, for example, death has always played a highly prominent role.[4] The same
is true for literature. A great many writers and poets have engaged
intensively with the subject of death. Then there is the so-called "self-
help literature," which prominently features books on dying and
death.[5] We may even say that there is a certain "verbosity" about
death nowadays.[6] In any case, the "repression of death" so often
described in the past is no longer present to many thoughtful people.
There are more and more women and men who think about a dignified dying and deliberately consider their own death, view it with
eyes open, and discuss with their families what should be done if
they succumb to dementia or fall into an extended coma. Others are
actively engaged in the hospice movement.

That movement, beginning at the end of the 1960s, says quite
rightly that we need hospices, palliative care stations, and specific
services that can provide time and attention to those who are dying,
because our ordinary hospitals and the people who work there
are not in a position to enable the dying to have a dignified death.

Dr. Michael de Ridder, who practices in Berlin, writes against the background of decades of clinical experience:

> Our hospitals, with few exceptions, are the very stone-and-steel opposites of what a human being needs at the end of life. The way they are built and equipped, as well as the dispositions and abilities of the mostly overworked doctors and nurses, are not designed for indulging a human life approaching its end with care and concern. Instead, they act like more or less perfect machinery, conveying to the sick, and most certainly to the dying, the feeling of being sand in the gears. They instil helplessness, dependency, and also something that calls into question the success of much therapeutic effort: existential terror.[7]

Is it any wonder that in light of this situation a third of all Germans have already considered taking their own lives if they should come to need comprehensive care, and that a high percentage of the population (there as in the United States) favors "assisted suicide"? But all this is not only fear of a situation in which we are radically dependent on the help of others. It seems that many of our contemporaries are increasingly fascinated by the idea of deliberately planned suicide. Doesn't it make sense to celebrate one's own death as a last "free act"?

It is not only that there have long been clinics in Europe in which physicians assist the dying with appropriate means. It is not only that there are organizations like the Hemlock Society to which one can apply to kill oneself and that offer counseling, presence, and assistance for suicide. No, there are also more and more books and films that describe in minute detail how seriously ill or aged people prepare for their departure and then celebrate it in a well-staged ceremony.

For example, a couple's suicide is portrayed: how they clean their apartment and put flowers on the table so that their death will be "festive." Then they put a notice on the bedroom door saying that they died by their own free decision. The man brushes his hair and slips on his best pajamas. The woman applies rouge one more time and dons her prettiest negligee. The necessary tablets are counted, crushed, and dissolved in liquid. Before the fatal glass they take a little food and some anti-nausea medicine so that their stomachs will not vomit out the poison. Everything that has to be done and taken into account is on their carefully composed "To-Do List." Anyone may read detailed instructions in the internet, or in the corresponding advice literature.

All this is delivered to our homes nowadays, as a book or a film—and we are into it. There are, of course, many reasons—besides simple voyeurism—for the macabre desire to watch others kill themselves in the media. Since there are almost no taboos left in our society (sexuality has long since become completely public and is marketed, down to the tiniest detail), this is an opportunity, perhaps, to break one of the last that still remains.[8]

Such suicides are still more desolate when they are not fiction, but reality, with family members looking on. A seventy-seven-year-old woman in Munich was diagnosed with Alzheimer's disease. She then decided to take her life at home, with her family around her. After the suicide the city authorities at first made a complaint against the family for neglecting to attempt to save her, but the action was quickly dismissed. The disposition of the case was described by the Public Prosecutor's office on 30 July 2010:

> On the evening of 28 February 2009 the children of the later deceased came to their mother's apartment. First they talked and ate together, then the later deceased took anti-nausea medicine. About half an hour afterward she swallowed some tablets, after which they all drank champagne together. In about ten minutes the later deceased felt weary, brushed her teeth and put on her nightgown, then went to bed. One after another the accused went to their mother and took their leave of her. When, about half an hour after midnight on 1 March 2009, her breath became shallow and irregular, the accused sat by their mother's bed and held her hand. Around 12:41 the absence of breath and pulse signaled that death had occurred. No attempts were made to save the deceased.[9]

We may wonder what was going through the heads of the family during this death. Sorrow, sympathy, concern, happy memories?—or perhaps also, in the background, some less noble thoughts? Or was it perhaps the theory praised by a number of Greek and Roman philosophers, that human freedom culminates in the ability to choose and shape one's own end?

That idea is attracting more and more adherents. Is not this very self-chosen "departure" a sign of human dignity? We could not decide to come into this world, but we can determine our own departure, and in doing so we can be free. Precisely that is said to be the greatest privilege of the human, distinguishing us from the beasts: that we can "lay hands on ourselves."

Of course, there is something else at work in this ideology of freedom as well. There is a growing interest in overcoming old age—and of course that is connected with the fact that we are collectively aging, living much longer than people in previous centuries. We see before us a lengthening period of our lives in which our life-force slowly but inexorably declines. Arthur Schopenhauer described that in masterly fashion:

> In old age, passions and desires, together with the susceptibility to their objects, are gradually extinguished; the emotions no longer find any excitement, for the power to make representations or mental pictures becomes weaker and weaker, and its images feebler. The impressions no longer stick to us, but pass away without a trace; the days roll by faster and faster; events lose their significance; everything grows pale. The old man, stricken in years, totters about or rests in a corner, now only a shadow, a ghost, of his former self. What still remains there for death to destroy? One day a slumber is his last, and his dreams are ———.[10]

The long line represents, for Schopenhauer, the complete nothingness into which the human being is extinguished. To him (and incidentally, he was strictly against suicide) this dissolving into nothingness was something utterly positive. It is appropriate to the human, is absolutely in accord with human nature—because human beings, like plants and other animals, are part of Nature's eternal cycle.

That, apparently, is how many people today also feel, though with a different rationale. "Natural" or self-incurred death simply puts an end to an old age whose burden has grown greater and greater. People get tired. We have had it with politics and politicians; we don't want to turn on the TV. We can't even read very well anymore. Going out on the street demands an enormous amount of caution. Short-term memory gets worse and worse, and long-term memory is less and less reliable. Our brains are getting foggy. We can't remember names or recognize faces. Our children are living their own lives and don't have much time for us. More and more of our friends have died. So why fear death? It is part of life. It is, in itself, already a "salvation" from the burdens of old age. The question of "eternal life" is irrelevant; after all, we've had this life, sometimes beautiful, sometimes unfair. But now it is coming to an end, and that is all right.

Feelings like these are also reflected in the headings of obituaries; for example:

> Death may also come as a friend
> to those who are aged,
> whose hands can no longer hold fast,
> whose eyes are weary,
> whose voices only say:
> Life was beautiful.
> But now I've had enough.

"I've had enough"—that is an ancient motif, very popular in Baroque poetry. Anton Ulrich von Braunschweig's "Dying Song" begins with this sigh:

> Enough! My dull senses
> long to go to where my fathers sleep.
> After all, I have a perfect right.
> I've had enough! I have to seek repose.[11]

The song repeats "enough!" seven times and ends with a humble, yet grandiose, command: "Enough! Therefore let death be mine!" However, the song not only speaks of a life grown weary because of an ever-increasing burden, and not only of a desire to sleep forever. Instead, the person who here longs for the sleep of final release at the same time places his whole life in God's hand:

> So, Lord, accept my soul,
> which I surrender to your hand and care.
> Inscribe it in your book of life.
> It is enough! that I lie down to sleep.[12]

That is the profound difference between this attitude and that of the mere longing expressed by many of the aged in our society: simply to fall asleep and be extinguished forever. The poet of the Baroque era wanted to die in order to be with God.

Reinhold Schneider (1903–1958), in his *Winter in Wien*, asserts that falling asleep and being extinguished has always, in principle, been the normal human desire according to Nature. He says that the question of "eternal life" is linked to a very particular set of historical circumstances, culminating in the appearance of Jesus. Apart from that, the question of eternal life has seldom existed, and today it is disappearing again:

> The whole of Christian culture, with all its charisma, is sustained by the seriousness of this question. But is it essential to humans? Is it indispensable? No. Neither the pre-Socratics nor the Stoics proposed it; innumerable hordes of peoples come and go without suffering from it.[13]

For Schneider, then, the desire for immortality is not an essential feature of the human. While it is true that within Christian cultures there has been a longing for eternal life, whole peoples had previously "handed themselves over to death" and never sought eternity. In today's society, he asserts, Christian preachers are suddenly confronted again with the fact that "the question of immortality is lapsing into silence."

What should we think about this cultural-historical thesis? It sounds attractive. Reinhold Schneider could have quoted Friedrich Nietzsche (1844–1900), who, looking back over his life and work in *Ecce homo*, his last major book, wrote almost triumphantly and with braggadocio:

> "God," "the immortality of the soul," "salvation," a "beyond"— to all these notions, even as a child, I never paid any attention whatsoever, nor did I waste any time upon them,—maybe I was never *naïf* enough for that? I am quite unacquainted with atheism as a result, and still less as an event in my life: in me it is inborn, instinctive. I am too inquisitive, too incredulous, too high spirited, to be satisfied with such a palpably clumsy solution of things. God is a too palpably clumsy solution of things; a solution which shows a lack of delicacy towards us thinkers—at bottom He is really no more than a coarse and rude *prohibition* of us: ye shall not think![14]

It seems that, with this, Nietzsche announced the end of the question of immortality. So was Reinhold Schneider right? No. He, too, felt and thought as a man of his time. He apparently could not see that the desire for eternal life can take the greatest variety of forms: for example, belief in reincarnation or the longing to sink back into the womb of the universal Mother Nature, or the idea of eternal return, or simply the forlorn hope of living on in one's descendants. Above all, he knew nothing of the epochal re-emergence of Islam we are now experiencing. For Islam, belief in the resurrection of the dead is taken for granted.

Reinhold Schneider was also unaware of the current neo-pagan esotericism in which the longing for something beyond is rampant and blooms in the most exotic shades. And Schneider was simply mistaken with regard to the ancient Stoa. Stoic teaching about the "last things" was by no means simple or unified. It oscillated between naked materialism and pious belief in the soul. Especially in middle and late Stoicism we find outstanding representatives who were convinced of the immortality of the soul; these include Poseidonius (135–51 BCE) and Lucius Annaeus Seneca (1–65 CE).[15] Seneca wrote to a mourning mother of the journey her son's soul would undertake after death:

> He has tarried a brief space above us while his soul was being cleansed and purified from the vices and rust which all mortal lives must contract, and from thence he will rise to the high heavens and join the souls of the blessed: a saintly company will welcome him thither.[16]

This idea was, in fact, a basic doctrine of Seneca's teaching. The immortal soul transits for a time through the air while it undergoes a process of cleansing from its faults. But then it enters the realm of eternal Being and abides among the "saintly company" of philosophers and sages.

No, here Reinhold Schneider was simply mistaken. The question of what comes after death was proposed with the fullest intensity millennia before Christianity; we need only think of Egypt. (See part 2, chap. 3 below.) And it has not been silenced even now. It emerges in the most varied forms over and over again, often hidden and in dubious guises. It belongs to the nature of humans, who reach for infinity in everything they do.

Therefore we may and must ask: What happens to us in death? What happens to our life, our "I," our consciousness, the history of our life? Is it all over for us? Is death followed by profound night, eternal sleep, and absolute nothingness? Is our self extinguished forever? Or is it followed by the life Christians describe in that worn-out but irreplaceable phrase as "eternal bliss"?

But not only that: we may and must ask about the history of the world. What will become of the countless people who have been degraded, tortured, raped, murdered? Will the injustice, lies, manipulation, suffering of billions of innocent people never be uncovered, revealed? And in turn: Will the endless efforts to discover truth, to ease the sufferings of the downtrodden, to improve the conditions of society ultimately lead to nothing, because not only do individuals die but whole nations and cultures vanish, and inevitable destruction awaits everything in the end? Or will there be a revelation by God of everything that has ever happened throughout history, and with it the resurrection of all history into God—into the love of God that creates justice?

PART TWO

What Israel Learned

1

Faith Seeking Understanding

The first part of this book opened our view to embrace a broad horizon of rituals, images, myths, and philosophical themes, of yearning hopes and cold denials. Truth be told, it was only a snippet. It could have been expanded endlessly. But even from this brief view it ought to be clear that this is an essential human question emerging from the depths of our existence and never silenced. It does not fall silent even when death is regarded as pure extinction. Even the defiant statement "we came from nothing and return to nothing" (which is most assuredly a confession of faith!) seems to vibrate with the question whether, just maybe, things could be different.

However, a look at cultural and religious history shows not only that the intense search for an answer never ceases but also that the proposed answers shimmer in all colors and travel in all directions. They move through endless stages between pious belief in the soul and radical skepticism. We encounter a great, sounding chorus that not only sings polyphony but emits shrill dissonances. It seems that there is no clear answer to the question of what happens after death even in the area of *human* possibilities, because here people are talking about something that no living person has ever experienced.* Can there be any answer at all to such questions?

---

* I will not touch on so-called "near-death experiences" in this book. They are remarkable, often even fascinating, but they, too, are unable to answer the

We might expect that philosophy would best be able to offer an answer. What does it mean, after all, that humans are questioning beings whose probing never ceases? And how is it that they are constantly seeking? They are longing for something, finally attain it—and no sooner have they done so than it is no longer enough for them. Or: Why is it that in everything they think, feel, say, and do they are constantly reaching beyond themselves and that they can only construct concepts against an endless horizon?* In everything they do they seek the infinite, above all in their passions and their longing for pleasure and beauty. Friedrich Nietzsche gave an almost perfect description in his "Drunken Song" from *Also sprach Zarathustra*:

> O man! Take heed!
> What saith deep midnight's voice indeed?
> "I slept my sleep—,
> "From deepest dream I've woke, and plead:—
> "The world is deep,
> "And deeper than the day could read.
> "Deep is its woe—,
> "Joy—deeper still than grief can be:
> "Woe saith: Hence! Go!
> "But joys all want eternity—,
> "Want deep, profound eternity!"[1]

Nietzsche is not referring here to Christian eternity but to the eternal return of the fulfilled moment. But that affirms what we have just said: human beings reach out incessantly after endlessness, however they imagine it.

The question is, however: What is this reaching out? Is it just unceasing unrest, constant drivenness, an eternal projection and redis-

---

question of "afterward" because those who have had those experiences arrived at a borderline and then returned.

*Concepts are only possible because a leap is made from the concrete "this" to the universal: more precisely, to endless realizations of the concrete individual. In turn, the recognition of a concrete, finite thing is only possible against an infinite horizon. These remarks must suffice here; let me refer to the major work of Joseph Maréchal, *Le point de départ de la métaphysique*, 5 vols., 3rd ed. (Paris: Desclée de Brouwer, 1944–63).

covery of the self? Is it only that biological drive that ultimately enables the permanent evolution of all living things? Or is it the human project created by God—the human being who is restless until she or he has found God? Augustine formulated it inimitably in his *Confessions*, which from beginning to end are a prayer to God, and he did so at the very beginning:

> "You are great, Lord, and highly to be praised (Ps 47:2); great is your power and your wisdom is immeasurable" (Ps 146:5). Man, a little piece of your creation, desires to praise you, a human being "bearing his mortality with him" (2 Cor 4:10), carrying with him the witness of his sin and the witness that you "resist the proud" (1 Pet 5:5). Nevertheless, to praise you is the desire of man, a little piece of your creation. You stir man to take pleasure in praising you, because you have made us for yourself, and our heart is restless until it rests in you.[2]

Thus Augustine tried to say from whence humans' unceasing restlessness comes. But his answer is theological, arising out of Jewish and Christian experience and presupposing God's speaking and a believing response to that speaking.

This book holds to the same position. What happens to us after death is something we can only know in faith, and it is only from faith that we can ultimately speak of it. I want to say that at this point, as clearly as I can. I am not writing as a natural scientist or a student of the history of religions or as a philosopher. I write as a Christian theologian, that is, as someone whose calling is to interpret the word of God. And that is why I want to emphasize again that as regards what happens to us after death we can know nothing except through God's own self and out of a listening faith. Christian tradition calls that "revelation."

Let the concept of revelation not be wrongly understood. How does God speak to the world? Not through loudspeakers set in heaven; not by dictating a book to a prophet; not by whispering softly in the souls of the elect and telling them things that no human being has ever heard before.* No, God speaks through the experiences of those

---

* It goes without saying that prophetic hearing as a medium of revelation is not excluded. It is only that such hearing, just like visions, arises out of the human

who follow God's ways. Such experiences may be associated with inner peace or unrest, consolation or lack thereof, finding the way or hopelessness, being made whole or remaining hopeless—depending on whether people open themselves to the self-unfolding truth of God or not.

The miracle that a whole people did not refuse God's truth but reached out for it over and over again took place in Israel. There, at the crossroads of Asia, Africa, and Europe, between the high cultures of Assyria, Babylon, Phoenicia, and Egypt with their dazzling religious systems—precisely at that crux that made it uniquely possible to see, to compare, to criticize, and to distinguish—there, just there, people had the decisive experiences with God that were then recorded, consolidated, continued, and repeatedly given critical testing in the book we call the "Bible."

The Old Testament constitutes by far the greater part of the Bible and is the mighty, always indispensable basis for the New Testament. The writings of the New Testament are only the last layer of meaning of the Old Testament, removing all ambiguity and bringing everything to its completion. Therefore in this second section we must, first of all, take a very close look at what Israel experienced in the centuries of its history.

But first, one more methodological pointer to what follows! This first chapter of the second section is entitled "Faith Seeking Understanding." That is exactly the title the great medieval theologian Anselm of Canterbury (ca. 1033–1109) originally gave to his *Proslogion: fides quaerens intellectum*. He did not invent the phrase, of course. It rests on statements that occur repeatedly in the works of Augustine: "Believe, that you may understand!" He in turn is referring to a saying in the Greek translation of the Old Testament, the so-called Septuagint (LXX). In the Septuagint version of Isaiah 7:9, contrary to the Hebrew text, we find: "If you do not believe, neither will you understand."

---

subconscious and hence does not exclude what the person has already seen and heard. Certainly God can make use of such natural phenomena to communicate. See Gerhard Lohfink, *Jesus of Nazareth*, trans. Linda M. Maloney (Collegeville, MN: Liturgical Press, 2012), 292–95.

What did Augustine and the medieval theologians mean when they cited this passage? They meant to say that it is only the experience of faith that makes possible a certain knowledge of anything having to do with God. However, that faith-experience must be able to justify itself to reason. That is precisely the method of this book.

2

Radical Worldliness

When we open the Old Testament and ask it what it knows about
death and what comes after death we first encounter a phenomenon
we had scarcely reckoned with. We find a profound skepticism about
all religious notions of the afterlife. Large portions of the Old Testament appear to know of no life after death. Death is the end. In 2
Samuel a woman sent by General Joab says to King David: "We must
all die; we are like water spilled on the ground, which cannot be
gathered up" (2 Sam 14:14). The Old Testament wisdom teacher
Qoheleth says it still more dramatically:

> Truly! the fate of humans and the fate of animals is the same; as
> one dies, so dies the other. They all have the same breath, and
> humans have no advantage over the animals; for both are vanity.
> Both go to one place; both are from the dust, and both turn to
> dust again. (Eccl 3:19-20)

Animals must die; humans must die: there is no difference. Human
life runs out, the spirit flees, the body returns to dust; everything
ends with death. The same message is found, for example, in Psalm
39. This petition of a sick person emphasizes twice that a human
being is but a "breath" (Ps 39:6, 12). And at the end of the psalm the

sick person pleads to God: turn away your punishing gaze, so that I may breathe quietly for a little while longer:

> Hear my prayer, O LORD,
>> and give ear to my cry;
>> do not hold your peace at my tears.
> For I am your passing guest,
>> an alien, like all my forebears.
> Turn your gaze away from me, that I may smile [once again],
>> before I must depart and be no more. (Ps 39:13-14)

So real life ends with death. Of course, as was the case everywhere in the ancient East and in antiquity, there was still the realm of the dead, the underworld, *Sheol*. But if we look more closely we see that *Sheol* is the place of nothingness. There is no life there that is worthy of the name. Christoph Barth once wrote, in a study of the individual psalms of lament and thanksgiving: "Dying does not mean ceasing to be, but rather ceasing to live."[1] That hits the nail on the head. We could also speak of a shadow-existence. The book of Job calls the underworld a place "[of no return] . . . a land of darkness and the shadow of death, as murky as the deepest night" (Job 10:21-22).

In the underworld the connection with the living is snapped. Those who have sunk down into *Sheol* have no further share in Israel's history. Even their own history is broken off and flown away. The dead know nothing more, says Qoheleth:

> Whoever is joined with all the living has hope, for a living dog is better than a dead lion. Also: the living know that they will die, but the dead know nothing; they expect no more reward, for the memory of them is lost. Love, hate, and jealousy of them have already perished; never again will they have any share in all that happens under the sun. (Eccl 9:4-6)

But most dreadful of all is that in *Sheol* the human being is no longer able even to praise God (Pss 6:6; 115:17; Isa 38:18). Such a one is far from God, and God, too, is at a distance (Ps 88:6). It is true that the Old Testament can say of a man who has died that he has gone "to his people" or "been gathered to his people."[2] The formula indicates the collective consciousness of early Israel: all are members of a long succession of generations, but being gathered to the ancestors still does not mean that the dead person has really achieved community with those gone before, certainly not a life with God. The primary intent is quite simple: the person's bones now lie where the bones of his or her ancestors are buried. They are in the family tomb.

Certainly those still living received consolation and even a feeling of security from the thought of being someday buried where parents and ancestors rest. Probably there was even a sense that one wanted to die and be buried in the land promised to the ancestors.[3] And yet: anyone who is in the grave is on the way to the underworld, and there is no more life in the grave with the bones of the ancestors than there is in the underworld. In Psalm 143 an individual prays, and with that person, as is always the case in the Psalms, all of Israel implores:

> Answer me quickly, O Lord;
>   my spirit fails.
> Do not hide your face from me,
>   or I shall be like those who go down to the Pit. (Ps 143:7)

Those still living, who have been saved from crisis, behold the face of God. That is: they live in profound communion with God. In the "pit," that is, in the grave and the underworld, that communion ceases.

What is decisive is that this sober assessment of death corresponds to a radical "worldliness" in Israel's stories, prayers, and theology—in short, throughout the Old Testament. Real life happens here, in this world. The place for humans is in the history that is happening now. This is the place for blessing, joy, and praise of God. Community with God remains entirely bound to earthly life. The happiness a person in Israel desires from God is a long and satisfied life, many children, rich harvests, great flocks and herds, joyful festivals, and protection from foes. In Psalm 144, for example, the blessing that people hoped to receive from God is described very palpably:

> Then shall our sons in their youth
>   be like plants full grown,
> our daughters like corner pillars,
>   cut for the building of the temple.

Our barns are filled,
  Overflowing with produce of every kind;
  our sheep increasing by thousands,
    by tens of thousands in our fields,
and our cattle are heavy with young.
  There is no breach in the walls, no exile,
    and no cry of distress in our streets.
Happy are the people to whom such blessings fall;
  happy are the people whose God is the LORD. (Ps 144:12-15)

That is what God's hoped-for blessing looks like. It is altogether earthly. But Psalm 144 also reveals the happiness that comes from being close to God: "happy are the people whose God is the LORD!" It is no different with Qoheleth.[4] After having tested all human possibilities and all of Israel's cultural traditions, indeed, those of the entire East, he advises his readers:

> Go, eat your bread with enjoyment, and drink your wine with a merry heart; for God has long ago approved what you do. Let your garments always be fresh; do not let fragrant oil be lacking on your head. Enjoy life with a wife whom you love, all the days of your vain life that are given you under the sun, because that is your portion in life and property, in your toil at which you toil under the sun. Whatever your hand finds to do, do with your might, as long as you have strength; for there is no work or thought or knowledge in Sheol, to which you are going. (Eccl 9:7-10)[5]

Make no mistake! What Qoheleth advises is neither indifference nor detachment. People must act vigorously, but in doing so they must connect to God. All of life's enjoyment must take place in the fear of God. People should enjoy their lives before God, especially in the days of youth; they should be of good cheer, keep their minds free of anger and resentment, and protect their bodies from illness—but after death it is all over, and people will return to the dust from which they came.

But doesn't the Old Testament contain a hope for the future after all?—a hope that there will come a day when God reverses every circumstance?—that a time will come when justice will be established at last, the oppressed set free, the poor raised up, the suffering rescued, the sick healed, the sorrowing consoled?—a time when God will change the fortunes of God's people and give peace to Israel both within and without?

That future hope does exist. It runs throughout the whole of the Old Testament, and especially the prophets. It is true that prophetic preaching always contains diagnosis: the uncovering of the deep wounds in the people of God, the denunciation of injustice, enslavement, and exploitation. But prophetic speech also involves the promise of salvation: God's rule will be established in Israel; God will create justice and give peace. Then the wolf will lie down with the lamb (Isa 11:6). Then the land will be full of the "knowledge of the Lord" (Isa 11:9). Then even Nature will reflect salvation and bring forth abundant fruit (Ezek 36:33-36).

But all that only confirms what has been said, because in the first place it all takes place in the realm of this time and place, in this world, on this earth, in the land of Israel. If the images of peace, justice, and blessing seem to surpass the measure of normal experience, they are still located in the sphere of earthly history.

Certainly we may ask about the extent to which images of ultimate peace and absolute justice are already on the way to transformation, from earthly immanence to transcendence. But the criterion for such questions can only be death and the overcoming of death, and in that case it is the fact that an abundant wealth of blessing for coming generations in Israel is not the same as the destruction of death, most certainly not the same as the deliverance of the dead of previous generations. No, it remains the case that even the prophetic promises first of all affirm the radical worldliness of Old Testament thought; even those promises, in their time, acknowledge no life after death.

3

Dissociation from Faith in the Hereafter

Obviously the question is now: Why is the Old Testament so reticent about life after death? Why are major parts of the Hebrew Bible averse to any idea of a blessed hereafter? Why is there this overpowering worldliness in the text of the Old Testament?

To answer this question we must first refer to the world of ideas within which many of the peoples of the ancient Near East and the Mediterranean realm moved. *Sheol*, with the shadow existence of those dwelling there, was not only part of Israel's world of ideas: for example, Hades, the underworld, also belonged to the ancient Greek worldview. Awareness of the impossibility of achieving eternal life was even the principal theme of the very ancient Mesopotamian epic of Gilgamesh. The hero Gilgamesh seizes the plant of immortality from the sea floor—but while he is asleep it is stolen by a snake. Only the gods possess immortality; human beings are mortal—unless they are raised up as heroes and placed among the gods.

What is unusual in the Old Testament is not the idea of *Sheol*, which also existed elsewhere, but that the world of death and the underworld was at first kept so consistently separate from God.[1] The spheres of God and of death had nothing to do with one another. In this way death was de-sacralized and de-divinized.[2] Precisely here, at this point, we find the deepest root of the distancing between Israel and its neighbors, together with their religious systems.

Consider, first of all, the Canaanite religion! In Canaan, as for all the other nations around Israel, death was itself a divine power. There was a god of death, a ruler of the underworld named "Mot." Death had its proper sphere of power, which even projected its own mysterious fascination. People sought to enter into the realm of death's power by means of spells and magic. Necromancy (the invocation of the dead) was practiced all around Israel. It was profoundly tempting to try to force the spirits of the dead to present themselves, to make use of them, and through them to discover one's own destiny.

First Samuel 28:3-25 tells the eerie tale of such an invocation of the dead in Israel. Saul, the anointed king of Israel, tries to learn the result of an imminent and decisive battle with the Philistines from the medium at Endor. But what he learns is about his own death. The dead prophet Samuel comes to Saul from the underworld—as an old man, wrapped in his robe—and tells him nothing other than what he had already told the king (1 Sam 15:26-28).

The Old Testament tells of this invocation of the dead as a warning. What King Saul did is utterly condemned. But that in itself shows that the practice of invoking the dead must have been widespread in ancient Israel. It is only in the theology of the Old Testament that such invocation is first rejected (Lev 19:31; 20:6, 27; Deut 18:9-13; Isa 8:19; 65:4). The people of God must not participate in such things, even though the world of the dead was always fascinating and enticing, because for Israel's prophets and theologians death was not a separate realm of divine power and the underworld was not God.

Reverence for the ancestors was also part of the attraction exercised by the world of the dead. It played an extraordinary role in many ancient religions. The dead ancestors were regarded as "agents of power" or power brokers: that is, the well-being or woe of the tribe depended on them. Often they even took the place of gods. They were honored; people prayed to them; people sacrificed to them.

There was certainly such a cult of the ancestors in Canaan, within the framework of the "family religion" that was common in antiquity. Appeal was made to the names of dead parents and ancestors. Animals were sacrificed for the dead of the tribe, and drink offerings were poured on the earth, the place of the dead.

Did that also happen in Israel? Some indications within the Old Testament textual tradition seem to point to it,[3] but they are disputed. More consequent is that thus far archaeology has produced nothing to show that there was anything like cultic worship in Israel at the tombs of the dead.[4] It is true that we find vessels for food and drink in Judean tombs; these were to provide sustenance for the dead. But that is "care for the dead" and does not signify a cult of the dead in the sense of real ancestor worship. And we most certainly cannot speak of any "divinization" of the dead. So it remains true in this case also that Israel's faith is this-worldly. Its God is a "God not of the dead, but of the living" (Mark 12:27).

We are still in the process of distancing the Old Testament from Canaanite religion. That distancing reveals itself on another point as well: when, beginning in the thirteenth century BCE, the groups from which Israel would later emerge were forming in Canaan, at first they could only settle on the not-so-fertile heights because the Canaanites continued to occupy the more humid lowlands, where they lived from commerce and the products of the land. But the land's fertility depended on the coming of the rains between November and February. The harvest was always in danger. Every year the vegetation withered in the heat of late summer; for Nature that summer heat was a kind of "death." Would the winter rains bring salvation? Would the fields and pastures again soften into lush life?

In view of such "rain tillage" it is no wonder that Canaanite religion was primarily a fertility cult. In its mythology the drying up of vegetation in the late summer and its revival in spring represented a dying and rising deity named Baal.[5] All fertility was condensed and symbolized by Baal. He was a storm god from whom came dew, rain, and thunder, so it was believed. When Nature died, so did Baal, or rather, when Baal died, so did Nature. But why did Baal die?

The myth said that Baal fought with Mot, who was not only the ruler of death but the god of summer heat and drought. So the rain-god Baal fought with the heat-god Mot—and lost. He had to descend to the underworld. But Anath, the goddess of love and war, brought Baal back to his mountain palace and buried him there. In his own palace the "cloud-rider" Baal returned to life—and the autumn rains began at once. Nature revived.[6]

The cult imaged the death of Baal in a loud lament, as people in Canaan participated in a ritual of vegetative fertility rhythms and, through their lamenting of their dead god, secured their own fertility and that of the land. At the same time, by entering into the vegetative rhythm they took control of the crisis of their own mortality: if the death of the fertility god is holy and pregnant with hope, so one's own death is holy and not without hope.

It is clear that Israel must have recoiled against such a cult and the assurance of life associated with it, because some of the groups out of which Israel was formed believed in the god YHWH, superior to and creator of the world. In the Canaanite myths, by contrast, creation and new creation were natural, annual events. New life arose out of the natural cycle. This kind of renewal of life, which was also associated with sexually symbolic rituals, could only be rejected by the wiser heads in Israel.

But note: only the wiser heads! We should by no means assume that the sharp distinction between YHWH and Baal was drawn everywhere in Israel and from the very beginning. Many Old Testament texts, especially the stories of Elijah in 1 Kings 17–19, show how long it took before the real Israel separated itself from the Canaanite religious world and its seductive fertility myths. It must have been a hard struggle, one lasting for centuries—a battle over theological distinction and clarity. But, at least in the final version of the Old Testament, that struggle had been concluded and the separation completed, clearly and definitively. Gods that arise, die, and rise again were completely unacceptable to Old Testament faith. People who held to that faith wanted nothing to do with that kind of life-security.

Thus far we have been looking at the Canaanite period, but in considering Israel's separation from it we have to look primarily to Egypt. Israel was constantly confronted by and fascinated with Egypt. Of all its neighbors it was the land of the Nile that possessed the most excessive cult of the dead. No people were so obsessed with death and afterlife as were the ancient Egyptians. "Death must have continually preoccupied the Egyptians—with the construction of pyramids for kings and huge burial monuments for high officials, with the decoration and outfitting of these tombs, cenotaphs, and commemorative chapels, with the preparation of statues, stelae, offering tables, sarcophagi, wooden coffins, and Books of the Dead, with the procurement of mortuary offerings and the conducting of mortuary rituals."[7] Nowhere in the ancient world was there such a fully established belief in the afterlife.

It is true that in early Egypt eternal life was reserved for the Pharaoh, whose corpse was mummified and the tomb chamber filled with precious burial gifts. In its midst stood a statue of the Pharaoh. Artistically shaped figures called *ushebti* were placed there as well; they were to serve the Pharaoh in eternal life.* The tomb itself involved an extensive layout. From the Third Dynasty (2740–2670 BCE) onward, pyramids were erected over the tombs. All this served to secure eternal life for the Pharaoh, who would enter into the circle of the gods as an immortal divine monarch.

Alongside the official state cult, ancient Egypt gradually developed (beginning during the Eighteenth Dynasty, 1530–1292 BCE) something like a "personal piety." The assurance of an afterlife, at first reserved for the Pharaoh, was democratized. Now all who lived rightly and could pass through the "judgment of the dead" could become immortal gods in a life after death. Egypt became a state in which immortality was better organized than anywhere else. There was a cult of tombs such as we can scarcely imagine. Preparation for the afterlife became one of the principal pillars of Egyptian religion, as countless inscriptions attest. Thus on the tomb statuette of a woman named Ipy, from the Ekhnaton period (fourteenth century BCE) we read:

> Your body is protected,
> your heart is satisfied.
> Nothing evil will touch your body
> and all will be well with you.
> Your flesh will not decay.[8]

* Normally the *ushebti* were up to ten inches high, but there were also more monumental figures. Originally they embodied the deceased. They were deposited in the funerary chapel, thus ensuring the symbolic presence of the dead person. From the Eighteenth Dynasty onward they increasingly took on a different function as aides to the deceased in the afterlife.

The faithful in Israel saw or experienced all that up close, and they knew that such a mythicizing of death, such entrancement with the afterlife could not be God's will, because it drew attention away from this world, which was God's goal, and fixed it on another. It replaced trust in God with concern for one's own eternal fate. Most certainly, every YHWH-believer had to reject the Egyptian idea of "becoming gods." Therefore Israel—insofar as it remained true to its own proper experiences of faith—could not accept a piety of the afterlife on the Egyptian model. For the time being it remained without a belief in the afterlife and had to live purely as a this-worldly people.

4

Security in God

Israel—or at least its prophets and teachers—maintained the rejection of a life after death for centuries, admitting no hope for a future life on the Egyptian model. But did this strict refusal arise only out of a critique of Israel's religious environment? Was it only revulsion at the experience of foreign cults, a close look at them, a comparison and self-distancing? As important as all that must have been, it does not touch the depths of the this-worldly faith of the people of the twelve tribes.

What was decisive was Israel's insight—already hinted at previously—that its God was a God for this life, a God who willed and desired this world. The world was God's creation, God's plan, God's joy, which God would not abandon in spite of the chaos created by humans. God's love for the world was revealed in love for God's people, who were to be a blessing for the whole world (Gen 12:2-3).

Again and again God had led the ancestors, protected, sustained, and delivered them. The mightiest of those experiences of deliverance was Israel's liberation from the power of Pharaoh, the exodus from the slave-state, Egypt. The Exodus was Israel's foundational memory, the ground of its existence. When the liberation from Egypt was narrated in worship (Deut 26:5-10), Israel brought its later, contemporary experiences of deliverance into the great narrative. God not only freed this people way back then; God liberates and delivers now as well. The primal experience of the Exodus was the ultimate reason why Israel could concentrate on this life, this history, this world.

Always alive in Israel's "cultural memory" was the knowledge that it was sheltered within the hands of God. God was in its midst, standing by the people's side and not letting Israel fall. God had entrusted Israel with a land—a beautiful and precious land flowing with milk and honey. Again and again this fundamental trust in God was put into words: in many narratives, but above all in the Psalms. And in the pleas and thanksgivings of the Psalms we behold a striking phenomenon: here the later faith in resurrection was already antici-pated. Of course, it was not yet put into words *as faith in resurrection*. The formulations are cautious and reserved; everything remains suspenseful, and yet behind many verses of the Psalms lies the knowl-edge of safety in God that is without limit and therefore has no need of expression in phrases like "resurrection of the dead."

Psalm 49 is altogether exemplary in this regard. In and of itself the Psalm speaks, altogether within the sense-framework of Israel's wis-dom literature, of the absolute end awaiting all human beings—the wise as well as the foolish. In particular it is the powerful and wealthy who would like to be able to buy eternal life from God with their money (after all, everything in life is for sale as far as they are con-cerned); they have to get it out of their heads

> that one should live on forever
> and never see the grave.
>
> For it is evident that even the wise die;
> perish together with the fool and the dolt
> and leave their wealth to others.
>
> They suppose their houses will stand forever,
> their dwelling places from generation to generation,
> for they named lands their own.
>
> Mortals in their pomp will not last the night;
> they are like animals that are silenced. (Ps 49:9-12)

All must die and pass into the underworld, even the insightful and wise. Many wisdom texts speak this way, as noted. But Psalm 49 continues in a different trajectory.[1] Beginning at v. 14, it points to the exposure to death on the part of the rich who cling to their property and trust not in God but in their lands and wealth. It is only from them that, in the end, everything will be taken away:

> Such is the fate of those who trust in themselves,
>> and those who hang on their words must follow them.
>
> Like sheep they trot down to Sheol;
>> Death shall be their shepherd;
>> and the righteous shall rule them in the morning . . .
> But God will ransom me from the power of the underworld,
>> for he will receive me. (Ps 49:14-16)

"But God will ransom me." The rich and powerful in Israel cannot buy themselves out, in spite of their great wealth, but the one praying the Psalm, who is poor and disenfranchised, will be ransomed by *God*. Such a one will be brought to and received by God.* Here, suddenly, there emerges a hope that the poor who trust in God will not be subjected to the same fate as their rich exploiters. God receives them. The statement is still very reserved, but it is utterly confident. All this is much clearer in Psalm 16; we need to look at the whole of that Psalm:

> Protect me, O God, for in you I take refuge.
> [2] I say to Yʜwʜ, "You are my Lord;
>> You alone are the joy of my life."
>
> [3] As for the "holy ones" in the land, the "noble ones"
>> in whom I took delight:**
>
> [4] Those who choose another god multiply their sorrows;
>> their drink offerings of blood I will never again pour out
>> or take their names upon my lips.

---

* Instead of "will receive me" one could also translate "will carry me away" (like Enoch or Elijah).

** Author's translation of this disputed verse, based on the Münsterschwarzach Psalter. The NRSV "As for the holy ones in the land, they are the noble, in whom is all my delight" inserts a finite verb ("they are") that is not in the original text and changes the meaning. See the explanation below.

> ⁵ O Lord, you are my chosen portion and my cup;
>   you have cast the lot for me.
> ⁶ The boundary lines have fallen for me in pleasant places;
>   I have a goodly heritage.
>
> ⁷ I bless the LORD who gives me counsel;
>   in the night also my heart instructs me.
> ⁸ I keep the LORD always before me;
>   because he is at my right hand, I shall not be moved.
>
> ⁹ Therefore my heart is glad, and my soul rejoices;
>   my body will also rest secure.
> ¹⁰ For you do not give me up to the world of the dead,
>   or let your faithful one see the Pit.
>
> ¹¹ You show me the path of life.
>   In your presence there are fullness and joy;
>   in your right hand are pleasures forevermore. (Psalm 16)

At the very beginning of the Psalm, in v. 3, there is a translation problem. Who is the subject? Probably not the devout "holy ones," possible models in faith (as in Ps 34:10), but more likely the Canaanite gods who were so fascinating to many in Israel. They were addressed as "lords," as "noble," even as "holy." But however we interpret this difficult verse, it is still clear in what follows that the person praying the Psalm has abandoned the gods of the land and no longer sacrifices to them. This person clings to YHWH, the God of Israel, and YHWH alone. And those are not just empty words; behind them stands genuine experience: the God of Israel has become the psalmist's whole joy.

We have to look carefully at how the words are chosen. In and of itself this psalm could be interpreted altogether in terms of this world, as speaking of a happy existence only here, on earth. The psalmist, or the one praying the Psalm, has received everything that could be desired: land (v. 6), health (v. 9), joy in abundance (v. 11). Not seeing "the Pit" would simply mean that God will always deliver this person from dangerous situations.

So we could interpret the Psalm completely in terms of earth and immanence. But if we look more closely we can see that the psalmist speaks out of a confidence that extends beyond the borders of death. Nothing is said about enemy threats, dangerous illness, or violent death. This is about death itself. The one who prays the Psalm knows that a community of life with YHWH cannot be lost; it is so profound that it lasts beyond death.

But whence this assurance? It certainly does not rest on dreams of the afterlife or speculations on eternity; rather, the psalmist always sees the face of God, who constantly accompanies her or him. So the one who prays this Psalm is already living now, in this life, out of an experience of the sheltering presence of God. For such a person death is no catastrophe.

What is special about Psalm 16 is that it shows that Israel's faith remains altogether earthly, but at depth it is open to an action of God that encompasses even the realm of death and the underworld.[2] The psalmist lives in profound confidence that God will not abandon her or him, even in death. People who pray this Psalm know that they can trust in God absolutely. Other texts reveal the same attitude: for example, Psalms 22 and 73. Here again, nothing is said about a "resurrection of the dead," and yet they reveal a profound confidence that the devout in Israel are always sheltered in God.

In essence, none of this depends necessarily on text passages that speak of salvation beyond death. What is decisive is the enduring basic conviction in Israel that speaks through countless texts, such as the following:

> O LORD, your faithfulness reaches to the heavens,
>> your trustworthiness to the clouds.
> Your righteousness extends as far as the mountains of God,
>> your judgments press as deep as the great primeval flood;
>> human and animal you continually rescue, O LORD.
>
> How precious is your faithfulness, O God!
>> so that all people take refuge in the shadow of your wings.
>> (Ps 36:5-7)[3]

That is complete security, here in this text derived from the breadth of the world, from knowledge of God's faithfulness to creation—security that no longer needs to ask about "afterward."

So we may say that on the one hand Israel's long silence about resurrection was based on the fact that faith in YHWH was incompatible with the Canaanite cult of the dead and the Egyptian obsession with the afterlife. But on the other hand that silence arose out of the knowledge that the God of Israel *willed* the earthly world. It was God's will, God's desire, God's creation—and God's will was not for some kind of world-behind-the-world. It was this earth. Israel was profoundly convinced of that. Hence its skepticism toward all cults whose gaze was fixed on an afterlife outside this world! Such fidelity to the earth was, of course, only sustainable as long as the people could trust in the faithfulness of their God.

5

Faith in Resurrection Begins to Sprout

Then, in the margins of the Old Testament, so to speak, a belief in the resurrection of the dead was put explicitly into words. But that belief did not fall suddenly from heaven; it had long been growing in the context of Israel's experiences of deliverance.[1] Building on these, we find increasingly clear formulations in the Old Testament expressing the certainty that God's saving fidelity extends beyond death. That takes place, as we have seen, in the Psalter above all. From that point of view it is inappropriate to assign the theme of "resurrection" exclusively to so-called "apocalyptic."* Even when, in what follows, I speak of four examples from Old Testament "apocalyptic" texts, the "thing itself" meant by resurrection began to emerge in Israel's thought much earlier.

1. The book of Isaiah contains a text, within the complex of chapters 24–27, that speaks directly of the overcoming of death. These four

---

* "Apocalyptic" is a slippery concept. Should we define it in general terms with reference to crisis situations or base it on apocalyptic literature? If we begin from the Old Testament and Judaism, the most refined form of "apocalyptic" presumes that this eon will be destroyed with unspeakable sufferings and God will create a new eon (see, e.g., 4 Ezra). But many forms of the idea prior to or taking shape alongside these are also assigned the adjective "apocalyptic."

chapters come from a relatively late period; they are certainly not from the time of the historical Isaiah. They no longer look only to Israel, or only at the foreign nations; they refer to the world as a whole. In any case, the focus and mid-point of the events described in Isaiah 24–27 is Mount Zion, and thus Jerusalem.

A world-judgment will come when God will call to account the kings of the whole earth (and their peoples with them; Isa 24:21). At the same time God will enter into divine royal rule in the sight of all the world (24:23). The destruction of everything hostile to God comes with this entry into rule (25:6-7).[2] It is precisely in this context that we find Isaiah 25:8, which says that for Israel death will be destroyed once and for all. God does what was unattainable for the Canaanite god Baal.[3] God "swallows" death forever. That is: God destroys the dreadful power of death. The text does not yet speak of a *resurrection* of Israel's dead or of an *afterlife*. Everything that happens takes place on this earth.* But it speaks directly and unmistakably of God's over-coming of death:

> [God] will swallow up death forever. Then the Lord Yhwh will wipe away the tears from all faces, and the disgrace of his people he will take away from all the earth. Truly, the Lord has spoken. (Isa 25:8)

2. The quoted text still leaves the fate of the dead of earlier generations completely open. The answer comes only at Isaiah 26:19—another part of the text complex of Isaiah 24–27—where Israel is told:

> Your dead shall live, my corpses shall rise. Those who dwell in the dust shall awake and sing for joy. For the dew that falls on you is a radiant dew, and the earth will give birth to the shadows. (Isa 26:19)

---

* We cannot suppose that all the resurrection texts of early Judaism speak of a resurrection to transcendence in the strict sense. The dead can also be raised to a life in the messianic reign or a life on a renewed earth. However, existence on this new earth can also be described as such a miracle that it has transcendent features.

Who speaks in this complicated text is a matter of dispute. Is this God speaking to Israel, or the voice of a prophet? And is the same voice speaking in the first sentence as in the second? I will leave all that open, because the meaning is clear in any case: this is about Israel's dead. The "shadows" and the "dwellers in the dust" are the dead who are leading an amorphous existence in the underworld. They will awaken, arise bodily, and praise God.

The metaphors of dew and light are important for our discussion. These are images of God's creative power. The very first thing God did in creating the world was to speak light into being (Gen 1:3-4). No light, no life! And in Palestine the dew is absolutely necessary in the rainless months if the plants are not to dry up. The quantity of dew is also much greater than in central Europe or North America. The awakening of the dead is thus regarded from the perspective of creation. What God created, preserved from chaos, and repeatedly delivered—this God cannot allow to end in death.

Of course, we may ask whether this is not just a way of talking in a transferred sense about the preservation and protection of the people of Israel, whom God constantly raises up from perilous and life-threatening situations—or is the text really talking about those who have already died? The answer seems to be that throughout the whole text complex of Isaiah 24–27 the subject is the events of the end time; hence the text must be speaking of the eschatological raising of the dead. But it is an awakening of the dead for life on a renewed earth.

3. The book of Daniel then speaks even more clearly. Its historical background is this: Antiochus IV of Syria (d. 164 BCE), in the course of his Hellenization policy, had banned the worship of YHWH and ordered the great sacrificial altar in the Jerusalem Temple to be repurposed, by means of an addition, as an altar to Olympian Zeus. The book of Daniel calls this addition—in apocalyptic code—the "abomination that desolates" (Dan 9:27; 11:31; 12:11). On December 6 in the year 167 BCE the Jerusalem Temple was dedicated to Olympian Zeus. However, it was not only Antiochus IV who supported these procedures; part of the ruling class in Jerusalem itself approved the alteration of the ancient faith within the context of Hellenistic culture.[4]

What that group, and Antiochus IV, had not reckoned with was the strong opposition within a portion of the people who refused to allow their faith in the God of their ancestors to be taken away from them. The result was a bitter resistance, the martyrdom of faithful Jews, and the battles of the Maccabees against the Syrians and the Hellenistically oriented Jews in Jerusalem.

It was during this period that the book of Daniel was written. Its intention was to shift attention to God as the Lord of history in this time of Israel's need, which was seen as an eschatological crisis. The author of Daniel could not avoid the question of what would happen to those who had died for their faith. Daniel 12:1-3 says, in apocalyptically colored language:

> "There shall be a time of anguish, such as has never occurred since nations first came into existence. But at that time your people shall be delivered, everyone who is found written in the book [of life]. Many of those who sleep in the dust of the earth shall awake, some to everlasting life, and some to shame and everlasting contempt. Those who are wise shall shine like the brightness of heavenly festivals, and those who have led many to righteousness, like the stars forever and ever."

We have already seen the belief that the dead become stars in the heavens represented among the Greeks and Romans, but in our text it is only an aid to expression. In reality the text speaks here of faith in the resurrection of the righteous on the basis of Israel's previous experiences of deliverance ("at that time your people shall be delivered"). Nor is this about a resurrection to transcendence: the place of new life is this earthly world renewed by God.

This faith, then, is not speculation, nor does it drop from heaven. It arises out of history—out of the living experience that God repeatedly delivers God's people from its crises. Certainly a great deal remains open in this text. What about the righteous among the Gentiles? Do only the chosen of Israel rise, or does something similar happen beyond Israel as well? And does the resurrection include all of Israel, so that every Israelite rises—the faithful in a new, restored world, the apostates in a kind of hell? All that is really clear is that this is about a promise for all those in Israel who have endured in the face of persecution and trials. God remains faithful to them, and so at least the true Israel will be saved.

4. At this point we need to point at least briefly to another Old Testament text, namely, Ezekiel 37:1-14,[5] which contains a vivid description of a vision of the restoration of the people Israel. The prophet sees a vast field of dry bones, scattered over a great plain. God orders him to promise life to the bones and summon the spirit of God upon them. The prophet obeys and sees how the bones come together, are covered with flesh and skin, how spirit enters them and they arise: "a vast multitude" (Ezek 37:7-10).

What is the purpose of the vision? It promises nothing less than the gathering and return of Israel from the Diaspora to the land of their ancestors (37:12, 14), and thus the revivifying and restoration of the people (37:11). And yet it is all described in images that show clearly how the "resurrection of the dead" was imagined, perhaps already at the time when the book of Ezekiel was edited and most certainly in the subsequent era in Israel: opening of graves (37:13), revivification of the flesh by the Spirit of God (37:8), and purification from all uncleanness (36:25).[6] That is more or less exactly how the resurrection of the dead was later painted. In fact, this text from the book of Ezekiel has repeatedly inspired and nourished ideas about a "bodily resurrection" in both Judaism and Christianity.[7]

At the end of this chapter we will consider one more text, from outside the biblical canon. In all probability it originated in Palestine in the time after the destruction of the Temple in the year 70. The work that contains this text bears the name of the Jewish philosopher and theologian Philo, but it is not his. Its title is *Biblical Antiquities*. We may suppose that pious Jews in Israel at the time of Jesus imagined the resurrection of the dead as this text describes it. It is God who speaks:[8]

> But when the years of the world shall be fulfilled,
> then shall the light cease
> and the darkness be quenched:
> and I will quicken the dead
> and raise up from the earth them that sleep:
> and Hell shall pay his debt
> and destruction give back that which was committed unto him

> that I may render unto every man according to his works
> and according to the fruit of their imaginations. . . .
> And the world shall rest, and death shall be quenched,
> and [the underworld] shall shut his mouth. . . .
> And there shall be another earth
> and another heaven, even an everlasting habitation.[9]

Thus the day will come when this age of the world reaches its end: then death will be destroyed and the dead will arise to judgment. They come from the underworld where they have been staying. Then there will be a new heaven and a new earth—though it remains open whether this new world will be pure transcendence or a transformed earth. Probably for the author the two were not mutually exclusive.

So we may conclude: belief in the resurrection was only put into words at a late period in Israel.* We have seen why this was so. Israel first had to separate itself from its neighbors' cult of the dead and self-securing of eternal life. Only when Israel was firmly anchored in this world could it take a new step and formulate the idea of a God-given resurrection in which the shadowy existence in *Sheol*, the "land of dust," would be overcome. But the roots of those formulations, found in the margins of the Old Testament in Isaiah 24–27, Daniel 12, and Ezekiel 37, were much older. Those roots were Israel's experiences of deliverance.

---

*There is another text complex on the subject of "resurrection" in 2 Maccabees (see 7:9, 11, 14, 23, 29, 36; 14:37-46). It comes from the second century BCE and is not part of the Hebrew Bible, but is found in the Septuagint and the Roman Catholic canon.

6

Israel's Enduring Discovery

Isaiah 25–26, Daniel 12:1-3, and Ezekiel 37 thereafter played an important role in Israel's belief about resurrection; however, not everyone within Judaism accepted belief in a resurrection of the dead. For example, in Jesus' time the leading social class in Jerusalem, the group of so-called "Sadducees," rejected it (see Matt 22:23) because it was not stated in the Torah, the "five books of Moses." Even today there are groups within Judaism who leave the question of what comes after death completely open. To them it seems an unimportant issue. What matters is only a faithful life according to Torah.

One example of "leaving the question open" is found in the Jewish "Eighteen Benedictions," also called *Amidah* or *Tefillah*. At the very beginning of the benedictions we find:

Blessed are you, L-rd, you revive the dead.

The prayerbook of the German Progressive Jewish congregations has retained the original text in Hebrew but in the German version has deliberately changed it to read:

Blessed are you, L-rd, you give life in the face of death.

This is intended to accommodate all those who pray, even if they do not believe in a bodily resurrection. In substance the formulation returns to Israel's original experiences of deliverance: believers hope for rescue from situations of mortal danger and restoration to the fullness of earthly life. Still, the formulation remains open for greater things.

But even where, in Judaism, hope for the resurrection of the dead is a matter of course, we must pay attention to the significance of that hope. Take, for example, the *Kaddish*, one of the most important Jewish prayers. It is not only a prayer for the dead; it describes the center of Jewish existence: that God's name be hallowed *in this world*. The text reads:

> Exalted and hallowed be God's great name
> in the world which God created, according to plan.
> May God's majesty be revealed in the days of our lifetime
> and the life of all Israel—speedily, imminently, to which we say
>   Amen.
>
> Blessed be God's great name to all eternity.
>
> Blessed, praised, honored, exalted, extolled, glorified, adored,
>   and lauded be the name of the Holy Blessed One, beyond all
>   earthly words and songs of blessing, praise, and comfort. To
>   which we say Amen.
>
> May there be abundant peace from heaven, and life, for us and
>   all Israel,
> to which we say Amen.
>
> May the One who creates harmony on high, bring peace to us
>   and to all Israel.
> To which we say Amen.

In this principal prayer of Judaism, which has many things in common with the Our Father, the resurrection of the dead is not mentioned. The prayer is only about this world: that God be exalted above all others on this earth. And how is God honored? by the hallowing of God's name by the whole company of Israel, which repeatedly speaks its "Amen" in this prayer. But the hallowing of God's name takes place through the transformation of the world, and that trans-

formation comes about—as is presupposed—through the keeping of
the commandments, that is, by following Torah. Thus and in no other
way will God's reign, the realm of God's rule, come to be. Thus and
in no other way does God give peace to the world.

The case is similar with the "Eighteen Benedictions," the second
central prayer of Judaism, discussed above. It is about right knowledge, repentance, healing the sick, protection from persecutors, the
deliverance of the people, the restoration of Jerusalem, the coming
of the Messiah—that is, about the will of God in this world. The final
part of the prayer reads:

> . . . may it be good in Your sight to bless Your people Israel at
> all times and in every hour with thy peace. Blessed are You, O
> L-rd, who blesses Your people Israel with peace.

As we have said, the idea that God gives new life to the dead appears
only in a marginal sense in the Eighteen Benedictions: not within the
benedictions themselves but only in the solemn praise of God at the
beginning of the prayer.

It should be clear by now that Israel, from Isaiah 26 and Daniel 12
onward, that is, from the time of the first formulations of belief in the
resurrection of the dead, has never surrendered its piety of this world.
It is not finished with and superfluous. It has been made more precise,
but never retracted.

This means that Christian faith must hold to Israel's loving devotion to this world. It must not be spiritualized to its detriment. Everything Israel knew and knows about death and life retains its place
in Christian belief in the resurrection of the dead. It would be a dangerous mistake to say that, because the church's faith in resurrection
simply knows more than ancient Israel knew, those older ideas about
life and death are outmoded. No, anyone who wants to know what
resurrection really means must accompany Israel on the whole journey on which it has been led. Christian theology must continue to
carry Israel's this-worldly thought within it. But what does this preservation of Israel's knowledge look like in the concrete?

To begin with: Death is not the supreme festival of human freedom.
It is the darkest and most dreadful side of human life. It puts a radical
end to it. Its horror stares us in the face when someone we have loved,

who has accompanied us through life, one day lies before us cold, silent, and with a bloodless countenance.

Biblical Israel took death seriously, with all the love for reality that is native to it. Nothing was retouched, nothing prettified, nothing repressed. They knew that there is no physical immortality. There is nothing naturally eternal in the human that rises up to the stars. If there is immortality, it can only be the gift of God. In and of themselves, human beings are dust.

When, accordingly, Catholic and Anglican churches place ashes on the foreheads of the faithful on Ash Wednesday as the priest says "Remember that you are dust and to dust you shall return," that quotation from Genesis 3:19 is not a pretty flourish that furnishes a stylish opening to the Lenten season. The imposition of ashes is fundamental. The penitential season before Easter begins with the insight that those assembled are nothing but dust—the dust of dead stars. Christians owe that insight to Israel's sober-mindedness. It was faithfully maintained by that little nation and its theologians in the face of the excessive cult of the dead practiced by the nations around it. Without that insight from Israel there would be no Easter joy.

Furthermore: Christians will always bear ancient Israel's joy in this life within their hearts. They must never desire to escape this world in order to be with God or make Christianity a mere religion of the afterlife. Christians are only with God when they are totally in this world; they only do the will of God when they love this world, help to build it up, and refuse to dream of worlds behind the world. Otherwise they deserve Heinrich Heine's ridicule in his verse epic *Deutschland. Ein Wintermärchen* (1844):

> A little maiden sang to the harp;
> Real feeling her song was conveying,
> Though false was her voice, and yet I felt
> Deep moved at hearing her playing.

> She sang of love, and she sang of love's woes,
> Of sacrifices, and meeting
> Again on high, in yon better world
> Where vanish our sorrows so fleeting.

> She sang of this earthly valley of tears,
> Of joys which so soon have vanish'd,

Of yonder, where revels the glorified soul
In eternal bliss, grief being banish'd.

The song of renunciation she sang,
The heavenly eiapopeia,
Wherewith the people, the booby throng
Are hush'd when they soothing require.

I know the tune, and I know the text,
I know the people who wrote it;
I know that in secret they drink but wine,
And in public a wickedness vote it.

A song, friends, that's new, and a better one, too,
Shall be now for your benefit given!
Our object is, that here on earth
We may mount to the realms of heaven.

On earth we fain would happy be,
Nor starve for the sake of the stronger;
The idle stomach shall gorge itself
With the fruit of hard labour no longer.

Bread grows on earth for every one,
Enough, and e'en in redundance,
And roses and myrtles, beauty and joy,
And sugarplums too in abundance.

Yes, sugarplums for every one,
As soon as the plums are provided;
To angels and sparrows we're quite content
That heaven should be confided.[1]

A Christian who takes seriously Israel's worldliness and its incorruptible view of life and history will be able to evaluate Heine's mockery—what is wrong with it, and what is right—and will join in his laughter.

It is true that there has always been some distancing from the world and even flight from it among Christians, especially when a secularism that divinizes the world becomes dominant, or when a contempt for this world derived from other religions has made its way into Christianity. But Docetism, Gnosis, Manichaeism, and many other types of other-worldliness are not based on biblical faith. They have penetrated Christianity from outside.

It is anything but accidental that all or nearly all the heretics and false teachers who have tried to render Christian faith hostile to the world have also attacked the Old Testament. They have sensed that Israel's implacable this-worldliness was an obstacle to them. How different was the case of Dietrich Bonhoeffer! He wrote in a letter from the Tegel prison in Berlin on the second Sunday of Advent 1943, about a year before he was executed on orders from Adolf Hitler,

> I notice more and more how much I am thinking and perceiving things in line with the Old Testament; thus in recent months I have been reading much more the Old than the New Testament. . . . Only when one loves life and the earth so much that with it everything seems to be lost and at its end may one believe in the resurrection of the dead and a new world.[2]

Finally: It is part of the fervent this-worldliness of the Old Testament that it is always concerned with the whole person: spirit and body, happiness and hard work, love and passions. A member of the people of God can be passionate because the people's God is also passionate. She can burn with anger, be aflame with love, and celebrate glorious festivals before her God—festivals full of joy and bliss. The verses of the Song of Songs swell with images of worldly love that then, within the Song, become images of the love between God and God's people:[3]

> Set me as a seal upon your heart,
>   as a seal upon your arm;
>   for love is strong as death,
>   passion fierce as the underworld.
>   Its flashes are flashes of fire,
>   a raging flame.
> Mighty waters cannot quench love,
>   neither can floods sweep it away. (Song 8:6-7)

All that has to enter into faith in the resurrection; otherwise it would be a bloodless misery. In part 4 of this book I will return to the subject. At this point I only want to make the point that Israel had to go through an epoch of pure worldlinesss so that its this-worldly thinking would remain an enduring inheritance for Jewish-Christian faith.

The way in which the Old Testament people of God slowly found its path to faith in an eternal life with God, through steady distancing from the religions of its surrounding world, was complex. If we contemplate this history we can also see the "outside" of revelation. We sense how revelation really happens: not through dictation from heaven but on the real basis of a people that entrusts itself to God and lets itself be led by God, ceaselessly observing, comparing, criticizing, sifting—at the same time repeatedly investigating its own history and, when necessary, seeing it with new eyes. That is the way of revelation. That is the only way in which God speaks to the world, and in that sense Christians also believe in the self-revealing, true, and only God.

PART THREE

What Entered the World in Jesus

1

Jesus' Preaching

It is probably clear by now how "revelation" took place in Israel: not as apocalyptic drama, not in a cosmic scenario with trumpets, lightning bolts, and other special effects, but as *discovery*—indeed, as discovery over long periods of time, as a process of deeper and deeper understanding—through the open eyes of men and women who entrusted God with their whole existence and allowed themselves to be led by God. Everyone with any understanding will know that such discovery has to be dramatically shaped and decked in attractive colors for the purposes of narrative. Events that take place over centuries cannot be told in any other way.

Israel's stepwise movement toward understanding was, however, not a mere intellectual approach to the truth that is God. God revealed God's own self by bringing Israel out from unfreedom in Egypt into a new form of human community of life in which there was to be freedom, mutual aid, brotherly and sisterly common life. Thus the catalyst and enduring basis for all discovery was a saving act of God—or, to put it in more general terms, a historical event through which God was shown to be the liberator.

Such events of deliverance then run throughout all of Israel's history. The Old Testament tells of them over and over again. It is true that a comparative and distinguishing perception and an analysis that distanced Israel from its religious surroundings played an important role. But the basis for all that perception and recognition was the historical reality, the history through which God spoke to God's people.

It would be exactly the same with Jesus, the culmination and pinnacle of all Israel's discovery of truth. In him also, God's reality was shown in historical happening, but now in such a way that in him God's word became "flesh," that is, real human history—totally, definitively, and forever. What Jesus said, God said. What he did was God's doing. Whoever saw Jesus saw the Father. The reality of God's own self had now become visible, palpable, touchable reality. The first letter of John expresses this incomparable experience when it says:

> We declare to you . . . what we have heard, what we have seen with our eyes, what we have looked at and touched with our hands: the *Logos* of life. (1 John 1:1)

What is decisive is that at this absolute pinnacle of all knowledge in Israel what had been discovered in all the previous centuries was in no way repressed, superseded, or made superfluous. Rather, it was taken up and affirmed—in that it was clarified and deepened by Jesus.

Recall once more Israel's sober and illusionless love for earthly reality that was described so fully in part 2 of this book. Israel's urgent attention to the world continues in Jesus. He by no means points to a world outside this one. He demands no divorce from the world. He does not offer pie in the sky. Rather, he proclaims the coming of the reign of God. We have to remember what that means. Jesus did *not* preach:

> This world is a bridge. No one sits down on a bridge. Hurry across the narrow bridge of this life to eternal life with God.

Later on, people put such words into the mouth of Jesus,* but he himself never talked that way. Nor did he preach:

---

* An Arabic inscription in the ruined city of Fatehpur-Sikri south of Delhi reads: "Jesus, on whom be peace, has said: 'This world is a bridge. Pass over it. But build not your dwelling there.'" For this supposed saying of Jesus see Joachim Jeremias, *Unknown Sayings of Jesus*, trans. Reginald H. Fuller (Eugene, OR: Wipf & Stock, 1957), 99.

This life is only appearance. Seek true being, true life, the other world.

And he did not say:

I proclaim to you the resurrection to come. Life in this earthly vale of tears is but a prologue, a test, the time of screening for eternal life after death.

No matter how familiar such echoes from particular marginal branches of later edifying Christian literature may sound, sayings like these do no justice to Jesus' preaching. Jesus announces the reign of God, and God's reign has a far broader scope than life after death.

We need to keep in mind that the Our Father, the model prayer Jesus shaped for his disciples, says nothing about death or the beyond or the resurrection of the dead. It prays for the hallowing of God's name and the coming of the reign of God. But how can God's name be hallowed? It is hallowed when Israel becomes a people that honors God.[1] The background lies in Ezekiel 36:16-28. And where is the reign of God supposed to come? In this world, naturally: on this earth, in this history. The evangelist Mark summarizes all of Jesus' preaching in a single saying:

The reign of God has come near. Repent and believe in the good news. (Mark 1:14-15)

Again, this very precise summary of Jesus' message says nothing about resurrection. In fact, the word "resurrection" appears only marginally in Jesus' sayings and discourses. For Jesus the resurrection of the dead is integrated into the much greater and more powerful theme "reign of God." But what is "the reign of God"? What is "God's royal rule"?

The reign of God is the final and ultimate coming of God's saving self-donation in this world. That is why the proclamation of the reign of God is "Gospel" (*evangelium*), that is, "good news." But because the world is resistant to God and God's Gospel, this coming of God is always also a judgment on it[2]—a judgment, however, that does not destroy but leads to decision, clarification that leads to the truth and builds up. The coming of the reign of God transforms the world and makes it what it was always meant to be according to God's will.

Thus "reign of God" or "God's royal rule" is an event that transforms the world. The reign of God "comes" in this world, and not just sometime or other. It comes now, for Jesus "announces" God's rule, "proclaims" it. Jesus' disciples are supposed, literally, to "shout out" its coming in the squares and streets.[3] But what is promised and proclaimed is not something still far away, in the nebulous future. It is near. It is about to happen. It is hastening.

Jesus can even go further; he can say: where God's rule is seen and accepted, it is already present. So there is tension between "already" and "not yet": the rule of God is certainly not yet established everywhere. It has not yet reached everyone and many do not grasp it at all. That is why we have to pray for its coming. But it is no longer far away, because in Jesus himself, his words and deeds, it is already present, and many are already following Jesus or turning to the Gospel.

To understand more precisely what God's royal rule is about, one must read Jesus' similitudes and parables,* which are all about the mystery of the reign of God. Certainly, after Easter these parables of Jesus were often applied to current events and the situation of the early church. That was very much justified: every proclamation has to bring the existing text into the present if it is to remain a living word. But historians also have the right to work out the oldest form of a text. In the case of Jesus' parables and similitudes that leads us again and again to the theme of the approach or even the presence of the reign of God.

Thus, for example, Jesus tells about a successful burglary. The thief is skillful; he knew how to get into the house. But the owner also made it easy for him by not securing his house adequately. First and foremost: no one was on guard. The original similitude, which is easily reconstructed,[4] ends with Jesus' victory shout: "if the owner of the house had known that his house would be broken into he would certainly have locked and guarded it. But he did not know it, and so the break-in succeeded" (cp. Luke 12:39).

---

* In technical terms, similitudes are based on real-life situations; parables are about "exemplary" or highly unusual scenarios. We commonly refer to them all as "parables."

The early church later interpreted this seditious similitude as referring to Jesus' return: Christians should be awake and ready to receive their Lord when he comes again. But originally the similitude was about the coming of the reign of God. It has already come. It has broken into the spaces of the old society. Of course, the world would have defended itself, secured itself against what was coming, and still it was surprised. The break-in succeeded.

Jesus certainly had no hesitation about illustrating the surprising arrival of the reign of God with immoral scenarios. Of course, Jesus is not a burglar, but he, and with him the reign of God, came as surprisingly and unexpectedly *as* a burglar.

The similitude of the treasure in the field works with completely different material. A day-laborer, while plowing, comes upon a buried treasure—probably a clay pot filled with silver coins. He covers it again with dirt, goes away rejoicing, sells everything he has, and buys the field (Matt 13:44). He is certain that, under the law, the treasure belongs to him. Here again, this is about the reign of God. It is valuable; it is beyond price. It is worth giving everything to obtain it. Whoever does so makes the best deal of her or his life—because obviously the day-laborer is not going to leave the treasure in the ground. As soon as he owns the field he will dig up the silver. So the reign of God is already present. We can already find it, already own it.

In still another similitude Jesus compares the reign of God to a mustard seed that grows into a huge bush (Mark 4:30-32). In Jesus' home region around the Sea of Gennesareth a mustard bush can grow to be as much as twelve feet tall, and the beginning is a tiny seed, no bigger than the head of a pin. So it is with the reign of God, Jesus says. At present it is not impressive, but it is already growing.

The similitude is not just about "small" and "large." It is just as important, we see, that Jesus chooses his material from the world familiar to his listeners. He takes it literally from the vegetable garden (see Mark 4:32). And of course that is no accident. Jesus wants to tell his hearers that the reign of God does not take place in the distant future, and most certainly not in an earth-shaking storm, but here and now, in the world you know, in your everyday surroundings—among you.

The similitude of the leaven (Matt 13:33) argues similarly, again using the secular, ordinary world. A woman kneads leaven into a great quantity of flour, covers the dough with a cloth, lets it rise—and in a few hours the leaven has transformed the whole mass of flour. Here again the contrast between the tiny amount of leaven and the large amount of flour plays a role, but there is something else as well: the leaven permeates and transforms the dough. That is how the bread rises and becomes tasty. In the very same way, Jesus says, the reign of God will permeate the world and transform it into something that "tastes" wonderful.

Of course, many of Jesus' listeners asked: Is all that really so? Then where is the reign of God? Doesn't the reality in which we are living look completely different? The poor are oppressed, the hungry are not fed, the sorrowing are not comforted, the weeping have nothing to laugh about, the rich don't think for a minute of sharing with the poor in the land, and the powerful are not being cast down from their thrones.

Jesus counters such objections with the similitude of the sower (Mark 4:3-9). This, the most realistic of all Jesus' similitudes, describes the "impossibility" of God's cause. The seed cast by the sower falls into a world full of enemies: flocks of birds descend on it and peck it up; rocky soil lets the sprouting seeds wither; thorns and thistles choke the grain even if it succeeds in growing a little. That is the reality, Jesus says. But it is not the whole reality, for part of the seed falls on good ground, the grains divide into several stalks,[5] and so, despite all the obstacles and enemies, a rich harvest is reaped.

In another similitude Jesus even tells of how the seed ripens *unstoppably* (Mark 4:26-29). Someone has sowed, and the seed sprouts: first the stalk, then the head, then the ripe grain in the head. The sower goes to sleep at night, wakes up in the morning, goes to bed again—the wheat grows "of itself." And then, one day, the harvest is ready. This similitude is about the inherent power of the reign of God. One must not use violence to bring it about, as do the Zealots, the God-warriors of the time. It comes without violence of any kind.

Of course, Jesus would not have been Jesus if he had not set some very different texts dialectically against the similitude of the seed growing of itself—similitudes that challenge people to be smart and daring in view of the coming of the reign of God, demand that they risk their lives and gamble everything on a single throw of the dice.[6] These include, for example, the story of the talents (Matt 25:14-30) or the one about the corrupt manager (Luke 16:1-7).

Surely it is clear by now what the absolute center of Jesus' preaching was: not simply the afterlife! Not simply heaven! Of course, Matthew's use of the phrase "kingdom of heaven" has been misleading, but in early Judaism the expression "heaven" or "the heavens" was a circumlocution for God. So "the kingdom of heaven" is exactly the same as "the reign of God" and "God's royal rule." For Jesus, it was all about the rule of the holy God here on this earth—a reign that, of course, is something completely different from human self-glorification. The reign of God has no other purpose than to lead creation freely into what God means it to be: a world of justice and peace—and all that not as an event that will only happen at the end of the world, but as an overturning of all circumstances, a revolution that began with Jesus, in the midst of Israel, and since then quietly and unstoppably changes everything.

Certainly the horizon of this reign of God is immeasurable: God's revolution also eliminates death and leads in the end to an eternal life with God. But it begins here, on this earth, and it is about this world because from the very beginning God's intent was nothing other than the world. From that point of view the "world" of resurrection can be nothing other than the perfected, healed, and sanctified world in which we now live. To misuse or deny that is to slander Jesus' message and corrupt it.

2

Jesus' Deeds of Power

Certainly, Jesus not only preached; he acted. He called disciples to follow him and sent them out to gather and unite all Israel in the reign of God. He ate with outsiders and sinners because the reign of God is for everyone. He forgave wrongdoers. He healed the sick.

All that corresponds precisely to his preaching. It mirrors the reign of God that is now coming. It shows itself not only in words but equally in striking signs. When John the Baptizer, in prison, sends emissaries to Jesus to ask him: "Are you the one who is to come, or are we to wait for another?" Jesus says to tell the Baptizer:

> "Go and tell John what you hear and see: the blind receive their sight, the lame walk, the lepers are cleansed, the deaf hear, the dead are raised, and the poor have good news brought to them." (Matt 11:4-5)

The reign of God, which comes with Jesus and fulfills what Israel's prophets had said, changes not only hearts and minds. When the reign of God comes, not only will blindness of hearts be taken away, but those who are physically blind will see again, those who are now crippled will be able to walk, the hard-of-hearing and the deaf will hear again. The reign of God changes all conditions, it transforms society and the world. Healing and saving, it encompasses bodies, too, and it even attacks death.

The degree to which this was about real conditions in Israel's society is indicated by the many lepers Jesus heals.[1] Leprosy shattered society in those times.* Lepers had to leave their villages, live separately, and keep healthy people at a distance by shouting "unclean! unclean!" before they could get close (Lev 13:45). When Jesus healed lepers he not only freed them from the creeping horrors of their disease but, above all, from social isolation.

Something similar is true of his healings of people who were "possessed."[2] Nearly every illness that people in those days could not explain was regarded as the work of evil spirits who—so it was imagined—entered through the apertures of the human body, took control of it, dominated and tormented it. The person affected—it was thought—was no longer master of himself or herself but was the property of the demon, driven and directed by it.

We smile at such ideas and forget how many illnesses even among us are not simply organic. Not infrequently they are caused by outward or inward pressures against which the victims are often helpless.[3] Evil can also play a role in such compulsions—lodged within the sick person, but primarily coming from what is demonic and chaotic in society. These things can literally "occupy" people and "take possession" of them.

The cases of the "possessed" whom Jesus healed must in many instances have been about such social pressures. They seized the sick person "from outside" and manifested themselves in compulsive actions. Even sensible people could be helpless in the face of such forces. Jesus gave these "possessed" people back their freedom. Christians today must finally learn not to stop their ears and feel ashamed when the gospels speak of Jesus' expulsion of demons; they need to understand the full vehemence and realism of his powerful therapies.

Still more important, however, is the fact that in Israel's understanding all illnesses, all suffering, and all individual crisis situations

* The Hebrew concept of *tzaraath* (Greek *lepra*) encompassed a number of skin diseases.

were already bound up with the sphere of death. Someone severely ill was already marked, had already moved closer to the underworld, was in the grip of the power of *Sheol*. Many texts of the Old Testament indicate that. In their prayers the sick, despised, and shunned could say:

> . . . the cords of the underworld entangled me;
> the snares of death confronted me. (Ps 18:6)

or:

> . . . my soul is sated with troubles, and my life draws near to Sheol. I am already counted among those who go down to the Pit; I am like those who have no strength left. (Ps 88:4-5)

Contrariwise, those healed of a severe illness could say:

> O LORD my God, I cried to you for help, and you have healed me.
> O LORD, you brought up my soul from the realm of death, re-stored me to life from among those gone down to the Pit.
> (Ps 30:2-3)

Thus in the Old Testament every serious illness is already death, being absorbed into the sphere of the underworld's power. It is only in this perspective that Jesus' many healings reveal their true face. When Jesus acts against sickness he is attacking death. When he heals he is already overcoming death.

This precisely is the basis for Jesus' raising of dead persons. The raising of Jairus's daughter (Mark 5:21-43) or of the young man of Nain (Luke 7:11-17) were consistent and continuous with what Jesus had already done in healing many others. Therefore it is a less-than-convincing compromise for many exegetes to regard Jesus' healing miracles as historical but to see his raising of the dead as free invention by the early church. That kind of exegesis separates texts that are profoundly connected—and then historical judgments are made on the basis of supposedly different narrative genres. There is a failure to understand what incurable illnesses, severe depressions, and compulsions that rob people of their freedom mean at their theo-logical depths: namely, that they are already morsels of death.

Overall, Jesus' mighty deeds reveal the same thing as his preaching: the reign of God, longed for and prayed for in Israel, is now present, and its intent is to change not only hearts and minds, but with them the real conditions in Israel—and through Israel, in the whole world. Jesus must have preached *and* acted with an unheard-of "authority" (Mark 1:22, 27).

3

Jesus' Powerlessness

The gospels speak, and rightly so, about Jesus' "deeds of power," for example in Mark 6:2, 5, and yet, at the same time, Jesus was powerless. The gospels speak of that, too. In this chapter I want to show that his powerlessness was not a marginal phenomenon that appeared occasionally and at random; rather, it was central and compelling. Jesus' powerlessness was fully harmonious with his message. But first, the facts!

Jesus was powerless against the multifarious calumnies his opponents spread against him. Because it happened again and again that he sat at table with so-called public sinners and the outcasts of society, they gossiped about him, saying he was a "glutton and a drunkard," a "friend of tax collectors and sinners" (Matt 11:19). Because he was unmarried there were whispers that he was a *castratus*, a eunuch. Jesus defended himself against these slanders by saying that there are people who have castrated themselves for the sake of the reign of God (Matt 19:12)—meaning those who are *voluntarily celibate* for the sake of God's reign. The worst and most demeaning thing said against him, however, was that he was possessed by the devil and that he expelled demons with the aid of the head of all demons (Mark 3:22). This was supposed to expose Jesus as a devilish seducer of

Israel and undermine trust in him—the trust, in particular, of the "little ones," the poor and uneducated, who followed Jesus.

So it is no wonder that in this very context we find the sharpest and roughest words we have received from Jesus:

> "If any of you put a stumbling block before one of these 'little ones' who believe in me [that is, if you destroy someone's faith in my mission], it would be better for you if a great millstone [*lit.: a donkey's millstone*] were hung around your neck and you were thrown into the sea." (Mark 9:42)

A donkey's millstone was a round stone weighing about a hundred pounds. It was the upper millstone, turned on top of the lower stone by a donkey walking around it in a circle. The "little ones" here are most certainly not children, but the theologically uneducated who ran after Jesus and put all their hopes in him. The reference may even be to Jesus' disciples. The "sea" is the Sea of Gennesareth. The hardness of the saying about the millstone shows how pressured Jesus was and how powerless he felt against the net of smears being laid against him.

But Jesus was also powerless when—apart from all the aspersions—he encountered deep-seated unbelief. One day when he came to Nazareth, the place of his origins where his relatives lived, he experienced curt rejection, and so he could not heal any of the sick people there (Mark 6:1-6).* Jesus' deeds of power were therefore not automatic. Their prerequisite was faith, trust, and a will to repentance. In the face of arrogant and narrow-minded people, Jesus was powerless.

He was also powerless when his disciples did not understand him and turned away. According to John 6:66, one day "many of his disciples" left him and no longer followed him. Judas Iscariot, one of the Twelve, in the end delivered him up to the Sanhedrin. Simon, whom Jesus called "rock," denied him, and all the rest of the Twelve fled.

---

* The historical situation is probably reflected accurately in Mark 6:5, "and he could do no deed of power there." The rest of the verse tries to rescue Jesus' divine power to work miracles.

Finally, Jesus was powerless before and during his execution. The Sanhedrin, the highest religious court in Israel, handed him over to the Roman occupiers, accusing him of being a political insurrectionist, and the Roman prefect, Pontius Pilate, had him crucified for the sake of his own career, because the Jewish side had threatened to complain to the Emperor about him. Jesus fell between the millstones of power, which were stronger than he. He had to suffer crucifixion, one of the most brutal and horrible tortures ever conceived by the human mind. As he was hanging on the cross, the ancient beam of destruction, the high priests and scribes mocked him:

> "He saved others; he cannot save himself. Let the [supposed] Messiah, the King of Israel, come down from the cross now, so that we may see and believe." (Mark 15:31-32)

Jesus did not descend from the cross. He was powerless, delivered up to his opponents. There was a false and erroneous form of Christianity that refused to accept that. As early as the second century the evil flower of Docetism put out its shoots. This was a belief that what hung on the cross was only the appearance of a body. Of course, the real Jesus was not miserably crucified, because the Son of God certainly could not suffer! Islam still maintains this Docetic heresy when it says of the prophet Isa (= Jesus) that he was confused with someone else, that Jesus did not die on the cross.[1]

For Judaism, too, a crucified Messiah is simply unacceptable. The great Jewish scholar Moses Maimonides (ca. 1135–1204) listed criteria with the aid of which one might distinguish the true Messiah from pretenders. Clearly, for Maimonides, success was among those criteria. No one can withstand the true Messiah; in his lifetime he will gather all Israel, lead it into freedom, rebuild the Temple, see to it that all Jews follow the Torah, and establish peace throughout the world.[2]

Fundamentally, this image of the successful Messiah includes force and violence—perhaps extremely sublimated, but there. Jesus is profoundly different from this image of what is messianic, and he is just as deeply different from Muhammad. Jesus experienced failures, powerlessness, weakness. He lost some of his disciples and he could not persuade his opponents. Jerusalem did not become a place of spiritual triumph; it is where they killed him. But above all: Jesus categorically refused to use violence.

Jesus' powerlessness was rooted in freedom. God takes human freedom with the utmost seriousness and will not manipulate it, not even through subtle moral violence, which, as we know, is much worse than open coercion. Every form of coercion is foreign to the reign of God. It is no accident that on many occasions Jesus unmistakably set himself apart from the Jewish Zealots, who wanted to bring about the reign of God by violence. The disciples he sent out were not allowed to carry weapons, or money, or a staff; they could not even be shod with sandals that might make it easier for them to attack swiftly or run away on Israel's stony paths.[3]

The absolute nonviolence* Jesus lived, and that he also demanded of his followers, resulted in powerlessness, to the point of apparent impotence. Jesus' powerlessness relies entirely on God and God's saving intervention, and for that very reason it is stronger than all weapons, all forms of violence, any and every need to overpower others.

Jesus' battle against the powers of death did not culminate in his avoiding death but in his complete surrender to human violence, to the point of utter helplessness. Yet he still relied on God without reservation as he was so horribly executed.** The "Apostles' Creed" in its current Latin and one English version reads:

passus sub Pontio Pilato,	He suffered under Pontius Pilate
crucifixus, mortuus, et sepultus,	was crucified, died, and was buried.
descendit ad inferos	He descended to the dead,

---

*Jesus' action in the Temple (Mark 11:15-19; John 2:13-22) is constantly adduced as a counterargument, but that was a sign-action that had absolutely nothing to do with the ideology of violence.

** "My God, my God, why have you abandoned me?" (Mark 15:34) is not a cry of dereliction, as is so often asserted, but the beginning of Psalm 22. Jesus prayed that Psalm on the cross as his dying prayer. The fact that he was really praying the Psalm is attested by his saying *eli atta* ("you are my God," Ps 22:11), which the bystanders heard as *eliyya ta* ("Elijah, come," see Mark 15:35).

Descendit ad inferos means Jesus' descent to the *inferi*, that is, "those in the underworld," or simply "to the dead." Such translations as "to the place of the dead" or "into hell" are not only inexact but false, because they make people who know very little of ancient Near Eastern thought or ancient mythology in general think of the realm of the gods (or devils) of the underworld. But at this point* the creed only means to say that Jesus suffered death to its fullest. In the language of his time that meant: to the deepest part of the underworld. It meant that he had to suffer death powerlessly, helplessly, and to its darkest depth. It was in that way and no other that death was overcome.

None of that contradicts Jesus' message about the unstoppable growth of the reign of God. That reign comes in the way God acts: for the most part quietly, and always *incognito*; we might also say: through a "quiet" revolution of which many are totally unaware. God does not touch human freedom. And Jesus was aware of the circumstances: he speaks about the silent and imperceptible growth of seed (Mark 4:26-29), and still more, he also speaks in his similitudes of the powerful forces of resistance against the reign of God (Mark 4:3-9).

Everything that has been said in this chapter will be important for parts 4 and 5 of this book. In death, every Christian and, indeed, every human being will at first, like Jesus, be thrown into an ultimate powerlessness. Death is by no means the high point of life at which one reaches the pinnacle of one's freedom. It is misery, suffering, and being handed over. But in that very way it means ultimate closeness to Jesus.

---

*Here we cannot go into the soteriological interpretations associated even in the ancient church with Jesus' descent to the underworld (liberation of the righteous who died before Jesus, etc.) and up to and including the theology of Hans Urs von Balthasar.

4

Jesus' Resurrection

From a purely human point of view Jesus' miserable death should
have put an end to his cause. "We find a whole series of charismatic-
messianic movements in the first and second centuries CE for which
the violent death of the leader meant the end of the movement itself."[1]
That was precisely the pattern according to which things developed
immediately after Jesus' execution. Many of the disciples had fled,
returning to their homes in Galilee (Mark 16:7). They were already
beginning to resume their former work (John 21:3). Jesus' disciples
in Jerusalem remained hidden within the city. We may well suppose
that they were all utterly appalled and profoundly disappointed,
perplexed, and subject to resignation as they hesitantly began to
return to normal daily life.

The Emmaus story probably reflects this mood very accurately,
namely, in the conversations of two disciples of Jesus whose hopes
have been destroyed, who are sorrowing, baffled, and simply going
away. They say to the unknown person who encounters them on the
way:

> [Jesus] was a prophet mighty in deed and word before God and
> all the people. But our chief priests and leaders handed him over
> to be condemned to death and crucified. But we had hoped that
> he was the one to redeem Israel. (Luke 24:19-21)

The unknown traveler penetrates their resignation, showing them that he is the risen Jesus. The encounter with him opens the disciples' eyes and causes them to get up right away and return to Jerusalem, where they learn that

> the Lord has risen indeed, and he has appeared to Simon!
> (Luke 24:34)

Luke's Emmaus story is based on a concrete Easter appearance (the name of one of the two disciples is given), but it is a literary consolidation of many other such appearances, all of them encounters with the risen Jesus. They occurred in the midst of everyday life, they were unexpected, they took place over a long period of time, happening to very different persons and against all hope. They had nothing to do with deceit or delusion, or with construction and speculation.[2]

There are a number of theologians nowadays for whom the fact that the gospels speak of "appearances" of the Risen One is simply embarrassing. They either say that there were no "appearances" in the strict sense, but only "disclosures," a category that might contain practically anything except the solidity of the things told of in the gospels and affirmed in what Paul says of himself (1 Cor 9:1; 15:8; Gal 1:15-16), or else they think of visionary phenomena that can be dismissed as purely psychogenic and equated with hallucinations or mass psychosis. *In this form* neither does justice to the events.

Those who find "appearances" embarrassing because the average enlightened person receives none and thinks they are "silly" show that they have no knowledge of the differences among cultures. There have been cultures in which visionary phenomena were widespread. Simply to dismiss those cultures (and with them, for example, Paul[3]) because we do not know of any such thing in our own experience is pure cultural imperialism.

Obviously visions and appearances always have something to do with the human unconscious, where so many things are stored: fears, longings, images of hope, and past experiences. Who can deny it? But God (and in this case the Risen One himself) can communicate, show, even reveal the divine self precisely by means of all these "human" things and what people have "made" in their deepest dimensions. In such cases it is God and the risen Jesus who are the real agents, but they act in such a way that human "action" is not suppressed. To deny this indissoluble interpenetration of divine self-communication and the human way of shaping it is to call into question the whole theology of grace, for grace always presumes nature and history. God acts, always and without exception, through secondary causes.[4] The principle of the doctrine of grace, that God's action does not destroy human action but makes it free,[5] must be taken seriously in regard to the Easter appearances. To that degree, of course, the concept of "experiences of disclosure" is not wrong, but that concept must not deny the historicity of the visionary phenomena. Otherwise it goes off the rails. Both historians and theologians can with good conscience conclude that the Easter appearances really happened.

The result of those appearances was that the motion of Jesus' fleeing followers was reversed and, at the latest by Pentecost, the next great pilgrimage feast, they were again gathered in Jerusalem. From then on they lived on the basis of those Easter encounters with Jesus. They preached and witnessed with their whole existence that "God has raised Jesus from the dead."[6]

At this point it is necessary to reflect more precisely on the content of the Easter experience of the first witnesses and the proclamation that resulted. For the Easter experience and the Easter message are foundational for Christian faith. What exactly does it mean to say "God has raised Jesus from the dead"? Not:

In Jesus the divine has broken through,

or:

In Jesus, the immortal has conquered death,

or:

His soul has freed itself from the body and risen aloft into the ether.

In antiquity, in the time of Jesus, all those things could have been hoped for and said, but they are precisely what Jesus' followers did *not* say. They were not Greeks, but Jews. And because they were Jews and knew the Scriptures they took death seriously—with that extremely sober attitude toward reality that we spoke of at such length in part 2 of this book. They could never have arrived at the notion that what was naturally immortal in Jesus had been maintained. They could not imagine simply a continued life of his soul, on the Platonic model[7]—a soul with which they could then have entered into communication. Jesus was executed on the cross, he was dead, he was buried (1 Cor 15:4)—and for them, as Jews, that was an unavoidable reality.

The Easter narratives in the gospels also show that the encounters with the Risen One were events completely unexpected by his disciples. They could understand the whole thing only as God's act of deliverance done for Jesus. As God had so often acted in Israel, liberating the people from Egypt and again and again rescuing them from death, so now God had rescued Jesus. But as we have said, that knowledge was not merely the fruit of theological construction or unconscious coping mechanisms; it arose out of the real experience of encounter with the Risen One.

The narratives of those encounters are remarkable for still another reason. They all contain features of a drastic, positively disturbing physicality on the part of Jesus. He walks with the two disciples to Emmaus (Luke 24:15), breaks bread with them in the house (Luke 24:30); standing on the lakeshore, he instructs the men with Peter about fishing (John 21:6), then broils the fish they have caught for their breakfast (John 21:10).[8] Elsewhere he shows the gathering his hands and his side (John 20:20), and invites the doubtful Thomas to place his hand in the wound in his side (John 20:27).

Such drastic physicality is alienating to us today. But we can see it as an attempt to do justice to the experience of the real physicality of the Risen One. The witnesses of the Risen One did not encounter a ghost, a soul detached from its body, but Jesus, raised by God and present to them with his whole history, with everything that made him who he is, with spirit, soul, and body. Here also the disciples remained faithful to the experiences and the sober-mindedness of Israel.

Rigorous insistence on the physicality of the Risen One saved Christian faith from succumbing to a basic dogma of many Greeks: that salvation is liberation from the body, and paradise is characterized by bodilessness. We find an especially revealing witness to this feature of ancient thought in the satirist Lucian of Samosata (second century CE). He depicts the bodilessness of the saved, who live on the "Isle of the Blest," as follows:

> For clothing they use delicate purple spider-webs. As for them-selves, they have no bodies, but are intangible and fleshless, with only shape and figure. Incorporeal as they are, they nevertheless live and move and think and talk. In a word, it would appear that their naked souls go about in the semblance of their bodies. Really, if one did not touch them, he could not tell that what he saw was not a body, for they are like upright shadows, only not black.[9]

Of course, Lucian's text here, as throughout his description of the "Isle of the Blest," drips with irony as the satirist mocks all these ideas. Still, the text is for that very reason a clear indication that for many Greeks embodiedness beyond death was unthinkable. The gospels of Luke and John tell of the appearances of the Risen One as deliberate contrast with this late Greek thought. The Risen One is *not* described as quasi-disembodied; he has "flesh and bones." He shows the disciples his "hands and feet." He urges them to touch him; in-deed, he even asks them to give him something to eat, and before their eyes he consumes "a piece of broiled fish" (Luke 24:36-43).

Anyone who, in the face of such a scandalous realism, begins to wonder what happened to the piece of fish afterward is starting out on the wrong track. Luke's shocking description is directed against every kind of false spiritualizing. The evangelist means to tell the readers that rescue from death is more than a mere spiritual event. The whole person is redeemed, not only her or his spirit. What is saved is not a bloodless soul but our whole life-history, our flesh and blood, everything we have been.

It was as such a "whole" that the first witnesses experienced the Risen One. They knew him as the one with whom they had traveled through Galilee, the one who had taught and led them. They experi-enced him as the one who had been crucified. Therefore the Risen One also bore the wounds of his passion in his body. He retained them as glorified wounds, because resurrection means that every instant a person has lived bears fruit in eternal life with God. That is why later Christian iconography always depicted the Risen One in his fully embodied self—with all the wounds that had been inflicted on him. That corresponded exactly to the shocking experience of the Easter witnesses, an experience they could never have invented.

One more important detail is that Christian liturgy, in the "Exsultet" sung at the Easter Vigil, locates God's action in delivering Jesus in relationship with the deliverance of Israel from the Reed Sea. This is *the* night—so the "Exsultet" song declares—in which the Israelites were rescued through the waters, and in which Jesus sprang up from the depths of death. It is true that Jesus' resurrection is something outside all history. It no longer takes place in space and time. But it transforms and summarizes Jesus' whole history before God and is manifested in the midst of history. To that extent it can be compared with and sung together with God's great foundational deed of deliverance for Israel.

5

The Firstborn from the Dead

The previous chapter was primarily about the historical backgrounds of Easter, as well as a central point of the Easter experience: the physicality of the Risen One. But a crucial point was not really addressed, namely, the imaginative schema or form within which the Easter event was grasped by the first witnesses. *What* was it that the disciples experienced in the Easter appearances; *what* was it that they saw as having happened to Jesus?

This question is not often posed,[1] because the answer seems so obvious: the disciples experienced Jesus as having been *raised from the dead*. In reality there is nothing obvious about it, because Judaism in Jesus' time possessed a number of different forms in which the disciples could have expressed their Easter experiences.

However, if we put it that way we are covering up a crucial issue. The first witnesses were not faced with the didactic question of how they should express or formulate their Easter experiences. Instead, the experience compelled them to speak. It came over them in their encounters with Jesus, who showed himself to them. When they said "God raised him from the dead" it was not some secondary formula but evidently a necessary and even imperative expression of what they had experienced in and through Jesus. Could they have experienced it in other ways? Of course!

For example, in the Old Testament and early Judaism there was an idea that the discipline of religious studies calls "being taken up" or "rapture." It is not so much an idea as a complex of ideas; we can describe it more or less as follows:[2]

A person who has received a special commission from God, who has been taken wholly into service by God and has lived an exemplary life before God is at some point taken up from the world by God and now lives with God. This "rapture" can be vividly described, as in the case of the prophet Elijah, who goes up to heaven before the eyes of his disciple Elisha (2 Kgs 2:11-12). But the taking-up need not necessarily be described; it can be briefly noted that the person in question was "taken" by God. For example, in the case of Enoch:

> Enoch walked with God; then he was no more, because God took him. (Gen 5:24)

What is decisive in the description or statement of a "rapture" is that "he was no more [= no longer visible]." Those taken up by God can no longer be seen or found, even if they are sought for (cp. 2 Kgs 2:15-18). There is no burial or tomb. Because the Old Testament says of Moses that "no one knows his burial place to this day" (Deut 34:6) there were also sayings in early Judaism about Moses' having been taken up, even though Deuteronomy 34:5 clearly says that Moses died. Evidently it was possible for the idea of rapture, which in itself denies the death of the one taken, to be secondarily combined with actual death. For example: the two mysterious witnesses in Revelation 11 are first attacked and killed by the "beast that comes up from the bottomless pit," but then they are given life by God and taken up to heaven in a cloud (Rev 11:7-12).*

What is decisive in the Jewish idea of rapture is that one taken up by God "remains" with God until sent back to earth in the end time. The rapture thus signifies that the person is kept in reserve for an eschatological function and at that time will appear to give witness. We can see how common such ideas were in Jesus' time from the fact that many of the people took Jesus to be John the Baptizer, taken up

---

*The motifs of (1) the presence of witnesses and (2) the cloud as vehicle show that, overall, this is a form of the narrative of "rapture."

to heaven and now returned to earth, or Elijah or one of the other prophets taken up by God (Matt 16:14).*

But what does this Jewish idea of "taking up," which is found in somewhat different forms everywhere in Greek and Roman antiquity, have to do with our subject of Jesus' resurrection? Why am I giving it so much space here?

For this reason: the genuine idea of "rapture" always, without exception, applies to an individual. Such an individual is chosen by God, is sent, is ultimately taken up from earth and preserved, hidden away in God—until that same individual returns to earth with an eschatological mission. How easy it would have been for the first witnesses to allow their Easter experience to be shaped by this pattern!—especially, as we have seen, since death could certainly be integrated into the "rapture" schema.

But the Easter experience was *not* one of Jesus' being taken up, nor was it expressed in that way. It is true that Luke closes his gospel and begins the Acts of the Apostles with a depiction of the last appearance of the Risen One that is influenced by the schema of "taking up": He describes an ascension of Jesus that is quite clearly a "rapture."[3] But in doing so he is merely making use of a literary tool for concluding Jesus' appearances in dramatic fashion—a literary tool that must not be confused with the genuine Easter experience. The Easter event was experienced and formulated as: "God raised Jesus from the dead." The very ancient Christian confession of faith that Paul hands on in 1 Corinthians 15:3-5 reads:

> Christ died for our sins in accordance with the scriptures . . . he was buried, and . . . he was raised on the third day in accordance with the scriptures, and . . . he appeared to Cephas, then to the twelve.

* At least in the case of Elijah and the other prophets it is quite clear that this can only rest on the idea of rapture. John the Baptizer is a more difficult issue. According to Mark 6:14-16 there was an idea in circulation among the people that Jesus was the Baptizer risen from the dead; Herod likewise shared that idea. But there is much to indicate that this Markan formulation reveals Christian influence. If the Jews of his time had really thought Jesus was the Baptizer come again, they could only have imagined it in terms of the rapture-schema. Those taken up by God return to earth *with an eschatological function.*

Paul then lists further eyewitnesses. Here and in the other early testimonies to the resurrection it is not said that Jesus has been taken up into the mystery of God but that he has been raised "from the dead."[4]

There could have been another model available for interpreting the Easter experience, or rather for receiving and internalizing it. Some scholars suppose that in Jesus' time Judaism entertained the idea that God raised martyrs from the dead immediately after death. They refer especially to the account of the martyrdom of the seven brothers and their mother in 2 Maccabees 7 and that of the two witnesses in Revelation 11, as well as to traditions associated with those texts.[5] If this idea can be verified, it means that martyrs did not have to wait for the general resurrection at the end of the world, but because of their testimony in blood they could be taken directly to heaven. That idea too (if it really existed) could have been applied to Jesus. As we will soon see, however, that did not happen.

But first let me point to a third possibility. People could have said: "God *exalted* Jesus to the place at God's right hand (and thus justified him against those who condemned him)." This saying about exaltation was *certainly* available; it was a very good biblical idea (cp. Isa 52:13 LXX; Ps 110:1). In fact, the exaltation saying was widely used in New Testament Christology, and very early[6]—but clearly as a secondary development of the statement of Jesus' resurrection.[7] The oldest Easter confessional formulae are not "Jesus has been exalted to God's right hand" or "God took Jesus [as a martyr] into heaven," and most certainly not "Jesus was taken up to God," but "God raised Jesus from the dead." Why is that so crucially important?

The answer is simply that rapture, being taken up as a martyr, and exaltation are always about an individual. But the resurrection saying is about a collective, namely, the resurrection *of the dead*. And above all, it is an eschatological statement. Resurrection *of the dead* meant, in the Judaism of that time, the beginning of the new messianic world or, apocalyptically, the end of history—but in any case a radical eschatological break. That is why the so common and familiar confession that God raised Jesus from the dead contains the statement that with *his* resurrection the end has already begun; indeed, with his resurrection the general resurrection of the dead has commenced.

Jesus' resurrection is by no means "an exceptional divine action" that simply serves to "legitimate" Jesus.[8] Rather: in Jesus, God began something that affects everything. Evidently both the collective (it is about everything) and the eschatological (it is about the end) are inextricably bound up with the experience of the first Easter witnesses.[9]

The earliest church was thoroughly conscious of the revolutionary character of what had happened. They called Christ "the first fruits of those who have died" (1 Cor 15:20, 23), "the firstborn among many sisters and brothers" (Rom 8:29), "the firstborn from the dead" (Col 1:18; Rev 1:5), and the "author of life" (Acts 3:15). Or they simply said that he was "the first to rise from the dead" (Acts 26:23).

Obviously that means more than a numerical sequence, more than an emphasis on Christ's dignity. It means the indissoluble bond between the resurrection of Jesus and that of all the dead (1 Thess 4:14); indeed, it says that all believers are already involved in the process of Jesus' resurrection (Eph 2:5-6). What that means, and how we ought to imagine it, we will see. It is no accident that the last and therefore the most important chapter in this book is titled "When Does Eternity Begin?"

For the moment we must insist that, precisely because the Easter event in Jesus, at its very origin, was experienced not as rapture nor as the reception of a martyr into heaven nor as exaltation but as resurrection from the dead, it is clear that the resurrection of all the dead, the return home and transformation of the world, God's *new creation* that is the goal of all history—all that has "already" begun in Jesus' resurrection.

6

New Creation

The last sentence of the previous chapter suddenly referred to a "new creation," now appearing alongside "resurrection of the dead." That was deliberate: resurrection is not a natural phenomenon due to human beings as a kind of biological inheritance. To put it differently: resurrection is not the pinnacle of a natural process in which the evolution of all living things necessarily culminates. The biosphere is *not* constantly becoming more subtle, more complex, more independent—until, in the human being as its highest product, it finally produces immortality by itself.

Likewise, synthetic biology will not achieve anything of the sort. When modern medicine creates the preconditions for today's humans, on average, to live to be older—soon significantly older than previous generations—that, of course, has nothing to do with immortality. Everything civilization and medicine can achieve would be a "defective" immortality that ought to make us shudder. "Resurrection of the dead" is something completely different. It is not naturally inherent in human physical nature. It is God's saving action, undeserved, pure gift. The word "new" in the phrase "new creation" indicates that.

The biblical phrase, however, speaks not only of "new" but of "creation"—and we need to pay attention to that, too. The new thing is brought into connection with what happened at the beginning of the world and continues: creation! But creation is the unceasing making of the world out of nothing. Christian theology recognized very early that it should not speak only of a divine act of creation "in the beginning." That is why it speaks of *creatio continua*, an unceasing creative act of God. God "constantly" calls creation out of nothing.

This creation out of nothing is not anyone's achievement. It can only be understood as the ongoing, unbroken action of the attentive love of God. From that point of view in particular it makes theological sense—in fact, it is necessary—to call the resurrection of the dead "new *creation*," that is, to bring it into relationship with the creation of the world, because that makes it clear that the resurrection of the dead is not something added, something that could be or not be; even though it is pure grace it is part of God's plan for creation. Creation, from the beginning, points toward its perfection, toward glory, toward being at home in God.

Thus the resurrection of the dead is not a natural event; it is God's pure gift. But the unceasing creation of the world is in itself utterly gratuitous on the part of God, the act of God's creative love. Once we have understood that, "creation of the world" and "new creation of the world in the resurrection" come together. In essence they are one connected event coming forth from the self-radiating love of God.

Incidentally, the concept of "new creation" is not a Christian invention. It is rooted in the book of Isaiah. The central statement of Isaiah 40–55 is that God is now creating something new in and for Israel. That is, through God's instrument, the Persian king Cyrus, those deported to Mesopotamia will be led back home—and with that, Israel begins a new existence:

> Do not remember the former things, or consider the things that are past. See, I am about to do a new thing; already it springs forth, do you not perceive it? (Isa 43:18-19)

At the end of the book the statement is intensified. There we find the promise:

> For I am about to create new heavens and a new earth; the former things shall not be remembered or come to mind. But be glad and

rejoice forever in what I am [now] creating. For I am about to create
Jerusalem as a joy, and its people as a delight. (Isa 65:17-18)

The text goes on to describe how there will be no more misery and
weeping in Israel, that people will no longer be driven from their
houses, that their work will no longer be "in vain," and that they will
not beget children for an early death. The "new heaven" and "new
earth" are thus altogether earthly, but they burst through everything
people are used to. They mean a world without injustice and suffering. The earthly history, being begotten and dying, goes on, but it is
now a "new" world, one in which there is justice and peace, consolation and rejoicing.

Jewish writings outside the Bible take up the promise of a "new
heaven" and a "new earth." They speak of the "new creation" God
will bring about.[1] However, the picture these authors draw of the world
is profoundly negative in its coloration. For some of the writings Israel
is under Roman occupation, Jerusalem is destroyed, the Temple a heap
of ruins. Apocalypses like *4 Ezra* and 2 Baruch were composed after
the destruction of Jerusalem.[2] Their authors no longer believe that
history will have a good end, and they draw a sharp distinction between the old world and the new, separating "this" and "the coming"
eons. In "this eon" God's promises cannot be fulfilled (*4 Ezra* 4:26-27).
"This eon," that is, the present world, is ruined and subject to death.
Therefore God will let this world be consumed in fire and will create
a new eon that will at last bring the longed-for justice and peace. Here,
then, the "new creation" of Isaiah is radically apocalypticized. The
"new" no longer happens in history but *beyond* all history.

The early church adopted a good deal of this apocalyptic radical-
ization: the final resurrection of the dead will bring about an end to
history. And yet the church, from its beginning, has maintained a
fundamental contradiction to all apocalyptic: "this eon" remains
God's good creation, in spite of all guilt and human-created chaos,
and God's promises will indeed be fulfilled in it.

In the famous eighth chapter of Romans, Paul does say that all
creation is subjected to decay and that to this day it groans in labor
pains. But in the same breath he says that it will be freed from its
slavery and futility and enjoy the freedom of the glory of the children

of God (Rom 8:18-25)—so not destruction and rejection of the old eon, as in the apocalyptic of books like *4 Ezra*, but liberation and deliverance. Creation will become what it was always intended to be.

And still more: in apocalyptic the new eon only arrives when the old one has passed away. The new eon, God's new world, presupposes the destruction of everything prior to it. But for Paul the old and new eons are interwoven. The old world, with its enslavement and unfreedom, is still present, but God's new world is already beginning in the midst of it. When Paul speaks of "new creation," astonishingly enough, he does not mean something that will happen sometime in the future or in the beyond, but rather the new life in Christ that has already begun for the baptized. Christians have already become a "new creation" through the Spirit of God given them in baptism.

> So if anyone is in Christ, there is a new creation. Everything old has passed away; see, everything has become new! (2 Cor 5:17)

So new creation through the life-giving Spirit of God happens already, in the midst of this history. The baptismal theology of the whole New Testament presupposes something similar: by receiving the Holy Spirit given them in baptism the baptized are already placed within the power-field of God's new creation. That is more radical than any apocalyptic could be. It is the radicality of the incomprehensibly new thing that has come with Jesus Christ's resurrection—and at the same time it is faithful to this present world, which is not despised but is brought home.

Thus there emerges anew in New Testament baptismal theology what appeared at the beginning of this chapter: the coming world of resurrection and the world in which we are now living are not two separate realities that have nothing to do with each other; both come forth from God's creative love, and God desires that there should be human beings, and for them a whole world. Both creation and resurrection are pure gift and are inseparably connected.

Here again the Christian message draws life from the incontrovertible basis of the Old Testament: everything is about *this* world and *this* creation. Redemption does not mean flight from the world and de-secularization; it is not a removal to a worldless beyond. It is healing and transformation of this present world, the leading of all creation to its goal.

To put it still another way: the resurrection of the dead is not a brilliant finale conceived by God, the great magician, for the amazement of the beholders at the end of the gala presentation "earth," and whose culmination will put in the shade everything that has gone before. No, it is giving form to that for which creation was intended from the beginning: to be a world before God, created out of incomprehensible and unjustifiable love, and always meant to find its way home to God. The resurrection of the dead is not a natural, physical event, but it is the consequence of the world's creation, its coming forth out of pure grace. And above all it is the consequence of the raising of Jesus from the dead, if it is true that he is the prototype and firstborn of all creation (Col 1:15-17).

PART FOUR

What Will Happen to Us

Now we begin the central part of this book. Everything I have said so far was only preparation, introduction, and a surveying of the terrain. Moreover, what has gone before was, in the main, historical information, whether about ancient belief concerning souls, today's ideas about the afterlife, or Jesus' preaching and New Testament resurrection theology.

But now the method must shift. From here on it will be impossible to argue primarily in historical terms; rather, for the most part we will be presenting a theological interpretation of our statements of faith. Here again, reason is always part of the process, though now its material is drawn from Christian faith.

A second preliminary remark: we can only speak of what comes after death in images. Every statement about the resurrection of the dead, just like every statement about God, is "speaking in parables." Theology talks of "analogous" statements, which means that, in whatever we may say about God and ultimate life with God, what we say is more different from the reality than similar to it.

But similar to what?—to the instants that revolutionize and enrich human life; to the moments of supreme fulfillment that are given us even now, and in spite of the horrifying knowledge of our own guilt. Such experiences are indispensable. If we could not refer to real experiences—our own and those of others—anything we might say about God and God's world to come would be meaningless and even impossible. We must always start with what there is in this world of experience of grace, fidelity, love, and commitment, of self-surrender and going beyond oneself. And still it is true that all these experiences are only shadows of what will happen to us in death. The "not-like"-ness is not only greater but unimaginably greater than the likeness.

Thus everything said in the next twelve chapters about the resurrection of the dead is a matter of images and parables, and we must constantly remain aware of this image-character of what we say. Often it will even be the case that the images and thought-models either augment each other or are mutually corrective. A closed system of eschatological images is neither possible nor adequate.

And finally, a third preliminary remark: everything said in this next, fourth section, without exception, is based in Jesus' resurrection. Christian knowledge of the *eschata*, the "last things," is nothing but an extrapolation of what happened in the resurrection of Jesus. Christian eschatology is not fantastic speculation that produces a richly detailed "geography" of eternal life. Ultimately it only interprets what happened with Jesus. More precisely: Christian teaching about the "last things" interprets what happened in the preaching, life, death, and resurrection of Jesus. His life, death, and resurrection are the starting point and center of all Christian eschatology.[1]

It is true that for the sake of simplicity I will often speak in part 4 of death as an encounter with "God." But then at the end, in the twelfth chapter, I will write in detail about the truth that the "place" of that encounter with God is the risen, or rising, Christ. Without him there is no resurrection for us, and most certainly no ultimate encounter with God's self. Let that be understood in advance so that this fourth section will not get out of balance. It must be embraced as a whole. The resurrection of Jesus from the dead is the first and fundamental premise for everything that has yet to be said.

1

The Ultimate Encounter with God

In order to speak of the human being beyond death or, better, *in death*, we have to have recourse to the concept of "encounter." In death the human encounters God, the unfathomable mystery of her or his life. The inner side of death is nothing other than encounter with the living God whom Scripture says heaven and earth cannot contain (1 Kgs 8:27). It is true that the human encounters God even before death, often without knowing it: namely, in her or his longing and joy, but also in lamentations, sorrows, and times of despair—and, of course, also in prayers and in service to those who need one's help. But in death the human encounters God ultimately and forever.

In all previous encounters God remained incognito and seemed silent, constantly withdrawing. All obedience seeking to follow, all words that tried to grasp God seemed to run off into the void. God remained the hidden God. Now God shows God's face.

It is impossible to describe how that will be, for this "no eye has seen, no ear has heard, nor the human heart conceived" (1 Cor 2:9). All those who pretend that they can easily describe and elaborate on this ultimate encounter with God make themselves ridiculous. They drag the infinite, immeasurable, incomprehensible God and the power of God's self-revelation down into a narrow and trivial thing.[1]

Still, we must somehow speak of the encounter with God in death. It must not be that Christians, faced with this decisive question of their lives, should fall silent out of fear of the ridicule of others or terror of the unspeakable. But how can we talk of it rightly and appropriately?

It is astonishing how austerely and sparely the gospels speak of that encounter. "Blessed are the pure in heart, for they will see God," Jesus says in Matthew 5:8. "Come, you that are blessed by my Father, inherit the kingdom prepared for you from the foundation of the world," says the world judge in Matthew 25:34. "Today you will be with me in Paradise," the crucified Jesus promises the terrorist who repents at the last second (Luke 23:43).* "They will see his face," it says in the last book of the New Testament (Rev 22:4).

One of the great theologians of the twentieth century, Hans Urs von Balthasar, summarized the ultimate encounter of the human with God—in fact, essentially the whole of eschatology—in three sentences:

> God is the "last thing" of the creature. Gained, he is heaven; lost, he is hell; examining, he is judgment; purifying, he is purgatory. He it is to whom finite being dies, and through whom it rises to him, in him.[2]

That says it all. Essentially, we need know nothing more. And yet faith must say more and dare not stop speaking at this point. But in what images, in what similitudes or parables? I will venture a voice from the liturgy of Easter that itself reaches back to an Old Testament psalm.

The church's liturgy for the morning of Easter begins, in its oldest form, not with jubilant choirs, not with trumpets proclaiming resurrection, and not with a blare of orchestral music, but with a tender chorale sustained almost by the melancholy of death. I am referring to the Introit, the "Opening Verse" of the Mass for Easter Sunday. It takes up Psalm 139. In its shortened form—omitting the antiphonal repetitions—it reads:

---

* Literally he is a "robber" or "bandit." That is what the Romans called rebellious Zealots who worked against the occupying power in Israel and ambushed Roman soldiers.

Resurrexi et adhuc tecum sum, alleluia.
Posuisti super me manum tuam, alleluia.
Mirabilis facta est scientia tua, alleluia, alleluia.
Domine probasti me et cognovisti me,
tu cognovisti sessionem meam et resurrectionem meam.

I have risen, and I am with you still, alleluia.
You have laid your hand upon me, alleluia.
Too wonderful for me, this knowledge, alleluia, alleluia.
O Lord, you have searched me and you know me,
You know my sitting down and my rising up.

Who is speaking? Who says "I have risen, and I am with you still"? Of course, it is the Risen One himself who speaks. And to whom does he say it? To whom does he say "you have laid your hand upon me; you have searched me and you know me"? The Risen One speaks to God. The whole Introit for the first day of Easter is part of a conversation between the risen Christ and the heavenly Father.

It is thrilling how the liturgy here, freely using verses from Psalm 139,[3] depicts the moment of Jesus' resurrection in the form of an address of Jesus to the Father—the first words, we might say, that Jesus speaks when he opens his eyes from the darkness of death and looks upon the face of the eternal Father.

Saying such a thing in human words attests to a great deal of audacity—even when the language of the Psalms is drawn on—for who can describe what happens when a dying person ultimately and forever encounters God in death? The liturgy dares to do it—at least as far as Christ is concerned—and sings it early on Easter morning with a positively reticent choral melody, cautiously and almost hesitantly.

Of course, this Introit song is Christian poetry, but it contains a central statement of Christian faith: the inner side of death is encounter with God's own self—in the case of Jesus an astonished encounter of the Son with the heavenly Father and, in our case, since we are sinners, not only a blessedly astonished but at the same time a shattering encounter with the absolutely Holy. And yet it is encounter, and indeed the sum and summit of all conceivable encounters. Death is encounter with the living, holy God and none other.

It is *God* who is our "place" after this life, says Augustine in his interpretation of Psalm 31:21—and for him that is decisively more than saying we are "in heaven" or "in Paradise," or "in Abraham's bosom."[4]

The Old Testament itself prepares us to see that God, when encountering humans in death, becomes *everything* to them, so that for each person there is nothing more except God. The one who prays Psalm 73 has cast bitter questions at God, but in the end confesses that, despite these questions, she has constantly remained with God. And as far as death is concerned, she is certain:

> You guide me with your counsel,
> and afterward you will receive me with honor.
> Whom have I in heaven but you?
> And if I am with you there is nothing on earth that I desire.
> My flesh and my heart may fail,
> but God is the strength of my heart and my portion forever.
>   (Ps 73:24-26)

This text does not yet speak of "resurrection" but of the certain knowledge that those who seek their pleasure, their security, and their future in God alone are "taken up" into the life of God "forever." It has always been seen that way in the church's faith-life as well. "God alone suffices," said the great Teresa of Avila. Christian doctrine speaks of the *visio beatifica*, the beatific vision of God after death, the eternal knowledge God gives of God's own self—and in that way of the ultimate encounter with God.

A look at the Old Testament itself shows that Israel was filled with the longing to see God. "Your face, O LORD, do I seek" (Ps 27:8) is one example of such longing, and "I shall see the goodness of the LORD" (Ps 27:13). It was customary in ancient Near Eastern cultures to carry the images of the gods in procession through the crowds at great festivals; then one could literally "see" the "face of the god," that is, the face of the statue of the god. The Old Testament took up that language, but filled it with new meaning:

> My soul thirsts for God,
> for the living God.
> When shall I come
> and behold the face of God?

My tears have been my bread
day and night,
while people say to me continually,
"Where is your God?"
These things I remember,
and I pour out my heart:
how I went with the throng,
and led them in procession to the house of God,
with glad shouts and songs of thanksgiving,
in the midst of the surging crowd. (Ps 42:3-5)

Obviously here looking at the face of God no longer means viewing a god's image. In the first place it simply refers to pilgrimage to Jerusalem and visiting the Temple. This is about encounter with the hidden God of Israel, the encounter with God's history. "Seeing God" thus meant, in a positive sense: being freed from trouble, rescued, coming to life.[5] Gradually, as the Psalm proceeds, the "beholding of his face" comes to mean much more: namely, abiding before the face of God for all time, even through and beyond death.

This lays the foundation on which Jesus will build, calling blessed those who have a pure heart, "for they will see God" (Matt 5:8)—the foundation for Paul's statement that the day will come when we will see God "face to face" (1 Cor 13:12).[6]

We should not think that such statements are obvious. In most archaic religions a person had to descend into the non-communicative underworld after death, or was "gathered" to the dead ancestors, to live on within the structures of the old family—but not before the face of a god. As far as the so-called "world religions" are concerned also, an encounter with God or a Godhead in death is anything but understood.

In Hinduism humans, when they die, move after an interval into the next incarnation. If an individual, after a long journey through newer and newer rebirths, finally finds salvation it is by coming to himself or herself—as a divine being.

In original Buddhism humans are not even permitted so much as to think of an encounter with the Wholly Other. Salvation is a lonely and painful getting free of one's own desires, and so of oneself. It is not the seeking of a partner and most certainly not the search for a divine partner.

Things are different in Islam, which enjoys a high degree of theo-centrism. A Muslim's whole life is oriented to God—in confession of faith, in prayer, in care for the poor, in fasting, in the pilgrimage to Mecca. Against this background it is all the more amazing that in the Qur'an, as far as life after death is concerned, the theocentric focus seems to be omitted. The afterlife is described as a beautiful garden; there is a fixed formula that recurs:

> God will admit those who obey Him and His Messenger to Gardens graced with flowing streams, and there they will stay—that is the supreme bliss![7] (*Sura* 4,13)

This formula appears about sixty times in the Qur'an,[8] usually with small variations but often with further expansions. These latter give a more precise picture of the content of the blessedness. The men received into the eternal gardens are greeted by angels, live in constant bliss, keep company with the prophets, are like brothers to one another, have everything they desire, wear green garments made of silk and brocade, are adorned with pearls and golden arm rings, recline on cushions or sit on sumptuous chairs, are surrounded by streams of the best water, of brooks filled with milk that does not sour, of rivulets of wine that does not inebriate. They rest in the shade under trees with low-hanging fruits, are surrounded by fragrant plants, eat from gold vessels, are served by boys like pearls, eternally young—and to all this Allah adds age-matched, large-eyed, lusty virgins ("houris"[9]) and pure spouses. "That is the supreme bliss" is repeated over and over.

And now for the crucial question: In all these good things that Allah bestows in the paradisal garden, does encounter with Allah himself play any part? perhaps in the phrase that sometimes occurs, "God is pleased with them, and they with Him"?[10] That is uncertain, because the formula need not be interpreted to mean a personal encounter. There is one lone text in which it is said that those who enter Paradise will see the angels "surrounding the throne" (*Sura* 39,75). But here again, everything remains open. Do they only see the angels? Contrast this with the plump and inflated images of earthly pleasures in which eternal blessedness is pictured, recurring throughout the Qur'an. An *encounter with God*, in person, is not clearly evident anywhere.[11]

A further observation: adoring praise of God plays a significant role in the Qur'an. Indeed, Islam's holy book begins with the words:

> In the name of God, the Lord of Mercy, the Giver of Mercy! Praise belongs to God, Lord of all worlds, the Lord of Mercy, the Giver of Mercy, Master of the Day of Judgement. (*Sura* 1,1-4)

But the fact that this praise plays no role in the multiple descriptions of Paradise betrays a strange disruption.[12] Paradise does not seem to be the real place for adoring God and thus of encounter with God, but is more like a gigantic and effective means of reward, providing private bliss and symmetrically corresponding to hell as an apparatus for punishment.

Please do not misunderstand. There can be no doubt that God is the absolute center of Islam, and mystical movements within Islam have also produced extended discussions about seeing God in Paradise.[13] But the Qur'an itself, as far as life after death is concerned, contains different emphases.

Certainly Christians should not be puffed up about this: Christianity, in the course of its long history, has revealed similar tendencies. In 1988–1990 Colleen McDannell and Bernhard Lang published their book *Heaven: A History*,[14] in which they showed that in the United States and in Europe since the eighteenth century there has been a notable stream of ideas about eternal blessedness in which God plays a rather minor role. Heaven is seen as a kind of continuation of middle-class life, often more like a family reunion. Being with one's spouse, children, relatives, and friends plays a crucial role. In heaven, as now on earth, there are work, mutual aid, child-raising, education, progress, amusement, and above all multiple love relationships. As in the Qur'an, earthly happiness is completely projected into heaven.

McDannell and Lang call this changed mentality, dominant especially in the Victorian era, the domestication of heaven.[15] Heaven was made cozy because many Christians became resistant to the idea that they would have to spend eternity playing harps, singing "hallelujah!" and meditating on the attributes of God. But the more profound reason, the authors say, was a new image of friendship, marriage, family, and love. People did not want to be deprived in heaven of these newly gained values of couple relationships and being at home in a nuclear family. They wanted not only to meet God there but above all to be reunited with the beloved and all those they had loved, and to take delight in them.

The "literary push to domesticate heaven" appeared especially in popular novels,[16] paintings, accounts of visions, the sermons of preachers in nondenominational churches and groups, in theologians' speculations pregnant with the spirit of the times, and in religious literature for the edification of the general public. McDannell and Lang are especially interested in this field. Elsewhere, above all in Roman Catholic teaching, the statement that it is the encounter with God, the *visio beatifica*, that is the basis of all blessedness remained intact. In later chapters I will address the unceasing question about human community in heaven—that is, "will I be with the people I have loved? will they be a part of my existence with God?" (See part 4, chaps. 6 and 12.) But at this point something crucial must be said as clearly as possible: death will be an encounter with God, and it is God who will be the human person's heaven or judgment. God will be everything for the person and there will be nothing else for anyone, really nothing else, except *in God*.

Above, almost at the beginning of this chapter, I referred to Paul's saying:

> no eye has seen, no ear heard, nor the human heart conceived, what God has prepared for those who love him. (1 Cor 2:9)

That we must steadfastly maintain. What Paul says here is a sword that cuts through all human fantasies about heaven. Incidentally, we find this same reticence about depicting heavenly glory in Rabbinic Judaism as well. It portrays the joys of the messianic time, but not of the world to come:

> R. Hiyya b. Abba also said in the name of R. Johanan: All the prophets prophesied only for the days of the Messiah, but as for the world to come, "Eye hath not seen, oh God, beside Thee."[17]

Similarly, *Sifre Deuteronomy* 356, commenting on Deuteronomy 33:29, tells how the assembled people of Israel asked Moses "Tell us what goodness the Holy Blessed One will give us in the World to Come," and Moses responds:

> "I do not know what I can tell you. Happy are you for what is prepared for you."[18]

That is a refusal to answer, similar to that of Paul and to what we find throughout the New Testament. Christian theology and piety should imitate this Jewish reticence and avoid all fantasizing about eternal life.

The question still remains whether there may not be experiences in life, even before death, in the life of every individual, that open our eyes and perhaps even sharpen our perception for what happens in death and beyond death. Rather than list a number of God-experiences that could be mentioned here I will refer to a single text. When the French mathematician and scientist Blaise Pascal (1623–1662) died, a carefully written scrap of paper was found sewn into the lining of his coat; evidently it had meant a great deal to him. This "Memorial," as it became known, describes the experience Pascal had on a particular day at a particular hour. It read:

> The year of grace 1654, Monday, 23 November, feast of St. Clement, pope and martyr, and others in the martyrology. Vigil of St. Chrysogonus, martyr, and others. From about half past ten at night until about half past midnight,
>
> *FIRE.*
>
> GOD of Abraham, GOD of Isaac, GOD of Jacob, not of the philosophers and of the learned. Certitude. Certitude. Feeling. Joy. Peace. GOD of Jesus Christ. *Deum meum et deum vestrum* [My God and your God (John 20:17)]. "Your GOD will be my God" [Ruth 1:16]. Forgetfulness of the world and of everything, except GOD. He is only found by the ways taught in the Gospel. Grandeur of the human soul. Righteous Father, the world has not known you, but I have known you [John 17:25]. Joy, joy, joy, tears of joy. I had departed from him: *Dereliquerunt me fontem aquae vivae* [They have forsaken me, the fount of living water (Jer 2:13)]. "My God, will you leave me?" Let me not be separated from him forever. "This is eternal life, that they know you, the one true God, and the one that you sent, Jesus Christ" [John 17:3]. Jesus

Christ. Jesus Christ. I left him; I fled him, renounced, crucified.
Let me never be separated from him. He is only kept securely
by the ways taught in the Gospel: Renunciation, total and sweet.
Complete submission to Jesus Christ and to my director. Eternally in joy for a day's exercise on the earth. *Non obliviscar ser-
mones tuos* [I will not forget your words (Ps 119:16)]. Amen.[19]

This memorial reports a real experience and is precisely dated. Pascal,
a scientist, noted it with almost the same precision with which he
documented an experiment. It is not a matter of theological insights
such as one may have on any given day, but of the shattering experience of a particular hour that changes everything, that one will never
forget. But this is not a universal human experience that every
religious person can have; it is, in the first place, a specifically *Judaeo-
Christian* experience with a prehistory, namely, the faith-history of
many generations. Pascal encountered Christ at a particular moment
in time, and in Christ he encountered the God of Abraham, Isaac, and
Jacob. That encounter filled him with a joy that revolutionized everything. At the same time it was an *ecclesial* experience; after all, it is no
accident that Pascal specifically names the saints of the day.

We have no right to somehow dismantle the words "Joy, joy, joy,
tears of joy," reducing them, for example, to a purely psychological
process. In that joy Pascal found peace, a peace that gave new order
to his life, reset it at another level, made it clear and unambiguous.
Pascal, deeply shaken, suddenly realized that he had previously been
separated from Christ even though he had long believed. He knew
that he had now truly found Christ, and God in him, and he knew it
with the utmost certainty. So Pascal repeated the word.

Many people have had similar experiences: for example, of suddenly standing in the presence of God and being unable to escape;
of feeling one's heart on fire; of a joy so deep that all other joys fade;
of inner peace and ultimate certainty. These experiences can be very
different. They can overpower a person or they can arise so gently
in one's heart that one almost misses them. But anyone can have them
in one form or another. They happen when one wills only to do God's
will and nothing more.

Those who have had such experiences will be able to believe that
at some point there will come an hour for which everything past will

have been only a prelude and anticipation: the hour of the ultimate and open encounter with God—the hour in which we finally know and are fully known. "There we shall rest[20] and see, see and love, love and praise."[21]

2

Death as Judgment

"There we shall rest and see, see and love, love and praise." So the previous chapter ended, but of course it was a look ahead. The encounter with God is not only celebration and completion. God is our judge. Anyone who wants to speak theologically about eternal life cannot avoid the subject of "judgment."

And why is the theme of "judgment" unavoidable for an honest eschatology? It is quite simply connected with the condition of the world, which does not need a long explanation. The daily news suffices: a defenseless woman raped by a dozen men, corruption involving millions of dollars, the shameless exploitation of workers in a textile mill, more than thirty innocent people blown up by a suicide bomber, the men of an entire village shot by religious fanatics, the use of devastating cluster bombs in a civil war with no end in sight—as I have said, the news of a single day, taken from eight pages of the newspaper. The misery of the poor still cries out to heaven (cp. Jas 5:4).

And just take a look back at the twentieth century: two world wars with unimaginable destruction and countless dead, lying propaganda in unheard-of quantity, manipulation of the masses, so-called state security forces, tortures, show trials, genocides, *gulags*, concentration camps, factory-style murders of six million Jewish men, women, and children—a terrifying list that could be lengthened and lengthened.

Because of the harrowing memory of all the refugees, those despoiled and starved, tortured, shot, and gassed, a will arose in the world to prevent repetitions of such outbursts of hatred. The twentieth was not only a century of inflationary murder; it was also filled with attempts, never before undertaken, to reveal injustices, create justice, and heal wounds.

The Nuremberg trials (1945–1946) of German war criminals from World War II saw the birth of an international criminal justice system that defined and codified older norms. Since then a number of courts have been set up, for example, to try the criminals from the former Yugoslavia (1993) and the genocide in Rwanda (1995). The climax of these efforts was the establishment of the International Criminal Court at the Hague by the Rome Statute (17 July 1998). It has so far been signed by 135 states and ratified by ninety-three.[1]

Something else that should be mentioned is that, probably for the first time in human history, great memorials have been established not for rulers and fallen "heroes" but for the victims of injustice. Jerusalem contains Yad Vashem, a museum for the history of the *Shoa*. The names and personal data of all the Jewish victims of National Socialism are collected there. Yad Vashem also documents the names of Jewish congregations that were dissolved. Murdered Jewish children are memorialized in a hall of their own. And throughout the whole world, especially in Germany, there are many places dedicated to the memory of the murdered Jews.

The many other victims of wars and injustice are also being memorialized. Their names are being brought together and a great many historians are working to bring war crimes and their background before the eyes of the public—at least in Western countries!

And yet, as right as it is to put war criminals on trial, and as necessary as it is to maintain the memory of the horror, everyone knows how little human jurisprudence can accomplish. A great deal will never be revealed, and even if it is, the victims are dead and their descendants are not in a position to grasp, even remotely, the magnitude of the evil.

Something else makes everything much less hopeful: the cry for justice rises to heaven not only because of crimes against whole peoples. The great dictators are produced and sustained by countless little tyrants and by everything that happens daily on a small scale and far from the public eye. Contempt for other people and misuse of power are not restricted to the monstrous crimes perpetrated in politics and the economy. The will to betray, dominate, and exploit others starts in the kindergarten classroom and continues in offices and bedrooms: men tyrannize over their wives, wives over their husbands, parents over children, children over parents, teachers over their students, students over their teachers, bosses over their employees, employees over their bosses. Very subtle methods sustain the exercise of power: cold silence, for example, or extortive tears, or putting whispered rumors in circulation.

These kinds of injustices are normally impossible of discovery by any human court of justice. They remain behind closed doors, almost never come to public attention, and they grow and wax from generation to generation. Those who have to endure such daily oppression get no memorials.

And things are even more complicated than that. Massimo Tosco, in an effort to make us reflect, writes about a fictional memorial plaque:

> Lord Juan de Porrés, generous beyond all measure, built this hospital out of love for the poor—whom he had made poor in the first place.[2]

Let us suppose that Lord Juan de Porrés was never aware that he was exploiting the poor. In that case the text means to indicate something hidden in which we are all involved: we do things we consider good—we may even think we are benefitting others—and yet at the same time we are entangled in evil we cannot see through. We live in harmful situations we do not even perceive and that pervert our actions, even our actions for good.

For example, we buy certain products from emerging nations that are only cheap because in those countries women, men, and children are exploited under inhuman conditions. The example reveals that there is more than just public evil. There are harmful situations and structures of injustice in every society, sustained by the personal guilt of people we do not even know. We enter into those situations as if it were a matter of course, not noticing that they are based on injustice, and we enhance them by our own actions—and all without any evil intent.[3]

I hope the readers will forgive me this long and winding approach. I want to make it clear that it is necessary for people to struggle unceasingly for justice in the world. The effort to create just societies, and above all a just world society, is a duty given to humans, and to the people of God above all, and it is altogether a part of the coming of the reign of God. But in this regard, and especially in this regard, the best and freest society always comes up against its limitations. Human courts are helpless in face of the immeasurable potential for injustice in the world; indeed, they are themselves involved in that injustice. Ultimately they are unable either to establish adequate justice or to uncover the depths of worldwide injustice, which is the result of human freedom for good or evil. Only God can reveal human history in all its dimensions. And only God can really, universally, and above all finally create justice.

Friedrich Schiller wrote, "the world's history is the world's judgment," and that sentence, usually quoted apart from its context,[4] contains much truth. The Swiss Reformed theologian Emil Brunner (1889–1966) emphasizes what is true in Schiller's statement, but remarks:

> Only we must not forget . . . that such judgments [*in the lives of individuals, the history of nations, and humanity as a whole*] betray their provisional character inasmuch as those who are the instruments of them involve themselves in new wrong in the very process of executing them, and so make a fresh judgment necessary. The French Revolution was the judgment on the *ancien régime*; Napoleon was the judgment on the degenerate revolution, the Holy Alliance the judgment on Napoleon, the revolutions of '48 the judgment on the Holy Alliance, and so on up to our own times.[5]

The truth remains that only God can ultimately create justice, and therefore there must be a divine judgment. Otherwise the world and its history would be a senseless perversity. A world in which murderers triumph over their innocent victims, in which the powerful and those who despise other people are always celebrated in history and the betrayed always remain so would be the ultimate absurdity. A world that is not judged would be a world without hope, without purpose; it would be worthless. Every religion that has considered the fate of the human after death has proposed that there will be a judgment. For example:*

The deceased must travel over a swaying bridge above a deep abyss; if they have lived very bad lives they will fall into the darkness. Or they must make their way over a narrow plank to the other side; for the righteous the plank offers a sure footing, but for the criminals it becomes a knife that cuts them in two. Or the dead must enter on a journey full of dangers that pose threats corresponding to their past lives. Or the human heart is weighed in a vast scale; the fate of those who cannot stand before divine justice is sealed.

In ancient Egyptian religion, which offers us one of the most developed judgment scenarios, the heart of every dead person is tested in a scale by a tribunal of forty-two judges of the dead, headed by Osiris. The husband of the goddess Ma'at, ibis-headed Thoth, is there to take notes. The heart to be weighed lies on one side of the scale and on the other side a feather that is the embodiment of Ma'at, the goddess of justice and the legal order. If the heart and Ma'at are equal in weight, the deceased withstands the test. Otherwise the heart is given to the goddess Ammit for destruction.[6]

Hinduism, as we have seen, also recognizes a system for judging right, or a right order of the world: it is provided for through the equalizing causality of *karma*, which makes the next rebirth to be in a better or worse form of existence, depending on the individual's previous way of life. However, this reveals precisely how problematic many religions' ideas about justice are: in the Hindu model all the Jews who were gassed in Auschwitz must have committed the most heinous crimes in their previous incarnation. Otherwise their *karma* would not have permitted them to be so ignominiously murdered. Their miserable deaths, and those of all the six million, were thus punishment for sins in a previous life—which is an absurd idea![7]

---

*Early forms of religion that stopped with a mere veneration of ancestors did not yet consider this question, or if so, only marginally.

In fact, all images of judgment in which the deceased must ultimately answer to a *system* of justice and be measured against it are problematic. Plank, bridge, knife, abyss, controlling guards, court sessions, panels of judges, and many other images familiar to the religions can very easily be understood as mere symbols of a mythical world system that is supposed to guarantee justice.

Here in particular the difference between this and Jewish-Christian thought is evident. According to biblical faith the deceased are judged not according to a system, but by the living God.[8] God alone is the source of all justice, all righteousness, not as its symbol, not as its embodiment, not as something God *has*; God *is* righteousness. God is pure and absolute righteousness and can will nothing else but that the world God has created out of love will become a just world reflecting God's own self. Certainly that realization was a long process—a history of freedom extending over thousands of years and only completed in the death of each individual and in the judgment of the world.

I say "completed" on purpose, because judgment does not happen only at death; it is happening in this life for each individual and just as much so in the life of nations. But, as we have seen, none of that can replace the final judgment at death. Only in death are all God's justice and righteousness fulfilled. But what is this judgment at death like?

Above all, it is *disclosure*. Before God, the absolutely Holy One, nothing remains hidden. Everything is revealed. Everything comes to light: the individual's concealed and private thoughts, the silent and hidden deeds, even the things that have never been spoken about, never reported, never judged—even things the perpetrators did not know about because they were buried deep in the cellars of their souls.

But what will then be revealed before God are not only "the purposes of the heart," the individual's secret thoughts and hidden actions (1 Cor 4:5), but also the driving forces in whole nations and cultures. What was it, exactly, that drove Germany, Austria, France, Great Britain, and Russia into World War I? It was not the mood of a moment that drove millions of people, nearly all of them baptized, blindly rejoicing into that madness; it was the powers of egoism, arrogance, hatred, and unfathomable stupidity, all of which had developed over long periods of time.

And what was it that brought forth the worldwide anti-Judaism that revealed its most hideous visage under Hitler? Who were the guilty? Did they not include those church theologians who, beginning in the second century,[9] again and again, and with increasing volume, denied that God's people Israel had been chosen by God, who "disinherited" Israel, so to speak, and accused it of responsibility for a "murder of God"?

Human history is full of such collective false judgments, often with fearful consequences. These, too, must be laid bare before the face of God. At this point we should also mention the collective actions of the helpers and toadies of despots. What would Hitler and Stalin have been without their countless helpers and the helpers' assistants?

At the same time, of course, we must also speak of all the good that has come from the united common efforts of many people, even whole nations. Think only of the solidary aid given today by many nations when a natural catastrophe occurs anywhere in the world: a development in human history that deserves immense respect. Or consider the selfless solidarity experienced today by countless refugees and asylum seekers—from many individuals, from many groups and organizations.

Thus encountering the living God in death means not only that sin and guilt come to light but also innocence and resistance to evil, the behavior of those who were merciful and did not exercise violence, who hungered and thirsted for righteousness, who preserved a pure heart and were peacemakers (Matt 5:5-9). Before God's face will stand the whole mass of good that holds history in balance: all the married couples who have remained faithful to one another, all the workers and employees who have done their daily work as they should, all the scientists and scholars who have worked themselves weary to measure the cosmos and tell its history, the tireless efforts of so many physicians, the integrity of many politicians, the tenacious battles of many lawyers and judges for justice, the unceasing patience of mothers and fathers in raising their children, the nonviolent discipleship of Christian martyrs, the faith of the confessors, the hope of the poor, the love of the saints, the yearning of the loving.

Then will also come to light that many of those who have committed suicide were, in their despair, seeking nothing but the meaning of their lives and the world, that many who worshiped their ancient inherited gods have, without knowing it, lifted their hands to the *one* God, and that many who denied God have in reality denied false gods and sought the *true* God—but God was not shown to them.

Also part of judgment is our astonished joy at the goodness in our own lives and those of others. Unfortunately, it is precisely this aspect that is often neglected in theology and preaching. Medieval painters and sculptors were still aware of it: they showed not only the horror of the condemned but also the laughter and radiance of those who are blessed in the judgment. What shines from their faces, certainly, is not pride at their own achievements; it is a joy saturated with the deep knowledge that their decision for the good was only possible out of God's grace. Therefore among the greatest artists of the Middle Ages and the Renaissance there is no exultation over the condemned on the faces of the blessed, but rather horror and sympathy. I see no other way, for example, to explain how Mary turns her face away in Michelangelo's gigantic fresco of the Last Judgment.

Now let me go one step further and speak not simply of the distress of the condemned *and* the radiant joy of the blessed, but of both together in the hearts of those who encounter God at death. Jesus' great parable of the judgment in Matthew 25:31-46 and the monumental paintings of the Last Judgment in the ancient churches must depict the two as separate groups: the damned at the judge's left, the blessed at his right.* But in reality it is most likely that both will be found in one and the same person, who at the judgment recognizes, with a blessed shock, all the good that God has done in and through him or her: the search for truth, the longing for the Wholly Other that transcends one's own life, the never-ruptured hope of still changing that life—and at the same time beholds, with horror, her or his failings: the good neglected, the bad example given to others, the illusions nourished in one's own heart, self-assertion, self-betrayal, all of life's lies: the whole history of our own sins.

---

* Of course, Matt 25:31-46 is the basis for all these depictions.

When we encounter God in death we will for the first time recognize with full clarity who we really are. God has no need to sit in judgment on us, to harangue us as human judges lecture the accused; God has no need to tell us "on this and that point you were a miserable failure; I have to mark this and this against you; here and here are your sins; I have to condemn you."

There will be no judgment in that sense. In our encounter with the holy God our eyes will be opened to behold our own selves. We will know who we are. We ourselves will judge and condemn the evil in ourselves. The encounter with God will become our own judgment of ourselves.

When theologians speak today of judgment at death or the so-called "Last Judgment," the concept of "self-judgment" plays a central role. Thus, for example, the Frankfurt systematic theologian Medard Kehl writes:

> God does not judge "from without" and imposes no punishment
> in addition to sins; rather, the naked encounter with the love of
> God we have wounded and scorned . . . judges us in the most
> painful way. We ourselves, standing in such a distorted relation-
> ship to God, are then our own court and sentence.[10]

So judgment does not mean that God (or Christ) presides over a terrifying scenario, speaking an implacable condemnation and in the end demanding retribution. Judgment does not mean that God pronounces words of judgment from on high, punishes, and demands penance, but that, in light of the absolute truth that God *is* by nature, individuals will be their own court of judgment. We will all pass judgment on ourselves.

Of course it is still too little to say only that in the face of the holy and living God we will judge ourselves. We will also pass judgment on ourselves in face of the "victims" we have created and who implacably rise before our eyes in death: the many we have not helped, even though we could have; the many we could have consoled and did not; those for whom we could have been models of faith and were anything but; the many we overlooked, disappointed, shamed, despised, or led astray and misled; the many we have exploited for our own purposes. In death they will all appear before us and stare at us—and they, too, will be our judges.[11] We must even suppose that when we encounter our "victims" in death we will undergo all the sufferings we have caused them.

And so the encounter with God in death will become an encounter with truth: the truth about God, about others, about the world, and above all the truth about ourselves. In that sense we can even hope for judgment, because truth is something in which we can rejoice. I hope for myself that for once clarity will appear in all the dark corners of my life: that, for example, I will learn what I have desired for my life at depth. I hope that confusions will be clarified and the tangled web of guilt and innocence will be unsnarled, that the true good will be visible, the ambiguous made clear, the only apparent good uncovered, and the evil in me exposed. I hope that everything that is pulling apart, scattering, and dividing my life will be gathered up and brought home.

Clarity in the face of the all-penetrating truth of God has to be something altogether liberating—and probably it is precisely in that clarity that the unimaginable mercy of God will be revealed. Now we must speak of that mercy.

3

Judgment as Mercy

In both the Old and New Testaments it is very often said that God judges the world "in righteousness," or "with justice." Statements about God as a strict, avenging judge run throughout the Bible.[1] But both Old and New Testaments also speak again and again of God's mercy—for God's people and for the world. Which is more basic? Which has more weight? God's judging or God's showing mercy? God's righteousness or God's pity?

That is the question often asked today; whole books have been written about divine mercy.[2] Theology and the magisterium are retrieving what they previously treated as a stepchild: the idea of God's mercy. How did it happen that Christians in previous centuries saw in God, and even in Jesus Christ, only the stern and threatening judge—and needed Mary, the "Mother of Mercy," as a balance?[3] Now the pendulum has swung to the other side. There is an almost excessive emphasis on the merciful, concerned, loving, motherly, gentle, sympathetic, compassionate, and tender God. What is going on?

Careful! It could be that the question of which carries more weight, God's justice or God's mercy, is becoming a completely false dichotomy. God is not a composite of various traits, sometimes threatening, sometimes merciful, sometimes just, sometimes gracious. God is completely and altogether mercy and just as completely and altogether justice—which means that God's justice is mercy and God's mercy is justice![4] All statements about God are, as we have seen, *analogous*, that is, the unlikeness to concepts in our everyday experience is unimaginably greater than the likeness. Therefore God's justice is not the same as human justice, and God's mercy is not the same as human mercy. So the title of this chapter could just as easily be "Mercy as Judgment" instead of "Judgment as Mercy."

The theoretical question of which has more weight, God's mercy or God's justice, is thus always in danger of leading us to speak about God in the wrong way. Here again we can learn from the Bible. Its great texts on the subject of "divine mercy" are not at all based on theoretical, timeless propositions divorced from any situation. They are always embedded in the dramatic history of God with God's people. The Bible does not simply speak stereotypically, as the Qur'an does, always with the identical formula regarding God's mercy.* Instead it describes how God's mercy breaks through in very different historical situations in the face of Israel's sinfulness and lostness.

For example, take Exodus 32–34. Israel has barely been liberated from Egypt and received the Torah at Sinai, God has just made an eternal covenant with the people, and there they are, dancing around the golden calf (the text's symbol for foreign gods; cp. 32:1) and singing "These are your gods, O Israel" (32:4). That's an end of that. Israel has revoked its faithfulness to God. The covenant is broken. God must punish. In what follows, God is depicted as wanting to create a new people of God, with Moses as its ancestor.[5] But Moses succeeds in persuading God to a change of heart by referring to the oath God had sworn to Abraham, Isaac, and Jacob (32:11-14). It is in this very context, shaped by the most heinous sin and the absolute forfeiture of salvation, that God has mercy, offers forgiveness, and reveals God's self definitively as

a God merciful and gracious, slow to anger, and abounding in steadfast love and faithfulness. (Exod 34:6)[6]

*Every one of the 114 *Suras* in the Qur'an begins with the formula "In the name of God [Allah], the Lord of Mercy, the Giver of Mercy!"

A great many other statements in Torah and prophets about God's mercy are intertextually related to this proclamation and thus show its extreme weight within the Bible.[7]

Also important for our question is the book of Hosea, which contains a passage introducing a long, wrathful speech against Israel in which the voices of God and the author alternate. The discourse extends from chapter 4 to the end of chapter 11. The introductory section reads:

> Hear the word of the LORD, O people of Israel;
>> for the LORD has an indictment against the inhabitants
>> of the land.
> There is no faithfulness or love,
>> and no knowledge of God in the land.
> No: swearing, lying, and murder,
>> and stealing and adultery break out;
> violence has been done in the land, and
>> bloodguilt follows bloodguilt.
> Therefore the land shall mourn,
>> and all who live in it shall languish;
> together with the wild animals and the birds of the air,
>> even the fish of the sea shall perish. (Hos 4:1-3)

No harsher judgment can be laid on the situation of God's people. These three verses are "a genuine summation of divine wrath."[8] God's wrath falls not only on the people in Israel; it affects the whole land, with its animals. Even the fish are perishing.

That requires explanation. God does not destroy the animal world out of anger at Israel's sins. Instead, the text assumes that sins always have *consequences*. Arrogance, the lust for domination, and self-indulgence destroy not only the human soul but, with that soul, the whole surrounding world of life, what we today call "the environment." The text here summarizes, including not only sin but also the real consequences of human sin within the concept of God's judging wrath.

However, God's wrath does not have the last word in the book of Hosea. By the beginning of chapter 11, God's anger has been transformed into mourning. God cannot forget God's first love for Israel, and in Hosea 11:8-9 God's whole attitude changes, as glowing wrath collapses and is transformed again into love. God puts an end to the judgment already in progress. The cosmic catastrophe threatened in Hosea 4:3 will not come about:

> How can I give you up, Ephraim? How can I hand you over, O Israel? [. . .] My heart recoils within me; my compassion grows warm and tender. I will not execute my fierce anger; I will not again destroy Ephraim; for I am God and no mortal, the Holy One in your midst, and therefore I will not come in wrath. (Hos 11:8-9)

So God's judging wrath does exist. God cannot simply ignore the injustice and evil in the world. After all, evil is an attack on God's creation, an attempt to destroy God's work. Most certainly, God cannot let injustice within God's people go on. Israel is supposed to be God's instrument of help for the world. Therefore it must act and create justice. That is what is meant by "divine wrath." It is a judging wrath aimed at justice; its purpose is to restore the world.

But as rational and plausible as "God's wrath" is when rightly understood, it collapses: "My heart recoils within me; my compassion grows warm and tender" (11:8). Thus the text makes it clear that human concepts are inadequate for understanding God, "for I am God and no mortal, the Holy One in your midst" (11:9).

This reversal from wrath to mercy, from judgment to salvation, is not something we find only in the book of Exodus and the prophet Hosea. There are similar texts in other prophetic books, and beyond them, throughout the whole Old Testament. God responds to the infidelity and rejection of God's people with fidelity. God's heart beats for Israel; God has no choice but to forgive. So Isaiah 54:6-8 reads:

> Can one forget the wife of one's youth? says your God. For a brief moment I abandoned you, but with great compassion I will bring you back. In overflowing wrath for a moment I hid my face from you, but with everlasting mercy I will have compassion on you, says the LORD, your Redeemer.

We could cite many similar Old Testament texts, but these must suffice. God's mercy always arises out of a situation marked by sinfulness and hopelessness.

Jesus knew all these texts and presupposed them in his preaching of judgment, which was often very severe and provocative. With him, as with the prophets, we find the proclamation of judgment.[9] But the underlying theme of his preaching links to the joyful message of Isaiah 52:7-10, the announcement of superabundant saving grace. In the parable of the lost son Jesus speaks of God's unfathomable mercy (Luke 15:11-32). That parable, like the Old Testament texts cited above, is related to a particular situation; here Jesus defends his attitude toward people who have failed—not only in faith,* but in their whole existence.** Like the father in the parable, he goes to meet them and receives them into the new thing now happening in Israel. The lost son has no need to atone for his failure; he does not have to work off the inheritance he squandered. Instead, his father unhesitatingly restores him to his full rights as son, and a feast is celebrated.

Is it permissible to apply the point of all these texts to our question about the human encounter with God in death? Why not? Can God, in the afterlife, treat history differently than in history itself, where God's true nature has been revealed in dialogue with God's people? Can God act any differently from Jesus? Can God act differently from the way, in human circumstances, every truly good parent acts toward his or her children?

And could it be that Jesus demands, for the behavior of the people of God, a limitless will to forgive, a will to pardon without reservation and without condition—and that God would be unequal to that standard of forgiveness? "Lord, if another member of the church sins against me, how often should I forgive?" Peter asks. "As many as seven times?" Jesus answers: "Not seven times, but I tell you, seventy-seven times" (Matt 18:21-22)—which means always, without measure, without condition. But since Jesus is the definition of God, God's image, the reflection of God's nature—what should we conclude from that?

---

* The younger son, as his occupation as swineherd shows, has turned to a Gentile for help. If he had had faith he would have sought help from a Jew or a Jewish community.
** The younger son is also existentially at the last extreme: he is not entitled even to the pigs' leavings.

There is one thing, at least, that the biblical texts in this chapter have shown, and that is why they were quoted. We dare not take the subject of "God's mercy" out of its context, and that context is always the most severe human guilt, which is not concealed or denied. For Hosea it was a guilty situation that could not have been worse:

> Everything that had been positive is denied regarding the inhabitants of the land: fidelity, love, knowledge of God. . . . They are blasphemers and betrayers, murderers, thieves, and adulterers; bloodguilt follows bloodguilt. The wrath this evokes can only bring an end to the universe.[10]

And yet God cannot give up on Israel, and the world with it. God's wrath changes to mercy. This dialectic between judgmental wrath and bottomless mercy, between necessary judgment and self-surrendering love must be maintained. We cannot speak of God's mercy in any other way.

But that means that whoever hopes for God's mercy must at the same time repeatedly enter into her or his own history of sin and never suppress or cover it up, or somehow mystify it. One may only hope for God's mercy and not make it a cheap matter-of-course expectation.

If we maintain this attitude, then it certainly could happen that, at the moment of our final encounter with God, divine mercy could become judgment—but a judgment that clarifies, purifies, and heals everything in us. Now we need to say more about that.

4

Purification in Death

Judgment in death means the complete laying open and clarification of everything in the human person. Can it also be purification and healing? Is there a "purification in death"? With this question we enter disputed territory—disputed among Catholic, Orthodox, and Protestant Christians.[1] The present chapter is, in part, an attempt to show that the differences among the confessions on this point need by no means be so sharp as they have appeared throughout history.

It could be that the quarrel over the purification of the human person in death—that is, over purgatory (Latin *purgatorium*)*—could have been eliminated from the outset if the discussion among the confessions had rested on a realistic anthropology, that is, an image of humanity in accordance with reality.

What, then, is that true human situation? Consider just any person, anywhere, at any time. Even a person who has chosen truth, righteousness, goodness, and reconciliation, or quite explicitly God, sees

---

* *Purgatorium* simply means "cleansing" or "purification." In the course of history the word was often also interpreted theologically to mean "place of purification." German developed the word "Fegfeuer" [cleansing fire], which was subject to a great deal of misunderstanding, while the Romance languages and English retained words derived from *purgatorium*.

aspects of himself or herself that are often frightening: aggressions, caveats, resistances, condemnable thoughts of all sorts. Such a person certainly does good and wants to do good—but perhaps that do-ing-good is plagued by self-affirmation, self-assertion, self-exaltation. Such a person certainly seeks truth but perhaps is also infatuated with the search itself or is capable of correcting it a little if it is to her or his own advantage. Such a one certainly holds for the dignity and sanctity of the human being, but now and then detects in the depths of the self a secret desire for violent deeds and shameless acts.

Those who regard themselves soberly know what kinds of conflicts, self-righteousness, self-assertion, and self-addiction, as well as anxiety, mistrust, hardness, self-betrayal, and existential lies are present within. There is, to be sure, a center of the person in which God's superabundant grace and human longing coincide. But that personal center, with its "gift of freedom,"[2] only governs certain layers within the person. Alongside it, often even beneath it, there are spaces haunted by darkness and ghosts—some dreams in the night betray their presence. The deep cellars of the soul (and each person's self-created environment) contain ancient burdens, the con-sequences of previous sins, even though those sins have been for-given. For every sin, even those already forgiven, has consequences that have to be worked out, but often are not: instead, they continue to develop their evil effects.

It may be that at this point married couples should speak up: those who love each other profoundly, have remained faithful to one an-other, stuck together through good and bad days, and yet can tell what kind of misunderstandings, wounds, sorrows, and lack of ap-preciation lie between them, as well as things that have remained unspoken and unmastered for many years—and all that in spite of the most profound affection, one that continues to grow.

It is no different in our relationship with God. The saints, in par-ticular, have always known this and have spoken openly of all that is resistant and self-glorifying in their inmost selves. The great John Henry Newman wrote in one of his letters that he had "cause to shudder" at his own weakness.[3] Finally, we should consider Jesus' saying: "Blessed are the pure in heart, for they will see God" (Matt 5:8). Which of us can say that she has a pure heart?

All this shows that the person who, in death, appears before the absolutely holy God is an unholy and ambivalent human being. For that very reason there are some slightly absurd aspects to the unending quarrel over whether there is "scriptural proof" for purgatory. Of course it exists—namely, in the fundamental biblical statement that God is holy and the human being unholy, that constantly becoming holy is part of the existence of believers, and that the unholy person cannot stand before God. The Bible speaks of that in a thousand places. But if someone wants to demand, as scriptural proof, a pithy and accurate all-defining concept, and with it a kind of dogmatic definition such as those found in theological dictionaries—then, in that case, there is no scriptural proof in the Bible for purgatory.

Anyone who has a notion of God's holiness and knows what human beings are really like must also know that in death there appears before God a person who must be profoundly dismayed at the abysses in his own heart that come to light in that moment; one who must be terrified at suddenly recognizing the wasted possibilities of her own life; one who must be shocked at the realization of what could have been done for others and was not done; who must recoil because he stands not only before an implacable judge but before an incomprehensible love that not only strikes to the heart but touches the depths of that heart. This encounter of the unholy human person and the holy God necessarily and unavoidably leads to a purification of the person that suffuses her or him "like" fire.[4]

We can try to describe this process. Theologians today speak of purification, cleansing, transformation, ripening, an ongoing process of becoming holy, a breakthrough to the human fundamental choice, an integration of everything in the person that has not yet been fully accepted and integrated.[5] But at the same time they know that they cannot describe the process adequately. Only lovers who have learned how their mutual love has gradually and painfully burned away their egoism will guess at what happens then.

But because all that can so easily be misunderstood, and because medieval popular piety so long painted it with exuberant fantasy and entire orgies of fire, some additional clarifications are needed here.

First of all: purgatory is not a place. It is true that countless visions and stories, even the most sublime poetry, depict heaven, hell, and purgatory as places, even places with various regions and divisions. They project an entire topography of the world beyond. But those who pass through death do not arrive at "places." Their only "place" then is God, or more precisely, the eternal encounter with God (see part 4, chap. 1 above). The purification that Christian theology speaks of is an *event*, not a place.

Further: this event no longer takes place in *earthly* time. Speculations about the various lengths of time required for purification would be just as much off the mark as notions of space in the afterlife. Those who, in death, leave behind them the realm of earthly time and history do not enter into another form of existence in which hours, days, months, and years pass by. There, existence is no longer conceivable in terms of earthly time. That is why Karl Lehmann says of the event in which the person is purified:

> It is a moment in the perfection of the human being through God's judgment. That encounter is not measurable in earth's time. Purgatory lies precisely in the momentary transition between death and perfection.[6]

Obviously even the word "momentary" is an image, something not really imaginable but simply a turn of phrase intended to exclude a period of earthly time.

So preachers ought not to talk about the "length" of purgatory and thus awaken false ideas in their audience. Instead of introducing the category of time they should speak of differing intensities of purification: the event of purification in death will look different in the lives of those who have steadily practiced examination of conscience, sorrow over their own egoism, repentance, reconciliation, turning to God and the neighbor than it will in those who drifted through life.

Much more important is the following insight: the purifying process I am speaking of here is not a "punishment." It is true that for centuries the Roman Catholic Church spoke of the "expiation" of the punishment for sin in purgatory. The German catechism of 1936 still read: "The souls in purgatory are those of the deceased righteous who have yet to atone for their sins." Similarly, in the catechism from 1955 we find: "[the poor souls in purgatory] must suffer the punishment due for their sins."[7] But such expressions could only evoke misunderstanding.

God does not punish and does not make people do penance.[8] God
sanctifies, purifies, and heals. The *Catechism of the Catholic Church* (1993)
quite rightly avoids the concepts of "atonement" and "expiation" in
its section on purgatory.[9] Anyone who describes purgatory as a place
of torture or a kind of "cosmic concentration camp"[10] is describing God
as a disgusting and terrifying sadist.

The following is also important, especially for the dialogue with
Protestant Christians: the process of purification we are speaking of
here arises—just as does the New Testament concept of "sanctification" or "making holy"—from God's grace. It is only the mercy and
love of the God who gives God's own self in Christ on the cross that
enables human beings to become holy to the depths of their selves.
Thus purification in death is not a self-achievement or self-deserving
of blessedness; it is gift.[11]

Of course there can be no sanctification that is not accepted and
lived.[12] But that has already taken place in the human person's freely
lived life *on earth*. If the fundamental decision of that life was open
to goodness, truth, and justice, if it was in fact immediately directed
to God and God's will, the arms of the dying person are already
opened to cleansing, healing, and sanctifying grace. Then, in death,
the "fundamental decision" of one's earthly life, ripened through
grace, comes fully to light and makes the person capable of receiving
the gift of purification.

Decades ago, the Catholic theologian Ladislaus Boros advocated
the thesis that death opens for the human person the first opportunity
to decide with the totality of her or his whole person, and now at last
in unimpeded and complete freedom, for or against God.[13] It is true
that this "final decision" is partially rehearsed in the many "previous
decisions" in life that prepare for it, and yet it stands "above them."[14]
That final decision may even "revise"[15] all prior decisions in life. Thus
death, as the boundary of life, becomes the consummation of ultimate
freedom.

As beautiful as that sounds, this position does not take death seriously: its debasement, its powerlessness, its poverty, its suffering. And
when Boros considers it possible that all the decisions of a lifetime
can be "revised" in death he calls into question his own statement that
the decision in death is the fruit of all previous decisions.[16]

We must reject any relativizing: the arrival of death puts an end to all free decisions pertaining to this life; it allows for neither revision nor repentance—not even "in borderline cases."[17] Only in this way are the weight of history and the force of worldly existence preserved. Only in this way does earthly life, with its shifts and changes—often so difficult—its defeats and victories, maintain both its seriousness and its dignity. Here, in this life, decisions are made for God or at least for truth and the good—and it is out of the sum of these many small and great decisions that the "yes" to God in death can come to be, a "yes" that is now totally and forever open for God's purifying, healing, and hallowing love.

This takes nothing away from what Protestant Christians rightly consider so important, the justification of the human person *by God alone*.[18] Let me say again: purification in death is pure grace, just as every free decision for God during earthly life was pure grace. But there must be purification in face of the holy God. If we were to say that justifying grace simply covers up everything in the person that is hardened and resistant and pays no attention to it, justification would be no judgment on sins but something like magic: what is evil in the person would be conjured away or sugar-coated by God.

That cannot be. God does not deal with creation so casually. God desires the purification and transformation of creation, not the covering over and dressing up of what is resistant to God. For human beings that purification is searingly painful, and at the same time an unspeakable joy. There is deep pain over one's own unholiness and an endless joy at arriving wholly in the light of God, both intertwined and united.

Let me close this chapter with a pointer to what is to come: the process of purification is not a lonely, isolated event between God (or Christ) and the human person who now arrives before the judge. The process of purification has an ecclesial dimension.[19] We will speak of it in detail in part 5, chapter 1 ("Genuine Care for Our Dead").

5

And What about Hell?

We have already taken leave of the idea that God punishes people for their sins. But we have to keep repeating: the notion that God demands compensation, that God punishes, takes vengeance, requires penance by torturing people and causing them anguish is absolutely unworthy of God and a gruesome caricature. It is not God who punishes. People punish themselves.[1]

But aren't there many, many Old Testament texts to the contrary? Doesn't it speak all too often of violence—and in fact of violence emanating from God, perhaps even combined with words like "recompense" and "vengeance"? Don't those praying the Psalms beg in many, many places that God take revenge?[2] Doesn't Israel ask God in Psalm 79:12 for "sevenfold return" for the destruction of Jerusalem and the Temple?

But things are not so simple, because the background here is something different from what our Western culture calls "vengeance" or "reprisal."[3] In our society someone who exacts revenge is acting outside the law, withdrawing from social control and legitimation. That person surrenders to rage, strikes back, takes revenge, gets even. But when the Old Testament speaks of God's "vengeance" or "retribution" it means what we would call "restoration of right order":

God brings things back into balance, restores the order of law in the world. God heals the injustice done to the poor and oppressed and helps them to obtain justice. In particular regarding Psalm 79 we should say that when it asks for "sevenfold" retribution on the Gentiles its concrete meaning is:

> The barbaric actions of the conquerors, for whom literally nothing is sacred, neither the Temple nor the corpses, are judged as such a fundamental offense against the order of law that YHWH, for the sake of his own divinity, can no longer accept it. The psalm, with its appeal to divine wrath, cries out for God's justice as the guaranteeing force of a *world order* and as a court of justice especially for the victims.[4]

Thus when the Bible speaks of God's "vengeance" and "retribution" the expressions move within a different world of ideas than ours, and yet they are part of the language of law and justice. Injustice incurred will be compensated, justice restored, the poor and deprived will be helped. And this "restoration of justice can be expressed in metaphors of violence."[5]

Of course this in no way resolves the problem of hell, because in the minds of many Christians it was hell that signaled the possibility that God will restore the broken order of justice in the end and square the books on the fearful crimes in human history—with eternal punishment. But would that really be a settlement, a recompense, and one worthy of God? The problem presented by the existence of hell is the final damnation associated with it. Can God, whose nature is pure love, allow a part of humanity to suffer eternal hell, eternal torment?

Today's theologians raise many questions here, such as: Can ultimate beatitude, the feast of eternal happiness with God, really exist if at the same time—before the eyes of the blessed—some portion of humanity lives in eternal torment? And still more basic: Has God achieved the purpose of creation if part of that creation has definitively become a hell? Would that not mean that God's creation is a fundamental failure, and that creation's history of salvation and redemption has ultimately fallen short of its intended goal?[6]

It would appear that the New Testament speaks clearly on this question. There we read of the "day of wrath" (Rom 2:5), the lake of

fire (Rev 20:15), "eternal destruction" (2 Thess 1:9) of those who had
no pity on Jesus' starving and persecuted disciples[7] and therefore
have been thrust by the world's judge into "eternal fire" (Matt 25:41).
We could go on listing such passages, but how should we approach
these texts?

First, we should notice that none of these statements is in the form
of declarative, *informative* language.[8] They are all intended to ad-
monish and warn, and more than that: they are meant to frighten, to
shatter the icy shield of human indifference. Jesus can say:

> If your right hand causes you to sin, cut it off and throw it away;
> it is better for you to lose one of your members than for your
> whole body to be thrown into hell. (Matt 5:30)

If such a text is seen merely as evidence for the existence of hell it has
not been read rightly. Instead, it ought to lead one to appreciate the
vast responsibility that falls on Jesus' followers with the coming of
the reign of God. The reign of God is a matter of life and death; this
is about all or nothing.[9] Human beings can use the freedom that
comes with the reign of God for the sake of God's cause or misuse it
against God. Here, as in many comparable texts in the Bible, it is a
question of the sharpening of responsibility.*

Of course, saying that is still not enough. The expressions about
hell in the New Testament are to be read within the much greater
framework of other texts that speak of God's universal will for salvation: God "desires *everyone* to be saved" (1 Tim 2:4); "the grace of
God has appeared, bringing salvation to *all*" (Titus 2:11); Jesus Christ
"gave himself a ransom *for all*" (1 Tim 2:6); God desired "through
him . . . to reconcile . . . *all things*" (Col 1:20); the exalted Christ will
"draw *all people* to [himself]" (John 12:32); "one man's act of righteousness leads to justification and life *for all*" (Rom 5:18); "God has
imprisoned *all* in disobedience [in order to] be merciful to *all*" (Rom
11:32). It is striking how often the key word "all" is repeated in these
and other texts. God, says Scripture hyper-obviously, desires the

---

* Therefore, for example, the statement in Augustine's *De civitate Dei*, XXI, 12
that the number of the damned who receive punishment is much, much greater
than the number of those saved by grace is irresponsible and a theological
original sin. Augustine makes *performative* texts into *informative* ones.

salvation of all. That is certainly fundamental. But will God succeed? What if someone simply does not want it?

On the basis of the New Testament, one thing is certain: if someone is unwilling, God does not leave it there. It is with God as with a shepherd who goes after a wandering sheep (Luke 15:3-7) or a woman who seeks her lost drachma through the whole house (Luke 15:8-10). God seeks reconciliation with the unwilling as did a person who went to Jerusalem to offer sacrifice, but when standing before the altar remembered that a brother or sister in faith "had something against her or him" and "left the gift" before the altar and returned to be reconciled with the other party (Matt 5:23-24). The parable even leaves open the question of which of the two was responsible for the falling-out. For the one who interrupts the act of offering, what matters above all is reconciliation; without it there can be no worship. And do we suppose that God, who requires of us such a will to reconciliation, will not do everything conceivable to win back a single person?

If we follow this line within Scripture, then hell cannot be something God imposes on people. Hell can only be something that God does not want, in any case and under any circumstances. Then hell would be something a human being chooses for herself or himself. But is that possible?

Previous chapters have already used the phrase "fundamental decision," and it was clear from the context what should be understood by it: a person's many major and minor decisions consolidate themselves more and more into an attitude that shapes the basic direction of that person's life. That basic direction may be "covered over by layers of secondary decisions."[10] It is not always visible as such. It may be frayed at the edges. It may be combined with many ambiguities and dichotomies. It may be that the person concerned is not even aware of it. And yet it is there.[11]

If that fundamental option is directed immediately toward God everything is simple and clear. Then the human person, in death, stands finally before the one whose face she or he always desired to see (Ps 17:15). But there are infinitely many people who know nothing of the God of Israel and the church, who live, or have lived, quite contentedly within their particular religion, have lifted their hands in prayer to Ba'al, Amun-Re, Zeus, or Donar, who in times of need have called upon the god responsible for the situation or have worshiped natural forces and numinous powers. And there are those—their numbers are increasing—who grow up without any religion at all, who may be conscious atheists or agnostics, or neither agnostic nor atheist but simply people for whom the question of God is utterly foreign.

These people also make a fundamental decision, perhaps for goodness, truth, justice, humanity. They have sought the truth in various ways, and now they stand before the absolute truth, who has a face. They have desired the good, and now in death they behold what they have longed for as goodness in the one God, the absolute good. They have battled for a just society, and now they understand that in doing so they have reached out for exactly what is the will of the God of Abraham, Isaac, and Jacob. They have worked for peace, and now they stand before the God of Jesus Christ, who desires nothing other than a people who bring peace and reconciliation to the world.

But let us go still further: not everyone is a hero or a fighter with great goals. By no means do all seek the truth throughout their lives. And yet only God knows what there is within them of buried longing, hidden goodness, unconfessed search for a better world. In the judgment all these hidden things, and what has occurred only at depth within the person, will come to light.

Here we cannot avoid speaking also of criminals—those who tell lies on a grand scale, who manipulate, rob, rape, murder, destroy—including, of course, the criminals in the seats of power, in their expensive suits, unapproachable. Are they the best candidates for hell? Who would venture to enter a judgment here? Do we know what impels them to commit their crimes? or what is really going on in their minds, consciously or unconsciously? Mustn't we also reckon with the possibility that they are lacking all sense of guilt, so that their crimes take place on a sub-personal level? Do we know the innermost states of their existence, the space in which the fundamental decision of their lives takes place? Do they desire evil as evil?

And still the question of hell is not resolved. Suppose there were a person who fell through all these grids, who desires not good but evil—and desires it *because* it is evil; someone who does not want the truth, but lies, and lives a lie to the depths of his or her existence; someone who says "I am enough for myself. I am my own meaning.

I desire only myself, myself alone." It is certainly difficult to imagine such a person.[12] But novelists describe them, and poets speak of them as well. Scholars describe the aesthetics of the deliberately evil in literature as something that takes one's breath away.[13]

If there be such people who with the fundamental choice of their existence seek only themselves and reject everything else, God must leave them to themselves, to their own closedness-within-the-self. God cannot overpower them and certainly cannot assault them. Such a person would then really have nothing but his or her own self—and that, precisely, would be hell.

We can only hope that there is no such person, that even in such cases God's grace will prove victorious by tearing open the self-created prison of that person's own existence even before death. We can only hope that hell is empty or, better, that no one makes herself or himself a hell. But such statements remain on the level of pure hope. We do not know.

Hell remains a fearful possibility, which is why the Bible speaks of it. It would not be permissible to simply deny it theologically and replace it with a universal eschatological reconciliation. Those who want to banish from the world all talk of the evil, the horrors of which people are capable, and of the hells they prepare for themselves, do not make the world brighter and more human but only cloud its abysses. For talk of hell opens our eyes to the sweeping and consequential decision we confront day after day: simply to allow evil to exist in the world, to close our eyes to the suffering, injustice, and violence—or to work against the evil in ourselves and in society, with patience and in the spirit of the Gospel.

Talk of hell is required by the sober realism with which we must view history. Talk of hell is demanded by our gigantic responsibility. But it must always have a counterweight that is much heavier: God's absolute will for salvation.

6

The Whole Person

Previously this book has always spoken of the "resurrection of the dead," and that expression is quite correct. We find it many times in the New Testament,[1] and it has become a fixed element of the Christian language of faith. The so-called "great confession of faith"* says:

> We look for the resurrection of the dead
> and the life of the world to come.

However, the "great confession" appeared as an official formula only at the Council of Chalcedon in 451.[2] Before and after, the so-called "Apostles' Creed" played a much greater role. It is shorter, and in its essentials it goes back to the Roman baptismal creed, alongside which numerous similar confessions connected with other local churches also existed. In all these shorter creeds—if the resurrection is mentioned—the phrase is not "resurrection of the dead" but "resurrection of the flesh."[3] The Apostles' Creed reads:**

---

* "The Great Confession of Faith" is the now-common name for the so-called Nicaeo-Constantinopolitan or "Nicene" Creed.

** This is a literal translation of the Greek text. The elements "catholic," "communion of saints," and "eternal life" come from a somewhat later time but are also ancient (they are attested from the end of the fourth century).

> I believe in the Holy Spirit,
> the holy catholic* church,
> the communion of saints,
> the forgiveness of sins,
> the resurrection of the flesh**
> and life everlasting.

Why does the creed speak of "flesh" or "body"? What lies behind this formula, going back to the second century[4] and recited in Sunday worship to this day?[5]

"Flesh" in the meaning it has here sounds odd in our ears. When we hear "flesh" we think of butcher shops, menus, or a beach full of sun-seeking bodies. But in the Bible "flesh" often signifies more than "body" or animal parts. It can refer to human beings as such, everything they are, their whole existence. Important in our context is the biblical expression "all flesh," which means the whole of humanity or even all living things. "All flesh" is called to praise God in Psalm 145:21. "I will pour out my spirit on all flesh," says Joel 2:28. The emphasis in such usage can be on human vulnerability, weakness, mortality, and yet it always refers to the whole person: everything that makes it up, everything that belongs to it.

But what caused the early church to speak precisely of the "resurrection of the flesh/body"? It must have sounded crass and offensive to Greek ears—how offensive, we can see in a text by the enlightened philosopher Celsus (second half of the second century CE). He mocks the "idiotic teaching" of the Christians who believe in a resurrection of the body:

> It is folly on their part to suppose [in their faith in a bodily resurrection] [that the dead] will arise from the earth clothed with the self-same flesh (as during life); for such a hope is simply one which might be cherished by worms. For what sort of human soul is that which would still long for a body that had been subject to corruption? . . . For the soul, indeed, [God] might be able to provide an everlasting life; while [*cadavers*], on the

---

* "Catholic" here does not have its later confessional meaning. It means "universal" and refers to the church throughout the world.

** Original wording.

contrary, are, as Heraclitus observes, more worthless than dung.
God, however, neither can nor will declare, contrary to all reason,
that the flesh, which is full of those things which it is not even
honourable to mention, is to exist for ever.[6]

This text makes it abundantly clear why the early Christian baptismal confessions did not speak simply of the "resurrection of the dead."
It was obviously a point of conflict. At a very early period there were
types of Christian theology that despised the body and human cor-
poreality. Salvation was said to be removal from the world, escape
from the body, the overcoming of everything carnal and material.
Salvation meant precisely that the divine in the human would become
free of the body and elevated to a sphere of pure spirituality.[7] We saw
that kind of thinking in Plato (see part 1, chap. 2 above) and in a certain
type of Greek and Roman epitaphs. It shows itself also in a later Pla-
tonist like Celsus and indeed was widespread in antiquity.

But for the church, if it held fast to its origins in Israel and its ap-
ostolic tradition, such an idea of redemption was unthinkable. God
had formed human beings, with their bodily nature, their whole
materiality, with the Creator's own hands, and breathed the breath
of life into them (Gen 2:7). Therefore redemption must include the
body. But still more: Jesus Christ was the epitome of all redemption.
He was the original model for humanity as intended by God. In him
the *logos* of God had itself become human. Jesus was not only true
God, but also truly human. He did not have only the appearance of
a body, and he was not the epiphany of a god clothed in humanity.[8]
The Gospel of John says all that in one brief sentence: "And the Word
became flesh" (John 1:14).

It is equally important to assert that Jesus was always interested
in the whole person, not only her or his soul, as his acts of healing of
the frail and sick, the disturbed and traumatized, show.[9] He did not
preach "flee the world and overcome the body!" but instead proclaimed the reign of God that will change everything: body and spirit,
world and history. (Compare part 3, chaps. 1 and 2 above.)

Against this background in Jesus' person the keyword "flesh" in
John 1:14 is clearly seen to be directed against heretics who saw redemption as a liberation from body and evil matter.[10] Early Christian

theologians from then on spoke emphatically and repeatedly of the "flesh" of Jesus Christ and the "flesh" of the resurrection,[11] in order to defend what is genuinely Jewish-Christian against every form of contempt for the world and hostility to the flesh.[12] The sharpest and most concise formula is that of the North African Tertullian (second century CE):

> *Caro salutis est cardo.*
> The flesh is the pivot of salvation.[13]

What does all that mean in our context? It means that resurrection includes the whole human person and not only a part of her or him. It encompasses everything that makes the person: her joys and sorrows, his happiness and sadness—everything she has worked through in her life, and everything he has suffered—what she accomplished and what was given him—the great things she thought and the little things he did in daily fidelity—every hour she has endured—every tear he has wept—every smile that has passed across her face—in short: the whole history of the person's life. Because all that is connected with the body. Body and soul interpenetrate. The human person not only "has" a body but "is" body, and not only "has" a soul but "is" soul. The human can only be understood as a psychosomatic unity. When the Bible speaks of "flesh" it presupposes that very unity. Obviously the human person must be judged, purified, and made holy (see part 4, chaps. 2 and 4). But these things must happen in the person as a whole.

Certainly we need more precision here. What I have listed could be applied in its entirety to the individual: her or his private history, which would then be viewed in isolation and apart from the history of other people. But an isolated existence in that sense is impossible. Every individual is linked to others with a thousand threads: to parents, siblings, friends, neighbors, acquaintances, contemporaries. Above all, each of us is linked at depth with those we love. No one can be human without other people. No one can be an "I" without a "you." Individuality, being oneself, personhood do not exist without a living connection to others. Living as a person means "living in relationship." Existing means "experiencing others."

The resurrection of the flesh must incorporate all that. If certain books have become part of my personal development, my relationship to those books must rise with me. If a garden I have planted and tended has become part of my life, my relationship to that garden, my planting and care, must rise with me. If a beloved pet has been part of my life, my relationship to its dependence and fidelity will rise with me. But much more important: if another person has become my friend, someone who was always there and has always helped me, the "being together" with her or him will be part of my resurrection. Finally and above all: if two people have loved each other, shared their lives, if each has become part of the other, if, in the biblical phrase, they have become "one flesh,"[14] then resurrection will include everything they have given each other.

We could extend the examples almost to infinity; the biblical concept of the "flesh" includes them all. The Russian poet Yevgeny Alexandrovitch Yevtushenko (1932–2017) wrote a poem entitled "People." The second part can make clear what I am trying to say here:

> To each his world is private
> and in that world one excellent minute.
>
> And in that world one tragic minute
> These are private.
>
> In any man who dies there dies with him
> his first snow and kiss and fight
> it goes with him. . . .
>
> But what has gone is also not nothing:
> by the rule of the game something has gone.
> Not people die but worlds die in them. . . .
>
> Whom we knew as faulty, the earth's creatures
> Of whom, essentially, what did we know?
>
> Brother of a brother? Friend of friends?
> Lover of lover?
>
> We who knew our fathers
> in everything, in nothing.
>
> They perish. They cannot be brought back.
> The secret worlds are not regenerated.

And every time again and again
I make my lament against destruction.[15]

This state of being affected by the unique "world" that belongs to each person is a necessary precondition for understanding what Christian faith in the resurrection of the flesh means. Resurrection means that the whole person comes to God, the person with her first kiss and his first snow—the whole history of a life.

"Not people die but worlds die in them." Here there is an echo, in Yevtushenko as well, of the truth that to each individual belongs a whole world: that of parents, friends, and those one has loved with one's whole existence. For Yevtushenko, though, all that vanishes irretrievably. In Christian faith it does not perish; it is resurrected. Nothing is lost, not the tiniest memory. Everything we have experienced in this life, painfully and joyfully, will become the "material" of eternal life with God—but worked through, purified, transformed.

If this were not the case—if our whole past were not retrieved in our life with God, and with our past a piece of the world—then eternal life would be a new beginning foreign to us, a "beyond" in the bad sense, a world-behind-the-world that has nothing more to do with our life and history.[16]

Many years ago I noted down a sentence I saw painted in large letters on the wall of the dim entrance hall of a Christian retirement home:

Nothing travels with us.
What we here call earth,
Just as we came hither,
So we'll leave again.

The saying was not only a slap in the faces of the elderly women and men who spent their last years there, and were thus daily threatened with "departure." It was also fundamentally theologically false, because it was silent about the resurrection of the flesh, and it rejected earth. For the confession of a resurrection of the "flesh" does *not* mean only the human body but our whole history, that wonderful, venturous, convoluted history with its tears and ecstasies, its sorrows and blessings—it all "travels with us" into eternal life with God.

7

The Whole History of the World

The preceding chapter was intended to point to something that, essentially, we take for granted: that a human being is more than an isolated individual. One's incarnation, "becoming human," demands encounter with others. And even when we have "halfway" become human we cannot really be persons without the most complicated relationships to other people.

But we need to expand on that insight, for the many people each of us encounters in the course of our lives and who help us to become ourselves are themselves connected to many other people. Communication researchers say that every one of us knows about 150 people well, and each of those knows another 150 people well, and so on. And that mutual knowing is always also associated with mutual influence.

The researchers' thesis is valid. One need only count the names in one's address book, subtract all the purely business connections, and add the many people we knew in previous decades who no longer appear in our current address list. We truly do live in a network of relationships and interactions that continually expands beyond our acquaintances in both time and space. That network contains all the spaces and times of human history. Humanity is a unity in a much deeper sense than appears at first glance. I am connected with the person who first invented the wheel and so fundamentally changed the nature of transport beyond the travois previously in use. I am connected with that person because when I drive my car, and in countless other instances, I am living the results of that person's admirable discovery. I am connected with the people who invented the roof, because I live in a house that stays dry even in heavy rains. I am connected with the countless people who have contributed to making human language ever more subtle and flexible, because the use of language is my life. I am deeply connected with those who first had the genius to invent letters, because it is by reading and writing that I live.

We could go on and on with such examples, and they would show that we are linked not only to people who have made useful discoveries but also to the collective memories and objective spirit of whole epochs. We have to speak of an infinite network, without which we could not live. Moreover, it is becoming ever more intensive. The escalating growth of modern information technology must lead to an interweaving of humanity (both positive and negative in its effects) that was unimaginable even a hundred years ago.

What does all this mean for the resurrection of the dead? It means that resurrection can by no means be an exclusively individual matter. The individual who encounters God in death can do so only in union with all the dead throughout world history. This is so because the self of any individual does not exist without the others; she or he has lived from them, adopted their ideas or rejected them. Freedom is made possible for any human being through others, and each of us makes possible the freedom of others—or makes it impossible. Each of us has damaged or been deeply hurt by others. Therefore each of us can only be judged together with all those others.

Hence divine judgment on the individual must coincide with judgment on all, for the deeds of the individual are—whether in agreement or disagreement—tied to and networked with the deeds of many other people.[1] And of course networked not only with their "deeds" but also with their worldviews, interpretations of the world, and the guiding thoughts of many epochs. Those who lived in Germany in the time of the "Third Reich" lived *with* National Socialist ideology and were inevitably "perpetrators." There were any number of possibilities, each of them with sub-forms: (a) one could silently and submissively accept the ideology of "Volk, Reich, Führer";[2] (b) one could join the National Socialists by a free decision; (c) one could live in silent, secret "resistance";* (d) one could offer public resistance, which in almost every case would ensure one's death.

From that point of view it is no accident that the Bible always speaks of the "resurrection of the dead" in the plural—even in the case of Jesus. As we have seen, the New Testament calls him the "first fruits" or "beginning" of the general resurrection of the dead. (See part 3, chap. 5 above, "The Firstborn from the Dead.") The early Christians were convinced that Jesus' resurrection signaled the end of the world and that the resurrection of all, living and dead, would therefore happen in the immediate future.[3] Only when the end of the world did not happen was Christian theology faced with the task of bringing the "last things" for individuals and the resurrection of the dead at the end of the world together in a comprehensive system of ideas. It looked like this: the individual dies, but only her or his soul attains to God. The soul is individually judged and thereafter, supposing it has withstood the judgment (and, if necessary, after a limited time in Purgatory) lives in the full vision of God. Then, at the end of the world, there will be bodily resurrection and the general judgment. That complex of ideas dominated theology and popular piety for centuries. But—at least in the form in which it was usually expressed—it contained two problems:

1. The human body was thus devalued, and in fact made superfluous. For if the soul, after death, individual judgment, and purification, already lives in the full vision of God, then the later addition of the body is not at all necessary. The soul has already been existing in beatitude with God. What purpose is served by the later delivery of a body?

---

* The concept of the "Resistance" in dictatorships was created at the end of the 1970s by Martin Broszat, who derived it from the common medical concept. It refers to particular social groups' non-compliance with the ruling ideology, internal opposition, daily acts of resistance or civil disobedience exercised by those groups.

2. The whole construction for the most part assumed, without any particular reflection, that time goes on beyond death just as before: hours, days, years, centuries. The course of earthly history was precisely parallel to the course of life with God: the individual soul must wait until world history has come to an end and the resurrection of the dead takes place. The same theologians who knew that we can only speak in "analogous"* concepts of anything having to do with God suddenly made an exception for this "intermediate state": earthly time and "time" with God were the same, or at least "commensurable" with one another, that is, "comparable," or better, "measurably attuned."

Certainly we have to admit that the traditional complex of ideas just described perceived something quite right and even utterly important about the postulated intervening time: namely, the interwovenness we have spoken of at such length in this chapter. We are only "persons" through communication with others. Therefore in recent years many and very significant theologians have said that the individual person, even though already in the presence of God, can only be *fully and completely* with God when everything that ties her or him to others still living on earth has been purified and reviewed—for example, the suffering this individual has caused others. Joseph Ratzinger speaks of what remains to be done and completed in this sense as follows:

> We can ask whether a human being can be said to have reached his fulfillment and destiny so long as others suffer on account of him, so long as the guilt whose source he is persists on earth and brings pain to other people.[4]

He sees the review of events that is therefore necessary as lasting throughout history, because all people are mutually dependent and interwoven. Ratzinger speaks of the "interdependence of all" and explains it this way:

> Every human being exists in himself and outside himself: everyone exists simultaneously in other people. What happens in one

---

*For the concept of analogy see the introduction to part 4 of this book ("What Will Happen to Us").

individual has an effect upon the whole of humanity and what happens in humanity happens in the individual.[5]

Only "when the *passio* and *actio* of history have come to their end"[6] could those who have died before—even if they were already secure of their ultimate salvation—be completely finished and perfected. That in itself appears to be the theological justification for the idea of an intermediate state between the redemption of the individual and the judgment of the world at the end of history.

That makes sense and agrees with what I have said about purification in death (part 4, chap. 4) and the interwovenness of the many individuals. The problem is only that the "intermediate state" rightly demanded may again become associated with an unreflective time-scheme. The "between" called for with such persuasive arguments is often imagined in terms of *earthly* time, because the end of history is not yet, and therefore the "*passio* and *actio* of history" have not yet been completed.[7]

It is true that the working through of every kind of failure and evil that links us to other people is unavoidable. That review process takes place in the purification at death. To that extent there must be a "between" and a process of "interaction" with others, one that also affects the "body." But that process—as far as the perspective on what is beyond is concerned—may no longer be thought of in terms of *earthly* time, and it requires of the dead no "time of waiting" until history has reached its end, because precisely that would mean making the "intermediate time" of the process of purification parallel to and *commensurable* with the ongoing course of earthly history.*

Therefore we may posit that individual judgment in death and general judgment at the end of the world come together as one. They are not identical, but they cannot be separated, either in substance or in the

---

*So there is no objection to the formulations by those advocating a "resurrection in death" that say that the human being already risen in death must still "wait" until the whole of history has been completed, because this resurrection already completed in the death of the individual presumes the course of history to its end. But that "waiting" is an analogous concept, something we cannot imagine in positive terms. In no event does it presume an interval of *earthly* time, because in that case "waiting" would be used univocally.

sense of *earthly* time. And therefore the encounter with God in death is also an event that cannot be separated from the resurrection of all the dead. That is why I have spoken of the encounter of the "whole person" and likewise the encounter of the "whole of history" with God.

Of course such a statement presupposes a considered concept of time, something I will speak of at length in chapter 10 below. Beyond that, we must then also consider what is here called "interaction" between the living and the dead. (That will be the subject of part 5, chap. 1.) Current works on eschatological themes are fully aware of this whole problem field. Meanwhile, a great many Catholic theologians have begun to speak, though with a number of variations, of a "resurrection in death."[8]

It is true that there are two completely different approaches to the complex of ideas surrounding "resurrection in death."[9] One starts with the concept of the soul and asks: What, exactly, is the soul that encounters God in death? Does it have nothing to do with the body? Has it not internalized its whole body? And therefore is the "beginning" of bodily resurrection already present in the human encounter with God in death?

The other approach begins with a discussion of time. It asks: Is there such a thing as time in the earthly sense "in" or "after" death? At the very least, that "time" beyond death can no longer be commensurable with earthly time, and for that reason the "interim" before the general resurrection of the dead can likewise not be formulated simply in terms of earthly time. Therefore: resurrection is "in" death, though obviously even that "in" is an analogous and hence unimaginable idea.

8

The Whole Creation

We have seen what resurrection means: the whole person comes to God with everything belonging to her or him, the full and colorful history of a life. We have also seen that the story of every individual life is interwoven with the life-histories of many other people, and in fact with the developments and world of meaning of entire epochs. Therefore the history of all humanity must attain to God with and in every individual.

And yet those statements are still not adequate. Resurrection is something still more: according to the New Testament, with Jesus' resurrection begins what the Old Testament and early Jewish apocalyptic[1] call "new creation" or the creation of a "new heaven and new earth."[2] Jesus' resurrection therefore affects not only the human world but, together with it, the whole universe. It is not only human history that arrives at its goal in the Risen One; in him the entire cosmos comes to its perfection. That sounds like overreaching, but it is exactly what the New Testament says—and this chapter aims to demonstrate it.

To say that in the resurrection of the dead that begins with Jesus it is not only the *human being* but the whole *universe* that arrives at its purpose and end is to assert an unbreakable bond between the human and the cosmos. It is easy to see that the connection must be taken seriously: Planet Earth is part of the solar system; our solar system orbits in the center of the Milky Way; the Milky Way is one of many billions of galaxies; and the universe of galaxies has been expanding, since the "Big Bang" some 13.8 billion years ago, at an unimaginable and steadily increasing speed. Our planet is spinning around the sun somewhere within those imagination-shattering spaces. But what happened on this planet—so tiny in comparison to the universe—is breathtaking: life arose, organized itself with ever-increasing complexity, and finally became a home to the human spirit.

Biologists who study this molecular evolution say that primal bacteria, from which all the later organisms on our planet developed, must have emerged in hot pools or springs where they could breathe carbon dioxide and hydrogen; they were remarkably rich in metals. From these organic beginnings the human developed, in a long and highly complex evolution. We come from the matter of the earth and thus from the dust and gas of the stars. And we still draw life from the earth, the sun, and the waters. Human and cosmos, spirit and world belong inseparably together. A worldless humanity is unthinkable. "Matter and evolution form the prehistory of spirit or mind."[3]

The Bible is fully conscious of this tight connection between the human and the cosmos; we need only open up the first pages of the Old Testament to see it. Here we find an account of the creation of the world: heaven and earth, land and sea, plants and trees, sun, moon, stars, fish and birds, cattle and wild beasts. Then the human being is created as ruler and protector of all plants and animals. Finally:

> Thus the heavens and the earth were finished, and all their host.*
> (Gen 2:1)

"Host" (*zeba*)—that could mean the multitude of the stars (cp. Isa 40:26), and then, correspondingly, the teeming crowd of animals and humans. The Septuagint, the Greek translation of the Old Testament composed in the third century BCE, therefore had a certain license to say:

---

*NRSV: "multitude."

The heaven and the land and all their ornamentation (κόσμος; "cosmos") were completed.

And the humans in the middle of it all! This inextricable interweaving of the human with the rest of the universe is also visible in the Old Testament in that not only are people continually called upon to praise God, but so is the whole creation.

All angels and the heavenly host, sun and moon, fire and hail, snow and fog, mountains and hills, wild beasts and all cattle, creeping things and all birds, young men and women, all people, every creature, and even the depths of the earth

> let them praise the name of the LORD,
> for his name alone is exalted;
> his glory is above earth and heaven.

This enumeration runs throughout Psalm 148, which, together with Psalms 146–150, makes up the grand conclusion to the Psalter. These last five psalms are composed as an *eschatological look forward*; they are meant to say that the day will come when the whole creation will become praise of God. This finale closes the Psalter, which has previously spoken again and again of misery, strife, war, crisis, and death. In the end the universe will be pure praise: all creation including sun and moon, snow and fog, plants, animals, and humans.*

But how can non-human creation praise God? Obviously not by itself, but only because human beings again and again look at the world penetratingly, attentively, and with astonishment, appreciating the power and beauty of creation and making themselves its voice. They thus become the "mouth" of all creation before God. In just this way the human and the cosmos surpass all physical identities, becoming an ultimate and inseparable unity. When human beings, as the mouth of creation, become pure thanksgiving and praise, they have internalized creation; they become one with it and give it its spirit and meaning.

Hence the Old Testament is filled with the idea of the unity of creation. But it invokes that unity from a completely different perspective:

---

*Evil is then judged and destroyed: Pss 146:9; 147:6; 149:5-9.

it is true that humans can praise God and so make themselves the voice of creation, but they can also act *against* creation, and then they destroy not only themselves but the world in which they live—indeed, not only their immediate environment but the whole earth. Israel's prophets paint in broad strokes the ways in which chaos in society becomes chaos in nature.[4] For example, we read in Isaiah 24:3-7:*

> The earth shall be utterly laid waste and utterly despoiled;
> for the LORD has spoken this word.
>
> The earth dries up and withers,
> the world languishes and withers;
> the [exalted of the earth]** languish.
>
> The earth lies polluted under its inhabitants;
> for they have transgressed the laws,
> violated the statutes,
> broken the everlasting covenant.
>
> Therefore a curse devours the earth,
> and its inhabitants suffer for their guilt;
> therefore the inhabitants of the earth dwindled,
> and few people are left.
>
> The wine dries up,
> the vine languishes,
> all the merry-hearted sigh.

It appears that this apocalyptic text from the book of Isaiah is not about the land of Israel but the entire world of the nations. The earth dries up and withers because its inhabitants sin. "Human godlessness even destroys the order of the cosmos."[5]

This is precisely the backdrop in apocalyptic theology before which Paul is speaking in Romans 8:18-25 when he talks of the sighing and groaning of all creation. It is not only people who sigh and groan, but the rest of creation as well. It suffers birthpangs together with humanity. Mortality, futility, and emptiness still shape the world.

* Adapted from NRSV according to the author's translation.
** Author's trans., which sees here a reference to the upper social classes. —Trans.

As I have said, Paul is speaking here against the background of Old Testament apocalyptic depictions and those of early Judaism. All these texts arise out of a profound past history. They are two thousand years old, and in some cases much older. Besides, they are images and metaphors. And yet we can confirm these images today in horrifying ways. They are close to us and have become utterly real.

For decades we have seen how our environment, and the earth as a whole, is being exploited and destroyed—by gluttony, greed, and arrogance. Fields are being contaminated, rivers poisoned, the world's oceans littered with plastics, rainforests dug up, surfaces paved, countless species of animals made extinct, massive changes in the climate accepted with a shrug of the shoulders. In these last decades we have become aware, in an unexpectedly dramatic way, of the groaning of creation that Paul speaks of in Romans 8:22.

But I will not dwell on that. What I am about here is this: Romans 8 also reveals the inextricable connection between the human and the cosmos. Non-human creation[6] groans and sighs like a human being but, like humans, it is also in a state of anticipation.

And what is it waiting for? For liberation and redemption, Paul says (8:21). Then comes what is so astonishing and unexpected in this unique text: From what source does all creation hope to receive liberation and redemption? What is it reaching out for, so filled with sighs and yearning (8:19)? It is for the "revelation of the children of God" (8:19). And what is that revelation of the children of God? It happens in the resurrection, in the redemption of the human body (8:23, 29).

So Paul is looking to the resurrection, the revelation of what is already given to believers now, in this time, by the Spirit of God, as a kind of "earnest money." When this being-revealed then happens with the return of Christ, the liberation from the enslavement to mortality that lies upon the world and is the result of sin will take place finally and irrevocably—and that liberation will then include the whole non-human creation.

This makes it clear that resurrection is not something that creation can bring forth of itself, and not even highly developed humanity can do that. The resurrection of the human and the universe is a sharing in the resurrection of Jesus Christ. Therefore Paul writes in Romans 8:29 that God has destined all who love God

to be conformed to the image of his Son, in order that he might
be the firstborn of many sisters and brothers.

Within this compressed formula there is a sudden flash of the creation
account in Genesis 1: just as there, at the first creation, the human
being was defined as "image of God" (v. 27), so now in the new creation it is "the image of his Son," that is, of the Risen One. But we must
pay attention: "image" here is much more than mere external appearance. The "image" is the shining figure of the being, the nature itself.[7]
Thus Romans 8:29 intends to say that those who believe in God and
love God will, in the resurrection, take the same form as the being
and nature of Christ. Their resurrection is a participation—participation in Christ's Easter glory. But the section (Rom 8:18-30) goes
beyond even that: the believing and hope-filled person shares in
Christ's resurrection, and with believing and hope-filled humans, so
does the whole creation. It, too, will be liberated and redeemed.

The author of the letter to the Ephesians says the same thing in
different terminology and from another point of view when he writes
that God's plan "for the fullness of time" is to "gather up all things in
him, things in heaven and things on earth" (Eph 1:10). Thus all history
runs toward the exalted Christ—but not only all history; the whole
creation will be gathered together and receive its perfection in Christ.

The letter to the Christians in Colossae should be mentioned in the
same context. Its author writes about Jesus Christ in 1:15-20, in an
exalted style:[8]

> He is the image of the invisible God, the firstborn of all creation;
> for in him the universe, all things in heaven and on earth were
> created, things visible and invisible, whether thrones or dominions
> or rulers or powers—the universe has been created through him
> and for him. He himself is before all things, and in him the uni-
> verse holds together. He is the head of the body, [namely,] the
> church; he is the beginning, the firstborn from the dead, so that
> he might come to have first place in everything. For in him [God]
> was pleased to make the whole fullness to dwell, and through him
> God was pleased to reconcile the universe, whether on earth or in
> heaven, by making peace through the blood of his [Jesus'] cross.*

*Colossians 1:15-20; NRSV translation edited to match the author's.

The second part of this incredibly dense and theologically thick text[9] speaks of the crucified, risen, and exalted Christ, through whom God has bestowed reconciliation on the world. That goes back to the oldest Christology: Christ is the first, the beginning of the general resurrection of the dead—and that in itself is the basis for his all-surpassing dignity. In him, God, in the fullness of divine glory, has chosen to dwell (cp. Col 2:9), and through him and in him has reconciled the whole universe.

But very quickly there developed a Christology that took its starting point not from Christ's resurrection and exaltation but instead, in the tradition of some Old Testament wisdom texts,[10] from the creation of the world. Christ is the model for all creation—and therein lies his all-surpassing dignity. The text from Colossians 1:15-20 combines the two: Christ is the "firstborn of all creation" *and* "firstborn from the dead," that is, the beginning of God's new creation.

What is so special about Colossians 1:15-20 is that it speaks no less than four times about the "universe," or "all" (Greek *ta panta*).* What is that? Quite obviously it is not merely the *collected whole* of all creatures, but in a more specific sense the powers of the world that are in eternal strife. The author speaks of "thrones," "dominions," "rulers," and "powers" (Col 1:16). In the first place these are powers within society, but in the Hellenistic worldview there are cosmic forces behind these quarreling parties and mutually antagonistic nations. All conflict in the world derives from those powers through which our world is dimmed and enslaved to its innermost depths. In view of this situation, the author wants to tell the Christians in Colossae that all these evil forces in the world are powerless because not only is the universe "created for Christ" but through Jesus' death God has also bestowed an all-encompassing reconciliation—not only among humans, but among the cosmic powers, that is, reconciliation of the universe.

Thus Colossians 1:15-20 also says (though in an entirely different form from that in Rom 8:18-25) that the whole cosmos will be drawn into the glory of the new creation, because the universe has been created for Christ and will be reconciled in Christ. Thus Colossians 1:15-20 speaks not only of peace and reconciliation among human beings; it speaks of the goal of the whole creation.

---

* The NRSV renders this "all creation" or "all things."

Of course, these texts do not tell us how we should imagine the gathering and redemption of non-human creation, and we should not try to picture it, for it is unimaginable. We must only maintain that the whole cosmos will share in the resurrection that began with Jesus Christ. Thus the liberation of creation does not take place for itself and in isolation but, in a way beyond our minds' grasp, integrated in what happens to the risen Christ and, through him, to us humans.[11] We are not redeemed "from this earth" but "with it."[12]

Once we have grasped this, the call for the preservation of creation acquires an even more profound meaning, because it makes us humans aware of how we are interlaced with pre-human creation. When we act to protect the earth and all creatures we join with creation and make ourselves its speaking tongue before God. And then all the poetry that is now turning with ever-renewed fascination toward creation—and not only turning toward it, but re-creating it in speech—acquires a theological function. For example, when Matthias Claudius wrote:

> The hushed, black woods are dreaming,
> The mists, like phantoms seeming,
> From meadows magically rise . . .[13]

he was not *describing* the world but *interpreting* it, and not only *interpreting* it but *internalizing* it, and in that way *incorporating* it in the "known world" of human consciousness and so opening it to the resurrection. The same is, of course, true of all the great painters who depict the world and so bring it to its own identity; it is true of all musicians whose symphonies echo the rhythms of the world and history. Obviously what I am saying is true also for all abstract art: it does not image the world but creates new worlds—but *de facto* those new worlds are also reflections and interpretations of the world as it exists.*

But then all scientific research—from the work of molecular biologists to the calculations of astrophysicists—also acquires major theological significance, because the "measuring of the world" likewise

---

* This is shown, for example, in the fact that completely abstract paintings often, astonishingly and without any intention on the part of the artist, resemble microscopic images of the molecular world.

ties humanity more and more profoundly to the universe. If it is done properly it can amaze; but that amazement can be the beginning of praise, and through that praise in which the human incorporates everything else, from the structure of the atomic world through the silent forest to the spiral nebulae, a way is opened for bringing the whole pre-human creation into the reality of the resurrection. At first it is purely a path of knowledge. But amazement and recognition are the paths of the spirit, and by those very paths the universe is endowed with spirit and prepared for its resurrection.[14]

Obviously it is not only artists and scientists who know the world. In essence, every person constantly encounters what I am here calling "world." Each of us looks at it, senses it, tries to explain it, engages with it, works on it, cares for it, loves it—and in that way each of us internalizes it.

I am not asserting that that is all there is to say. Béla Weissmahr writes that in its perfection the universe will be the "personalization of all matter."[15] Joseph Ratzinger ventures to say that in the resurrection of the flesh "matter belongs to spirit in a wholly new and different way, and spirit is utterly one with matter." He speaks in this connection of a "universal exchange and openness" between spirit and matter and the "overcoming of all alienation." He writes: "Only where creation realizes such unity can it be true that 'God is all in all' [1 Cor 15:28]."[16]

It is a wonderful thing that there are such elevated statements; they show us the breadth of the biblical promises. Still, it seemed to me a good idea, at the outset, to follow the "lower" path of knowledge by speaking of the work of artists and scientists and, in fact, everyone, because that means taking the role of humanity in creation seriously—the role of humans who constantly seek to understand "world," study everything, name everything, assign a place to everything, bring everything into the picture, always strive for the whole, and in that way make it *their own*. What we have made our own cannot perish, because, as we saw, the resurrection incorporates the whole history of the human person and everything that belongs to it. (See part 4, chap. 6 above.)

Besides, the incorporation of the material world as described is founded on the principle of participation, without which resurrection is unthinkable: the pre-human world *participates* in the resurrection of the human because humans have internalized it. And—this is crucial—human persons, with everything they have internalized, *participate* in the resurrection of Jesus Christ. I will say more about this principle of participation below (chap. 12).

At any rate, this chapter should have shown that the creation of the world and its "last things" are intimately connected.[17] The world is created for resurrection because it is created for human beings—and human beings for Christ.

9

The City of Dreams

The Bible has a grandiose vision of the things we have been discussing in the last three chapters: it is the image of a gleaming city descending from heaven to earth. The Revelation to John ends with this vision;* it forms the end of the New Testament and thus of the whole Bible:

> Then I saw a new heaven and a new earth; for the first heaven and the first earth had passed away, and the sea was no more. And I saw the holy city, the new Jerusalem, coming down out of heaven from God, prepared as a bride adorned for her husband. And I heard a loud voice from the throne saying, "See, the tent** of God is among mortals! He will dwell with them; they will be his peoples, and God himself will be with them; he will wipe every tear from their eyes. Death will be no more; mourning and crying and pain will be no more, for the first things have passed away." (Rev 21:1-4)

Immediately an angel appears, sweeps the seer to the top of a high mountain, and shows him the miracles of the new Jerusalem, the eschatological city:

* Nothing follows it except the book's conclusion, Rev 22:6-21.
** Greek σκηνὴ, "tent"; cp. John 1:14. NRSV "home."

It has the glory of God and a radiance like a very rare jewel, like jasper, clear as crystal. It has a great, high wall with twelve gates, and at the gates twelve angels, and on the gates are inscribed the names of the twelve tribes of the Israelites; on the east three gates, on the north three gates, on the south three gates, and on the west three gates. And the wall of the city has twelve foundation stones, and on them are the twelve names of the twelve apostles of the Lamb. (Rev 21:11-14)

Then the city is measured by the angel before the seer's eyes, including its walls and gates:

The city lies foursquare, its length the same as its width; and he measured the city with his rod, fifteen hundred miles;* its length and width and height are equal. (Rev 21:16)

Finally the materials of the city's construction are listed: it is made of gold as pure as clear glass. The foundations of the city's wall are adorned with precious jewels and every gate is a pearl.

I saw no temple in the city, for its temple is the Lord God the Almighty and the Lamb. And the city has no need of sun or moon to shine on it, for the glory of God is its light, and its lamp is the Lamb. (Rev 21:22-23)

Whereas up to this point the vision of the heavenly city has been nourished by Old Testament texts, now the biblical allusions become even thicker:

The nations will walk by its light, and the kings of the earth will bring their glory into it. Its gates will never be shut by day—and there will be no night there. People will bring into it the glory and the treasures of the nations. But nothing unclean will enter it. (Rev 21:24-27)

These are allusions to the pilgrimage to Zion in the book of Isaiah,[1] and they are then continued with elements from Ezekiel:[2]

*Literally "twelve thousand stadia." A Greek *stadion* was about 185 meters or 607 feet.

> Then the angel showed me the river of the water of life, bright
> as crystal, flowing from the throne of God and of the Lamb.
> Between the street [of the city] and the river, on both sides, stand
> the trees of life* with their twelve kinds of fruit, producing their
> fruit each month; and the leaves of the trees are for the healing
> of the nations. Nothing accursed [by God] will be found there
> any more. (Rev 22:1-3)

The vision concludes with a renewed assurance of the healing
presence of God and of the Lamb—a presence that fills everything
with its glorious light. While at the beginning of the vision God's
presence culminated in the wiping of every tear from the eyes of
those belonging to God, so the vision concludes with the promise:

> . . . they will see [God's] face. (Rev 22:4)

The whole vision alludes again and again to sayings in the Old
Testament.[3] Many of the Bible's greatest words appear: creation,
heaven, earth, Israel, Jerusalem, the people, the nations, God, face,
glory. Image crowds on image, promise on promise—and all of it
under the auspices of redemption and fulfillment.

But no matter how the images come and go, *one* picture dominates
the whole vision from beginning to end: that of the city. Why that image
in particular? Why does the seer not describe an "isle of the blessed"?
or the blessed themselves, enthroned on clouds? or still better: an eschatological Paradise where calf and lion graze together and the
weaned child plays at the adder's den (Isa 11:6-9)? Then the whole
Bible would be framed by two Paradises: the lost one in the beginning
and the regained one at the end. But no: we are shown a city. Why?

In the first place, obviously, because of Jerusalem! For ages the city
of Jerusalem had been, in the Bible, the expression of the people of
God's deep longing. It had long since become the symbol for the
fulfillment of all promises, the hoped-for homeland, the epitome of
all shelter and beauty. One of Israel's pilgrimage songs reads:

---

*NRSV: is the tree of life. It is certain that there is a principal street, a river, and
rows of trees, but exactly how they are all related remains unclear in the text.

I was glad when they said to me:
"Let us go to the house of the Lord!"
Our feet are standing within your gates, O Jerusalem,
Jerusalem—built as a city that is bound firmly together.
To it the tribes go up, the tribes of the Lord,
to give thanks to the name of the Lord. (Ps 122:1-4)

This and many other Old Testament texts show that Jerusalem is the center and epitome of the people of God. The holy city that comes down from heaven and is called "new Jerusalem" is thus an image for eschatological Israel, the true people of God.[4]

The image is also that of a city because it represents a counter-image to that of Babylon, the city portrayed in chapters 17–18 as a whore. On the one hand, Babylon is the dreaded city on the Euphrates, the "devastator" of Israel (Ps 137:8) where, according to Genesis 11:1-9, people had sought out of pride to build a city with a tower reaching to the heavens—and then had to scatter because God confused their language. But at the same time Babylon is a secret cipher for the city of Rome in which the apostles and prophets were killed (Rev 18:20).

Revelation 12–22 must be read against this background of city-foundings gone awry. Now, at the end of time, the city succeeds. It is not established out of human *hybris* but comes down from heaven as a divine counter-project to every previous city. Its glory does not derive from theft, oppression, and violence; it comes from God alone. And it does not scatter people but gathers them (Rev 21:24).

But there is much more to this image of the city. We simply need to recall what a "new city" meant, from the time of Alexander the Great onward.[5] In late antiquity it had become the most progressive social construction, the subject of deliberate planning and future-oriented projects. Whole cities were meticulously planned on the drawing board, and mathematically calculated, before they were built. They had a quadratic shape, their towers were symmetrically arranged, the water supply and drainage systems were planned ahead of time, and the cities were furnished with broad processional avenues lined with columned arcades on both sides. The numerous new city foundations of the Hellenistic era were intended to express functionality as well as solemnity and beauty.

In fact, the city was the ancient symbol for society. Aristotle, who was the first to shape the concept of society, termed it *politikē koinōnia,* the "association of the *polis,*" that is, of the city.[6] We can see right away that much of this idea of the new city is reflected in Revelation 21–22, above all the quadratic shape, then the four towers at the four points of the compass, and finally the broad ceremonial avenue that leads straight through the city. The conclusion is unavoidable: with the image of the new heaven and the new earth, and that of the new Jerusalem, Revelation seeks to express that the perfection God will give to all history at the end is not merely of individuals who now find happiness and pleasure only for themselves. What God gives, rather, is a new society, what centuries of humanity have longed for and striven toward; it is society in its highest form. It is "encounter, assembly, and universal communication," for "the layout of the Hellenistic city and its architecture existed to be filled with life and can thus represent the community itself."[7]

Also part of this is that the new city is a "world society." It is international. All nationalisms are overcome. The prophetic promises about the "pilgrimage of nations" to Zion are fulfilled. That is: the peoples of the whole earth enter the new city with their "wealth" and their "treasures." The "wealth" is their gifts and tributes as guests, the things they bring according to Isaiah 60:5, 11.[8] We can expand on the idea by saying that it is the arts of the nations, their culture, their experience, their knowledge, the whole treasure of their history. Everything is brought into God's new world; nothing positive from the long history of humanity will be lost. The whole culture and science of the world, everything ever thought by human beings, everything they have longed for and worked on will be treasured within this city.

But what is crucial is that the nations bring their gifts to the people of God, the Israel of God, for the great vision in Revelation 21–22 makes that more than clear: this new city, this new society designed by God is the people of the twelve tribes, the true, eschatological Israel. The abundance of the number twelve indicates that: twelve towers, twelve angels, twelve foundation stones, twelve pearls, twelve thousand *stadia.* The people of God, with its prophets and saints, its apostles and martyrs, is the center of this new God-given society made up of all tribes, peoples, and languages, and yet it is no longer so, as in the "covenant formula," the basis of the Hebrew Bible, that "you shall be my people and I will be your God." Rather: "they will be [God's] peoples" (Rev 21:3).*

Something else should be noted: without Nature's sources of energy, society is unthinkable. And Nature is not absent from this great vision; here, in fact, the motif of Paradise comes into play, but *not* according to the model of "society *in* nature." Rather, here is "nature *in* society."** For it is not outside, surrounding the city or in its outer precincts, that the life-giving trees grow; they are in the middle of the city, parallel to the great avenue. There, too, flows the mighty river of crystal-clear water. So Nature is part of this new, God-given society, but it is not "outside," not uncontrolled and chaotic, but integrated in the city itself.[9] The fact that the sea is no more (21:1) means, in the language of the ancient world, that what is utterly chaotic and destructive in the world has been overcome and has no power any longer. The depiction in Revelation 21–22, like Romans 8, pushes us to imagine the redeemed and transformed universe not in isolation from Christ or from humanity, but utterly incorporated in the eschatological people of God, in God's new society.

At an earlier stage we saw that the resurrection includes not only individuals but the whole of history, in fact, the whole universe. Does the city here depicted also have a cosmic-universal character? It does indeed! Even its size implies it: each of its four walls is 12,000 *stadia* (1,500 miles) long. Hence, at least in the eyes of the author of Revelation, the city is as large as the civilized world surrounding the Mediterranean at that time. The new Jerusalem is not only a world city; the city *is* the world.

Furthermore, it is not only 1,500 miles in breadth and length—it is just as tall. For the people of the time those were cosmic dimensions

---

* NRSV: peoples. Unfortunately, some modern translations (beginning with the Authorized or "King James" Version) have chosen to use the singular at this point, but the oldest manuscripts have a plural here. The use of the singular is easily explained: the translators, or the scribes who wrote the manuscripts, were thinking of the Old Testament covenant formula.

** Here is another biblical confirmation of what was said above at the end of part 4, chap. 8.

beyond all imagining. This also makes it clear that the new city not only descends from heaven but extends into heaven, linking heaven and earth. So the whole universe is included. Probably the ancient readers understood the twelve kinds of precious stones as allusions to the twelve astrological signs; thus a set of cosmic motifs is also in play. The city, with its precious stones, mirrors the "order of the starry heavens."[10]

And still I have not yet spoken of the crucial point: the center of the city is not a temple square such as was a matter of course in every ancient city; instead, at its center are God and the Lamb. To say that there is no more temple is unheard of in the ancient Near East and for antiquity as a whole. It is also without example in the Old Testament. The book of Ezekiel allots an unusual amount of space (chaps. 40–44) to its description of the new, eschatological Jerusalem Temple—its obsession with detail is positively exhausting for the reader. Nothing like that in Revelation! All it does is repeat the old promise to Israel that God will dwell in the midst of God's people (Lev 26:11-12; Ezek 43:7).

So the new city has no temple; instead, God, the ruler of all, and Jesus Christ are at the center of the city. They are its glory and its light. That is probably meant to say that God in person is, with Christ, the temple in this city—and the whole city is nothing but a holy temple square. Because all its glory and all its light come from God, the city needs neither the sun in the daytime nor the moon in the night (11:23).

But that means that there are no more cosmic rhythms to measure time—the rhythms that, in fact, create time in the first place. The fact that the sun and moon no longer shine means that there is no more earthly time. The festival celebrated here is no longer under time-pressure. It has no end. And what makes possible this festival that has no evening? It is that the inhabitants of the holy city see God in person:

> they [eschatological Israel and, with it, the nations that have entered into and become sharers of Israel's dignity] will see his face . . . (Rev 22:4)

That blissful seeing is the absolute high point of what happens here. For that very reason the city needs no temple: the time of signs and symbols is past. God will become visible. Of course, the "seeing" means more than intellectual knowing. It means experiencing, being certain, sharing, loving.

At an important point in the overall vision—namely, at 21:2—the complex of images shifts in a way that at first seems alienating to us: the glorious city suddenly becomes a bride. We were just hearing about a city, and all at once we see a bride adorned for her bridegroom. We find that odd; for ancient people it was a matter of course. Cities were symbolized as women, or even goddesses: take the city of Athens, for example, symbolized by the goddess Athena, Rome by the goddess Roma. The Bible speaks of "daughter Zion" or "virgin Jerusalem."[11] That is the background here.

But the unexpected shift from the image of the city to that of the bride adorned for her wedding speaks, of course, not only about the youth and beauty of the city. The new city—as we now know, the new society of God, the eschatological people of God, all together, women and men—is not just enchantingly beautiful. Its inhabitants are all also entirely open, entirely receptive; they belong altogether to God, not only as individuals, but together. They have left behind all ambitions for power and all violence, but also all obstruction. They are pure surrender.

In addition, the quick shift of image (cp. also 21:9-10) indicates something else that is highly important: that the incomprehensible reality to be described in what follows is altogether "personal." While it will speak of stones, walls, and towers, of a street, a river, and trees, when the image of the bejeweled bride completely overlays that of the city there is no "dead" matter in the city any longer. All matter is then incorporated in the "personal" sphere, saturated with spirit—the human spirit and the Spirit of God.

We could linger long over everything portrayed in the image of the new city, but perhaps in the end we can only say that, if we take into account the book of Revelation as a whole, we see that the ultimate future of history is not catastrophe or the Paradise of the beginning; it is a new society that has passed through crisis, chaos, and persecution.

But above all: God is concerned not only with individuals but just as much with society. God is concerned not only with the soul but just as much with matter. God is concerned not only with creation but also with history. The weight of history is revealed especially in the motif of the pilgrimage of nations: the peoples come from everywhere with their precious gifts and enter into the new city. In short: God is concerned with the world as a whole.

Even the precious stones with which the foundations of the city wall are adorned speak of that wholeness: jasper, sapphire, agate, emerald, onyx, carnelian, chrysolite, beryl, topaz, chrysoprase, jacinth, and amethyst (21:19-20). These stones emit the glory of matter, and yet they are an image for the people of the twelve tribes. As universal as is the eschatological city, God's new society, and as much as it embodies the whole universe, its coming is not an event that takes place at all times and in all places. It is tied to concrete places and times: to the people of God and its history.

A final remark: when a book devotes long chapters to resurrection, judgment, purgatory, and hell, the reader is right to expect a chapter on heaven. This chapter about the city of dreams—this was the chapter about heaven.

10

On the Relativity of Time

As we have seen, the last book of the New Testament presents us with a city, the image of the perfection of the people of God and also of the gathering-together of history and the universe. But when will it happen, what the book describes? When will that perfection come to be? When will we see God in the assembly of all the saints, and when will God dry the tears from the faces of the peoples? When will there be no more misery and lamenting? When will God be "all in all" (1 Cor 15:28)?

I have already said something about this above in speaking of "resurrection in death," but that needs to be given more precision in this chapter. We will not be able to avoid "the strenuous effort of engaging with the concept," to use Hegel's expression.[1] Of course, we have to speak of the last things for humanity and the world in images, and those images can mutually relativize one another and sometimes even contradict one another, because images are only images. But at the same time we are obligated to examine and clarify all eschatological images and ideas, over and over again.[2]

The notion that time beyond death continues in the same or a similar way to its current within history is one that is urgently in need of clarification, and indeed of criticism. So this chapter is about the question: *When* do "the last things" happen—from the encounter with God to the resurrection of the flesh and the gathering of the whole universe?

It is odd that it is especially in the face of this question that the human mind proves itself unusually sluggish and crude. Most Christians, in thinking of the world beyond death, cling tenaciously to their ordinary idea of time. They do know that the idea of God seated on a throne (Rev 4:2-6) is a metaphor, as is the notion that we will be carried to God on the clouds (1 Thess 4:17), that trumpets sound at the resurrection (1 Cor 15:52), and that then the blessed will stand before God, clothed in white and with palm branches in their hands, singing psalms (Rev 7:9-10).

All those are images, metaphors. They should be taken seriously as what they are, and still they remain images. Every Christian is more or less aware of that today. Given the knowledge we have about such images and how we are supposed to deal with them, Christians also know that we cannot think of heaven simply within our system of spatial coordinates, because then it would have to be located somewhere beyond the moon or outside the Milky Way. Heaven does not have a place in the sense of *earthly* space. Everyone understands that more or less.

But when it comes to the concept of "time," thinking begins going awry. Earthly categories of time are applied unreflectingly to the world beyond death. Many still imagine God as existing in continuous time, parallel to the ongoing historical time on earth. They think that time goes on *there* just as it does *here*. Just as future events have not yet happened *here* and therefore have to be awaited, they have to be waited for *there* as well. For *us and our point of view* the perfection of the world has not yet happened—therefore it has not happened *there* either.

But can we really equate our experience of time here with that after death? Time, like space, is a way of looking at things, a means we use to understand the world. And that way of looking is bound up with our present world. We dare not presuppose either space or time as something absolute.

Even our "sense" of time can be very different. For a child, time never passes; for older people it speeds by. Africans, before they were overwhelmed by European civilization, experienced time differently than we do. But even the sense of time in Europe or America today only originated when clocks were invented, after which a clock on many a church tower showed the time consistently and exactly.* Then for the first time the hours and minutes became an iron and unrelenting rhythm—all the more so when pocket watches began to be made. For the great English physicist Sir Isaac Newton (1642–1726) all the laws of physics still played themselves out in a clearly defined space, and physical time ran simultaneously in every point of that space. Time, at least in Newtonian physics, and therefore in the consciousness of modern people, was something absolute.

But modern physics has destroyed the notion of the apparently absolute nature of time.[3] Time began 13.8 billion years ago, with the Big Bang. It would make no sense to speak of a time *before* the Big Bang, because there was no "before." Time, space, and matter only began to exist then. And what came after was not absolute time, as Albert Einstein's (1879–1955) theory of special relativity shows. Time is dependent on motion; it can run faster or slower. In a system in motion it appears to an observer at rest to be slower than in a resting system. In "black holes" time even stands still. For an astronaut who flies at high speed through space, time passes more slowly and the astronaut also ages more slowly. If the speed increases to that of light (which, of course, is impossible), time for the astronaut would stand still. So time is not an absolute. To use an image: there is no universal clock that could mark an absolute time for every possible position and all possible motions within the universe.

That alone simply forbids us to operate with *earthly* rhythms of time in speaking of existence beyond death. Theologians who still refer to time must be clear in their own minds that they are using the concept in an analogous sense, that is, that the dissimilarity to earthly time is unimaginably greater than the similarity. Hence the many quotation marks in this book whenever we speak of "time" after death. They are meant to signal: careful, please! Here we are arguing with a no-longer-descriptive analogous concept that is outside our experience![4]

---

*Of course, for a long while the time it showed was only that of the particular town.

Then can we say anything at all about our "temporal" existence beyond death? Only by negation!—that is, only by denying what *we* experience as time. And how do we experience time? We know it as a constant flow. What was just now present slips away into the past, and what was future is now present. The future is not yet, and the past is no longer. What we have is always only the minuscule "now" of the present that immediately and unceasingly becomes past. "Neurobiological measures of our subjective apprehension of the present only yield subjective quantities of time of different lengths between ca. 0.004 and 0.01 seconds."[5]

Certainly, Christian faith says that nothing is lost of all that sinks into the past. Resurrection obviously cannot mean that only a portion of a life or the last instant before death comes to God. Instead, resurrection means the arrival of the whole person before God—with everything belonging to her or him—with all his faith and all her hopes—with all the good she has done and all the guilt he has laid upon himself—with the heights and depths of her or his whole life. I have already spoken at length about that. (See part 4, chap. 6.)

The author of Revelation exemplifies this appearance-before-God of the individual's whole history by describing the risen Christ as the "Lamb" that was slaughtered and now stands as victor before the throne of God, the slit still in its throat (Rev 5:6). Jesus' death, his surrendering, atoning death, has become before God an enduring existential of his life.

The author of Hebrews does exactly the same with the formulation that Christ has entered the Holy of Holies with his own blood to effect everlasting redemption (Heb 9:12). But the gospels say the same when the Risen One appears to his disciples bearing all his wounds (John 20:24-29), or when the disciples at Emmaus recognize him in the breaking of the bread (Luke 24:35). Those are clear indicators that Jesus' whole history has come to God in his death and resurrection. Jesus thereby becomes the epitome of what happens to every one of us: in death the whole history of the individual is gathered up before God.[6] What does that mean for our question?

We can no longer assume that time passes in our existence after death, that there is a temporal "before" and "after," an earlier and a later, an *earthly*-temporal not-yet and an *earthly*-temporal at-last. To put it another way: we can no longer suppose that there will be a continuance of that flowing "now" that separates existence into many individual present moments, now-here, now-sinking-away. And yet we can and must assume that all the time of our life lived on earth will be "gathered" and "brought to its result in" our life with God. Every point in time, every "now" instant of our whole life will be brought together and become "finality." Our existence before God will become a single and final "now."

Even so, that full possession of the time once lived is, naturally, not eternity in the sense of divine eternity, because the new mode of human existence given by God has altogether to do with time: it was constituted by time—because everything that has been lived in the fragmentariness of earthly time as actual present will be brought in and gathered up. Our transfigured existence with God is "gathered time."

The basic premise of what has been said thus far follows *ex negativo*: our existence with God is *not* structured like our earthly existence: it does not take place in a time running from earlier to later. But that is by no means all there is to say. The definition *ex negativo* must go further, because up to now I have written as if the glorified life with God were only the static sum of time lived on earth, a "standing now" in which the human person's earthly history is finally and forever "gathered up."

Such formulations necessarily awaken the idea of a distinction between a dynamic *event* and the subsequent *result* of that event—between, in Latin terms, a *fieri* and a *factum esse*. In fact, we constantly make such distinctions as soon as we begin to talk about eschatological matters. For example, we speak quite naturally about the event of Jesus' resurrection and then of the consequences of his resurrection. We say, in the perfect tense, "Jesus has arisen from the dead" or "Jesus has been exalted to the right hand of God"—and suppose that the *event* of Jesus' resurrection was followed by the enduring *state* of being raised and exalted.

In reality we ought to question that distinction as regards the new existence in the presence of God. It does not describe the thing itself because it clings tightly to earthly ideas of time. This is precisely the time-scheme with which we organize the world that encounters us within earthly history. Event and result of the event, motion and rest, process and the state attained after the completion of the process are necessary ordering structures for understanding *earthly*-temporal reality. But for that very reason the scheme must not be applied naïvely and unreflectingly to existence after death.

If our new existence in the presence of God is a reality about which we can speak only by analogy, then in it the ordering system of course-of-events and result-of-events is elevated to a new kind of unity that we cannot imagine in any positive way. Concretely: existence with God after death can only be described in words not only as having been awakened (or raised) but just as properly as being awakened in a continuous sense—not only as definitive being-with-God but also as a "constant" coming to God, not only the *fruit* of the time lived on earth but also the *process* of being drawn into existence with God.

Christian theology, of course, has always known that we should not speak only of "eternal rest" but equally of "eternal life." Today's eschatology in particular emphasizes that our life with God is an event of unending dynamism—and rightly so! But the danger of such assertions is that most of them start, as if quite obviously, with a *condition* of the human person achieved by eschatological fulfillment and then secondarily describe that condition in dynamic categories. Thus, for example, Ladislaus Boros wrote:

> Our eternity will be . . . an ongoing entry into God. In heaven, everything that is static is translated into a limitless dynamic that propagates itself to infinity. Nothing is fixed or rigid in heaven. Fulfillment is eternal transformation, a condition of endless, unbroken vitality.[7]

As correct as such formulations somehow are, they run the risk of once again describing human fulfillment somehow as a historical and therefore temporal process containing a before and after, an earlier and a later ("everything that is static is translated . . ."). We can only counter that risk by making it clear that "time" beyond death is nothing but the "process" of being "drawn into" the entirety of earthly existence in its future "fulfillment," but in such a way that the process is always already its result, and the result still remains process. This paradoxical expression is meant to say that we cannot imagine the event, and for that very reason we must avoid converting it in our language to a pale, naïve-temporal imitation of earthly processes.

Thus the rightly demanded dynamic of heavenly life, the path "from glory into glory," must not be described as following from a condition, a having-arrived, that must first be attained; it must be made clear that the dynamic that is called for is nothing different from "arrival" in God's world.

To make this more palpable, we can say that Jesus is not only risen but enters "constantly" into his resurrection. He is not only the "Exalted One" but is "constantly" being exalted to the right hand of God. He not only sent the Holy Spirit; as the Risen One he is the "unceasing" donor of the Spirit that gives life. Correspondingly, after our death we not only stand before God but "eternally" arrive in the presence of God—and that is precisely how we go "from glory into glory." We must not speak of an "event" "after" death without continuing to be aware of the limitation, poverty, and complete inadequacy of our language.

Thinking through the "last things" from a negative perspective (*ex negativo*) brings us to a further insight that we urgently need to discuss at this point. If, for each individual, "being drawn in" to existence with God happens beyond earthly time, the same is obviously true for the whole history of the world. That is: even the "being incorporated" of the endless web of history of a whole in its fulfillment no longer takes place according to our before and after, no longer spread over millennia, but in an analogous "simultaneity" we cannot imagine.

For individuals this means that in death they experience not only their own "passing over" to God but "simultaneously" the "passing over" of the world and all of history. In "passing through" death, individuals experience not only the "gathering up" of their own individual histories before God but, simultaneously—linked by a thousand threads with the individual's history—the history of the world and all people.

We could also put it this way: when people die and thereby leave earthly time behind, they enter a "dimension" in which all the rest of history comes "simultaneously" with them to its end or fulfillment, no matter how many endlessly long eons of earthly time it may have passed through. Obviously the "simultaneity" in the description is analogous and not to be understood in the sense of earthly-temporal simultaneity; it is only that a before and after in the sense of earthly time-progression is excluded.

But just here the conflict arises. Inspired by many predecessors,[8] I presented the position just described in 1974 in my essay "Zur Möglichkeit christlicher Naherwartung."[9]* After that I was accused by some theologians of setting aside and idealistically passing over the whole history of humanity. It seemed to them to be only about individuals, and therefore nothing more than a kind of limited individualism that makes history just an empty spectacle. For how could the history of the world end already when an individual arrives in the presence of God while it is still in progress on earth?

I can only shake my head at such objections. Apparently their proponents are unable to free themselves from the perspective of earthly time with its before and after, earlier and later. Obviously, *from a perspective within history* time goes on and people die at completely different times. And obviously humanity is networked together, so that each is always also a part of the other. And obviously the perfection of the individual before God presupposes an interaction with those still living.

But those who argue that the history of the world cannot end "somewhere" while in reality it is still continuing on earth put historical time and "time" "after death" in what amounts to a geometrically parallel and thus commensurable relationship. That is: they have done for *time* exactly what everyone today would reject with regard to *space*: namely, locating the Christian heaven spatially "somewhere" above the earth.

But what is true of space is true also of time. There is not only the time-bound "perspective of those left behind," but also the one sketched here, that seeks to think of "time" after death,[10] a "time" that can only be conceived by analogy—thus not from the perspective of ongoing time and history but from that of "arrival" in the world "beyond" death. In that case no *earthly*-temporal distance can be placed between the "arrival" of the many individuals. Then the judgment of the individual cannot be separated in terms of *earthly* time from the "general judgment." Then the "fulfillment" of the individual and the "fulfillment"

* "Can Christians Expect the 'Second Coming' Soon?"

of the world flow "into one another." Then all who die in the grace of God rise from the dead "together" with Christ and Mary and all the redeemed of the world. Hans Urs von Balthasar rightly says:

> The vertical irruption of Jesus' Resurrection arising out of the horizontal flow of history (which according to Paul and John is the real promise and down payment of the resurrection and transformation of the world as a whole [1 Cor 15:17-23]) no longer permits us to expect the inbreaking of the new world to happen in the chronological continuation of a historical time running on toward its conclusion; rather, it happens in a dimension that is incommensurable to world-historical time.[11]

We can clarify the whole problem in terms of the creedal statement on Christ's return. The first Christians expected Christ's *parousia* in their own lifetimes. Paul thought that even those who had already died would rise from the dead and go to meet Christ's *parousia* together with those still living (1 Thess 4:13-18; cp. 1 Cor 15:51–52). Thus here Jesus' parousia is a public event taking place before the eyes of all humanity. It is the inbreaking of the risen and exalted Christ into this history.

Meanwhile, two thousand years have passed. The *parousia* of Christ has not yet happened in the form Paul expected. Will it still happen *in that form*? After all, billions of people have died since then, and billions are yet to die. If we imagine the *parousia* as a scenario *within history* or *at the end of history*, only a very limited portion of all humanity will be able to experience the event from an earthly perspective.[12] And then what was the point of it all?

But Christ's *parousia* is comprehensible and plausible if we do not simply transfer earthly categories of time to "time" in the presence of God. In that case all people without exception will "appear" before Christ, or rather, Christ will "appear" before them all—and this "in" death. What faith in Christ's return intended to say will then be really and completely true, but *not* in the form of an apocalyptic spectacle before the eyes of the tiny group out of the whole population of the world who are living at Point X in time. It will be entirely different: a "coming" to all people, without exception, who encounter Christ in their deaths "together" and "simultaneously."[13]

Obviously there are preconditions and circumstances to be considered within the overall event of "resurrection of the dead." We will rise from the dead "together with Christ"—and yet his resurrection is the ineluctable precondition and cause of ours. Christ is and remains the "firstborn from the dead."

We will rise "together" with Mary, the mother of Jesus—and yet her resurrection is an anticipation of our own, namely, through her believing "yes," spoken representatively for us all (Luke 1:38). In addition: Mary rises from the dead as the most perfected of all the redeemed. She is in any case "ahead of us" in that regard.

Finally: we will rise from the dead "together" with all the saints, and yet their faith has made ours possible and thus is a guiding gift for our own resurrection. Their purification in death also has a different "measure" than ours.

In other words: what Christian tradition has expressed in a purely temporal *before* and *after* was by no means false, but it is more appropriate not to express the thing intended in terms of *earthly*-temporal categories.

11

On the Endurance of the Soul

An old woman dies; the heart ceases to beat; brain function is extinguished. One organ after another shuts down. The blood obeys the pull of gravity and sinks slowly into the lower parts of the body. The dissolution of cells begins. *Rigor mortis* will soon follow.

The family members had sat by the bedside of the dying woman and held her hand. They are still there, and they begin to speak about her life and death, often glancing at the body. But the corpse lies pale and silent in the bed, completely uncommunicative.

What about everything this woman has done and suffered? What about the endlessly complex details of her long life?—its sorrows and delights, pains and joys, the simply infinite total of perceptions, observations, experiences, encounters, meetings, and insights? Above all: What about her personal efforts to change at least a small part of the world—in herself and around her? In short: What about her whole history?

In this major part of the book I have said that this very person goes to meet God and there finds her judgment, but also profound mercy; still more, that in the event of her death—on the inside of it, so to speak—she encounters God with her whole history. And I have said that *for her* there is no more earthly time, and the historical time of the world has already run out for her in the "moment" of her passage.

She has then "already" arrived at the resurrection of all the dead and the end of the world.

But what is this "she" I am talking about, who now encounters God and about whom it is impossible to speak apart from the personal category of "she"? Is there anything that bridges the immense gap between the cooling and decaying body and everything that has been said here about the resurrection of the person?

From the time of the ancient church, Catholic theology has spoken of the "soul" in this connection. The soul, we say, separates from the body at death, appears before God, is judged and purified; it must wait until everything resistant and unpleasing to God in it has been worked off, and it then will at last be "wholly" with God after the resurrection of the flesh and the general judgment.

But in the twentieth century there has been widespread objection by Protestant theologians to the doctrine of souls that is integral to this complex of ideas (and that, apart from the doctrine of purgatory, was still part of the teaching of the churches of the Reformation).[1] It was said that if the soul remains in this way, the darkness and implacability of death is trivialized: that to *somehow* die and yet to *somehow* go on living does not do justice to death or to the Bible, for according to the Bible the human being dies "altogether" and will be "altogether" raised up by God. This objection that the doctrine is unbiblical was joined with the accusation that the ancient teaching about the continued existence of the soul is a Greek construct, Platonic in nature, unreflectingly and hastily adopted by Christianity. In that teaching, it seems, the soul is the real person and really does not need the body, and that is itself not only unbiblical but un-Christian; therefore we must preach the "entire death" of the human, its total extinguishing, but also its total and undeserved awakening by God, "who gives life to the dead and calls into existence the things that do not exist" (Rom 4:17).

However, there was another motive behind this radical position. People wanted, at last, to escape from the immortality-pathos of the Enlightenment. In that period the immortality of the soul had nearly become a fundamental dogma, almost more important than faith in God. Now, finally, the power of the resurrection should be reclaimed as the work of God.

At first glance that radicality is quite plausible. Death as death is taken seriously, and the resurrection is given its due as real "awakening." The advocates of the whole-death hypothesis say, and not altogether unjustly, that the church's creed does not say "I believe in the immortality of the soul," but "I believe in the resurrection of the body."

Nevertheless, extremes call for closer examination.[2] Over time it became more and more clear that the idea of whole-death carried with it a difficult problem. To be brief: if the human being is wholly and completely dead and God then raises her or him wholly and completely, what about the continuity between the deceased and the one raised up by God? That is, if on the one hand everything is radically at an end and on the other hand there is an absolute new beginning, then the new person has nothing more to do with the old one. This new person is really not "raised" but created anew.[3] It *resembles* the person in every detail but is not *the same one*. It is a fabulous duplicate, a successful copy, a perfect clone, if you will, but not the person who previously lived; that one is and remains dead.

In order to avoid this difficulty people brought God's "memory" into play. It was said that, while the deceased is indeed dead, she or he lives until the resurrection of the dead in God's "memory." God's "memory" preserves her or his identity at the later resurrection of the dead. What can we say about that solution?

It is, of course, correct that everything "in God's memory" or "in the mind of God" can only be supremely alive and not something like a filed "document" on a hard drive. But if everything in "the mind of God" has supreme reality, must one not say that the dead person "lives" on in and through God? And if the deceased lives on in this sense would it not be better to go ahead and speak of the soul, which endures because it is created and loved by God,[4] the soul, which makes it possible for *this same* man or *this same* woman or *this same* child to approach God in death?

So there is much in favor of the idea that we should go on talking of the endurance of the soul in death, in accordance with the long Christian tradition. Without the endurance of what many centuries have called "soul" there is no identity between the one who dies and the one who comes to God in death. But then everything depends on an appropriate use and right understanding of the concept of "soul."

That is to say, it must be clear that the soul is not a blank page, not an unworldly abstraction without a past, but that it has internalized the whole history of the person in question. Everything has been impressed on it; everything is preserved in it. Every person, during his or her life, is not only a part of the world; in becoming a person (a process that extends even to death) the individual collects "world" unceasingly within itself because she or he engages with it, shapes it, marks it, inscribes it within the self—and does so by means of the body.[5]

For that very reason the soul is not a principle foreign to the body, free from it, or indeed hostile to it, something that is redeemed by finally leaving the body and matter behind; it is the epitome of what makes the individual person. It is not against the body but constitutes with it a profound unity, gives it its form, shapes it, ensouls and sustains it. Without its soul the human being would be nothing but a complex assembly of molecules. But biology shows us that those molecules are regularly replaced and sloughed off. What, then, constitutes the human identity—what makes one a person? Most assuredly not the material substance of one's carcass, but what makes that carcass a "body" in the first place, namely, the soul.

In this sense our contemporary theology is again asking about the soul and its identity-giving function between death and resurrection. It speaks with new insight and more appropriately of the soul that is not destroyed in death but takes with it everything that makes up and shapes the deceased,[6] all that "then"* will be purified and receive a share in Christ's resurrection. Certainly, after all that has been said, the question remains: Is the soul, thus understood, not still something immortal in the Greek sense, something that has no need of God's creative power but that remains alive through its own power: that, in short, is "immortal"?

That question must be taken seriously, because it is the primary basis for the objections of those Protestant theologians who fear that this means we are speaking of an essentiality in the human that endures even without God and thus perverts what Christianity means by redemption.

---

* Obviously this "then" is not meant in an *earthly*-temporal sense, which is why it is in quotation marks.

But a good theology of creation and grace can respond to those objections, for the soul is not something that has nothing to do with God and could exist "on its own" without God. Rather, the soul—to use an image—was breathed into the human person with the breath of God (Gen 2:7). But that means that it is part of the unceasing creation of the person by God. Without God, the soul, the person, could not exist for an instant.

Michelangelo's wonderful fresco in the Sistine Chapel in which God touches Adam with a finger and so brings him to life applies not only to the creation of humanity; it is true of our whole existence, from generation to the last breath, and indeed until our resurrection from the dead: the human person—or here we can just say the soul, as the person's identity—is at all times sustained and kept alive by God. Psalm 104 expresses this constant dependence of all life on God's creative power in this way:

> When you hide your face, they are dismayed;
> when you take away their breath, they vanish
> and return to the dust.
> When you send forth your spirit, they are created;
> and you renew the face of the earth. (Ps 104:29-30)

Joseph Ratzinger refers to this biblical statement when he describes the traditional concept of the "immortal soul" as a "dialogical" existence with God.[7] The soul's endurance does not come from itself; it is enduring because it is created, loved, led, and sustained by God, and because it is capable of and called to the knowledge of God. Martin Luther must have meant exactly that when he said:

> Where and with whomever God speaks, whether in anger or in grace, that person is surely immortal. The Person of God, who speaks, and the Word point out that we are the kind of creatures with whom God would want to speak eternally and in an immortal manner.[8]

It is as this "immortal" soul, thus understood—which is the repository of the person's whole history and therefore has also shaped and internalized the body—that the human being appears before the living God and receives a share in the glory of Christ's resurrection.

This takes nothing away from death's darkness. It remains a misery and a disempowerment. In its second Eucharistic Prayer the Roman Catholic Church remembers a deceased person by saying:

> Remember your servant N., whom you have called (today) from this world to yourself. Grant that he (she) who was united with your Son in a death like his, may also be one with him in his Resurrection.[9]

For those who believe in Christ, then, death is neither something natural and part of life nor a transition accomplished with great serenity, as Socrates showed his students; it is a dying with Christ. And Christ did not die a philosopher's death. We only have to read Psalm 22, which Jesus spoke in his suffering, as the prayer of one who is dying. The description of Jesus' death takes nothing away from the darkness of death, even though the church believes in the endurance of the soul.

It should be clear by now that I am speaking of the endurance of the soul in death because we have no other way of thinking about the identity between the dying person and the one raised by God. This is by no means a surrender of the thesis of "resurrection in death." That rests for me on the strict denial that beyond death there is still time in the earthly sense, that is, that "after" death a person must still wait for something *in an earthly-temporal sense.*

That by no means excludes the idea that there must be a transitional "process" between death and the resurrection of the dead in which the human person is purified and her or his resurrection takes its form from Christ. But that "transition," in which the soul is guarantor of identity, may no longer be thought of in earthly categories of time. It takes place "in" death.

12

On Participation

This book, then, says good-bye to the idea that the soul must wait with God in an *"earthly*-temporal sense" until the end of the world, until the judgment of the world, until the resurrection of all the dead, when it will finally receive its glorified body. The "in-between" that is rightly called for cannot be defined in *earthly*-temporal terms. Therefore the end of the world is present to the dying "with" death; the return of Christ takes place "in" death, the resurrection happens "in" death, and so does the judgment of the world. The church can no longer afford to uncritically offer naïve ideas about time when talking about the "last things," since those concepts of time have long since been shot full of holes by physics, and in fact have been abandoned.*

Above all, the church can no longer afford to banish the return of Christ and the resurrection of the dead from Christians' thinking, because a *parousia*, together with a resurrection of the dead, that has not happened in two thousand years of history and accordingly will

---

* This is a case similar to that of the teaching about creation: knowledge of evolution has compelled the church to rethink its idea of creation. Nothing of the biblical faith in creation has been lost in the process.

probably not happen in the next two thousand years lies in some kind of cloudy distance and therefore, in terms of consciousness, no longer exists (unless the church wanted to stoke notions of the imminent end of the world). But if resurrection and the encounter with the Christ of the *parousia* take place "in" death, then it would be possible to live in the same eschatological awareness as the early Christians[1]—and in that case we would have a strong basis and a purpose for a biblical *present* eschatology (see part 5, chap. 3).

Obviously we can only use images to speak of what happens to us in death. The idea of souls in a state of waiting over long periods of time was also an image, and was certainly justified as such. As we have seen, that idea gave a basis for thinking that the purification of the dead cannot take place separately from ongoing history.

When many theologians today speak of "resurrection *in* death," clearly that is also an image. The question is only whether for us today it is not the better, more appropriate image,[2] corresponding much more closely to our current knowledge of what time really is. That is why I had to speak at such length in chapter 10 of this section about the relativity of time. Conclusion: the deceased is no longer subject to earthly time but in death has "already arrived" at the resurrection of all the dead.

But precisely at this point an old problem arises with new poignancy, namely, that of continuity between the deceased and the person "raised" by God in death. That is why we had to speak also, in the preceding chapter, of the soul as the guarantee of personal identity. And yet a whole complex of difficulties for a right understanding of resurrection remains acute. That is the subject of this chapter. First let me list the problems to be addressed.

Previously I have spoken only about people who have a long history behind them during which they ripened into persons. I spoke of people who have become persons through encounter with others, constantly absorbing the world into themselves and internalizing it, while also producing a world. But what about infants who die, of whom we cannot say all that? An infant cannot yet speak, much less say "I." It has experienced the world only in the most limited fashion. It has not yet known anything about God and was certainly not yet in a position to make anything like a decision. Will that infant also appear before the face of God and experience what Christian faith calls "eternal blessedness"?

We can answer: of course! God loves all creatures and will bestow the fullness of divine love and care on that infant also.[3] That answer is certainly correct. But it cannot be used to gloss over a fundamental principle of resurrection: only that can be raised up that has happened in the history of the life in question. For that very reason the history of every person, every day and every hour in the life of an individual has immediate and serious significance for eternity. But what if there has been no personal development in the sense described?

Certainly it is true of every infant that it is already perceiving a hundred things. It listens hungrily, distinguishes the voices around it, knows those of its father and mother, is certain about what tastes good and what tastes bad, touches its mother's skin, grabs everything in reach with its tiny fingers, and above all it looks at the world with its big eyes, trying to recognize and distinguish things from each other. Can it be that God is not a blessing to that infant?

So let's really get down to basics! What about an embryo in an early stage that was unable to live and was sloughed off? That minuscule being does not yet have any sensations. Those may have begun rudimentarily, but nothing beyond that. Obviously we have to say of that embryo also that it is created and loved by God, and God cannot will that any part of creation should fall into nothingness. Here again, Psalm 146:6 says it rightly:

> [God] made heaven and earth,
> the sea, and all that is in them;
> he keeps faith [with creatures] forever.

To intensify the case: God will not allow even a just-fertilized and embedded egg to perish. But in what form does it exist before God in the resurrection? Can God make something that has no history, that has not even begun to exist as a sentient person, into a complete and fulfilled human being? In biological terms, can the zygote, the just-fertilized egg, live in the presence of God as a person with a developed will, intellect, and understanding?

Someone may say: "There must be some possibility with God even in such a case; it is only that we cannot imagine it." So let me sharpen the point even further: suppose we go back to human pre-history, the long phase of evolution in which hominization, the becoming-human of the human, took place. Everyone now knows that understanding and free will did not develop explosively from animal to human at some point during that long transitional phase. They developed over gigantic periods of time.

We can see this in the evolution of language. The mouth and pharynx had to evolve, slowly, to furnish an organic basis for developed language. There is no scientist who can put a finger on the exact point at which the human being was finally human.[4] Use of tools is not a criterion for defining the human, since that takes place also among our relatives, the great apes, and it was probably the case with our animal ancestors, too—for example, in breaking large bones with rocks to get to the marrow. There are even species of finches that probe for food by holding thorns in their bills.[5]

And language? Communication signals are common throughout the animal world, as is the transmission of information. We only need to think of the bees' tail-wagging dance that calls attention to the availability of food and even gives the direction in which the bees in the "audience" are to fly. There is also sector intelligence, often developed to an amazing degree. We may not even entirely exclude self-awareness among the higher animals.[6]

It is only reason and free will, rising above mere instinct, that we cannot presume to have existed among our animal ancestors. But did they suddenly fall from heaven? All this shows that the transitions from animal to human were fluid.

If we consider, as a test case, some "pre-human" or other on the way to being "early human," it is almost still an animal and almost already a human. This particular hominid has already lived a long time, has grown old and helpless. It has withdrawn from the herd and ends its life somewhere in a dark thicket between the forest and the savanna. Will it see God?

I have intensified the question we are dealing with to such a degree in order to bring the real problem to the fore. To repeat: what has not happened in the history of a life cannot become reality simply through "resurrection." That is the enormous power of the singular history of every individual human being. What has not happened *here* will not exist *there*. Good that was not done here, freedom not achieved here cannot be magically produced in the resurrection *from the deceased*.

For that very reason we must necessarily ask: What happens in the resurrection to the countless children who never had a chance to become developed persons? What happens to all the fetuses that are aborted? What happens to the countless beings in the intermediate phase of evolution that were no longer altogether animal but not yet quite human? This is not about the question whether they rise with the whole pre-personal world. A Christian may and must believe that God will not allow anything God has made to be destroyed. The question is whether they will rise *as persons* or somehow bound up in the world of the personal. And it seems to me that the concept of "participation" is important, indeed essential, for answering that question.

To make it immediately concrete again: an infant that lived a few days and then died had no opportunity to develop as a person and was completely incapable of an act of free decision. But it was—we hope!—loved by its parents. They wanted it, begot it, thought of it constantly, felt for it, planned for it, and did everything they could think of to bring it to a joyful birth. The newborn belonged to their thinking, willing, freedom—to their persons. It had become a part of their lives. Therefore that infant is with them before God; it is in their hearts and therefore is a part of their bliss and somehow shares in it. We cannot say more than that. The whole thing is part of the mystery of eternal life.

And what about the extreme case described above? What about the hominids who stood on the threshold of humanity? Here we can scarcely say that they were loved by later people and have their existence in that very fact. And yet it is by no means the case that they simply no longer exist. Science is extremely interested in them! Generations of paleoanthropologists have worked tirelessly to study unearthed bones, from *Sahelanthropus shadensis* to *homo neanderthalensis*, to discuss them, to put them in order in time, and to reconstruct in the best possible detail the form, abilities, and ways of life of these pre- and early humans. Knowledge of humanization has long since become part of our cultural memory and will therefore rise with us. (See part 4, chap. 8.) Pre- and early humans exist in that knowledge—not only in their essential form but more alive than we can imagine.

This all gives us a kind of grid. Extra- and pre-human creation cannot simply rise as *personal*, but it can rise *in human beings* insofar as the human marvels at creation, tries to understand it, studies it, and is fascinated by it. In this way humans internalize it and it can exist before God with and in them. Let us call this "participation." Without "participation" the miracle of genuine redemption of sub-human creation is unthinkable. But "participation" extends much further. Let me describe what I mean in four steps:

1. We have already seen that Paul speaks of the liberation of the "whole creation." (Cp. part 4, chap. 8.) Creation, subjected to emptiness and nothingness, awaits the revelation of the children of God (Rom 8:19-22). That is: the whole of non-human creation will be incorporated in what is given to believers in the resurrection.

These are bold ideas that Paul here formulates out of his Jewish love for the world. Nowhere else in the New Testament is it stated so clearly: the whole creation will then rise to the "freedom of the children of God" and share in their glory (Rom 8:21). What form that participation will take is something that must remain open. It is unimaginable for us, and even what I have said about "internalization" was only an attempt to come a little closer to the event.

2. It is easier to imagine the people of the resurrection sharing and communicating *with one another*. Here again we can—indirectly—refer to Paul, for there is no other New Testament author who so emphatically stresses Christian community and its "cooperation" or "togetherness" as Paul does. Christians should "love one another with mutual affection" (Rom 12:10); "live in harmony with one another" (Rom 12:16); "welcome one another" (Rom 15:7); "have the same care for one another" (1 Cor 12:25); "bear one another's burdens" (Gal 6:2); "always seek to do good to one another" (1 Thess 5:15); they are to live "with" and "for" one another, "rejoice with those who rejoice, weep with those who weep" (Rom 12:15). But above all, when other communities are in need of help they are to share with them in solidarity and "supply the needs [lit.: fill the empty hands] of the saints," that is, help fellow Christians in need (2 Cor 9:12).

But if mutual solidarity is essential already for Christian communities in this world, then most certainly for the community in heaven, for the church on earth is the mirror of the heavenly community and lives from its strength (Gal 4:26; Phil 3:20). If we can "rejoice with those who rejoice" already here, then we may most certainly do so in the "communion of saints." C. S. Lewis expressed that in his own way when he wrote that in heaven "every soul will be forever occupied with giving to the others what it receives."[7]

I dare to say it: I want one day to participate in the blessedness of the saints. I want to participate in the rapture of the great lovers; the patience of countless mothers and fathers that could not be shaken; the sagacity of countless holy women; the wisdom of the great doctors of the church, women and men; the courage of the martyrs; the love of those who followed Jesus with their whole existence. I want to "meet" Paul, Luke, Augustine, Thomas Aquinas, Francis, Theresa of Avila, Thérèse of Lisieux, Edith Stein, and many others, and "be with them." And of course I hope to see my deceased parents and siblings "again."

At the beginning of this theological section (see part 4, chap. 1) I said that, when the deceased finally encounter God in death, God will be *everything* for them, and there will then be for them nothing more besides God, and everything else only *in God*. What I have just said in no way contradicts that. Joy *in God alone* by no means excludes common joy with all those who are now a pure being-together in the presence of God. On the contrary: the happiness of being together with all those one has loved only enhances the bliss of seeing God— and the real "God alone" enhances the bliss of participation in the heavenly communion of saints.

In essence that dialectic is already realized in every Christian feast. No one can celebrate a feast alone; every one necessarily requires the gathering of a community. We see all the others, take pleasure in them and rejoice in being with them. And yet, if it is truly a Christian feast, the community does not celebrate itself but the mighty deeds of God. The feast acquires its brilliance only because those celebrating are oriented to something that is endlessly greater than themselves and by which they are completely sustained.

But how does what I am saying here accord with the statement that nothing can rise unless it was part of the history of the life in question, and for that very reason the history of every person, every day and every hour of that person's life, has such power for eternity? The statement remains true, but it has acquired a weighty addition: it is true that we can only bring before God in eternity what we have previously lived. But infinitely more will be "added to" us because we are allowed to participate in the communion of saints.

The Christians of the first centuries had an unerring sense of that. They wanted to be buried near the saints, especially the martyrs, so that they might participate in their fidelity to Christ. A gravestone survives that belonged to an unknown woman named Sarmannina; she was buried around 400 CE in the northern part of the former Roman fortress of Kumpfmühl in Regensburg.[8] The inscription on the simple limestone slab reads:

> To the blessed memory of Sarmannina, who rests in peace in the company of the martyrs.

3. We could say much more about the *communio sanctorum*, the "communion of saints," but this must suffice, because now we have to speak about the most important, all-encompassing, and all-sustaining form of participation, namely, the participation of human beings in the saving and liberating resurrection of Jesus. We are not only given a far greater abundance from Jesus; from him *everything* is given.

Here again we find the most considered statements in Paul's writings. He wrote a series of eschatological texts in which Greek *syn* ("together with," "united with") plays a crucial part.[9] For example:

> . . . and so we will be with the Lord forever. (1 Thess 4:17)

> For if Jesus—this is our faith—died and rose again, then God, through Jesus, will bring with him those who have died. (1 Thess 4:14)

> . . . we know that the one who raised the Lord Jesus will raise us also with Jesus, and will bring us with you [into his presence]. (2 Cor 4:14)

> . . . if we have died with Christ, we will also—this is our faith—live with him. (Rom 6:8).

> . . . we are . . . heirs of God and joint heirs with Christ—if, in fact, we suffer with him so that we may also be glorified with him. (Rom 8:17)

We can certainly read all these texts to mean that believers are gathered around the Risen Christ as his followers. But Paul means to say more than that. At the resurrection of the dead those who believe in Christ are not only gathered around the Risen One, and they are not only his disciples. Instead, they are united with him in such a way that they are "monomorphic," having the same form as he. That appears in the last of the cited texts, Romans 8:17: those who suffer with Christ are already living on earth in an inexpressible union with him, and that unity then becomes evident in their glorification. The letter to the Philippians says this even more plainly:

> Our citizenship [*politeuma*] is in heaven. It is from there that we are expecting the Lord Jesus Christ as our Savior. He will transform our vulnerable body that it may be conformed to his glorified body, by the power through which he can make all things subject to himself. (Phil 3:20-21)

In this text it is important, first of all, that, as so often in Paul, "body" (Greek *sōma*) means the whole existence, the whole person.[10] It is also important that Christ himself will effect our transformation to sameness with him. But above all: Christ's glorified existence is here not merely a model or pattern for the resurrection of believers. They, having been adopted in baptism into Christ's existence, have shared his suffering with him (Rom 8:17); now they will in the same way be incorporated in his glorification and receive a share in the "form" of his resurrection. This is real "participation," as suffering with Christ is real participation in his passion and is, like the Eucharist, participation (*koinōnia*) in Christ's suffering and resurrection (1 Cor 10:16).

4. Thus we have seen that in the resurrection the sub-human and pre-human creation shares in the glorification of believers; the believers in turn participate in and with one another and, above all, they participate in Christ's glory. And yet we are still by no means at the end. The New Testament continues this series of sharing-in and sharing-with still further, namely, by saying that Christ gives his disciples a share in his glory—and Christ himself shares in the glory of the Father. The Gospel of John in particular offers theological reflection on this blessed giving and receiving. Here is the crucial text:

> Father, I desire that all whom you have given me may be with
> me where I am, to see my glory, which you have given me be-
> cause you loved me before the foundation of the world. Righ-
> teous Father, the world does not know you, but I know you; and
> these know that you have sent me. I made your name known to
> them, and I will make it known, so that the love with which you
> have loved me may be in them, and I in them. (John 17:24-26)

What Jesus speaks of here will happen in the deaths of the disciples.
They will then no longer know *in faith*, but directly, face-to-face. They
will "see" Jesus' glory. Incidentally, here Jesus' eschatological return
has completely faded from the picture, as has the question of the resurrection of the body, and every thought of places or times. Jesus' disciples, when they die, will experience Jesus' glory directly and in its
wholeness. Everything is concentrated in that statement. Detailed questions of eschatology play no further part. The disciples will then be
forever where Jesus is, and they will see his glory (cp. John 17:5; 14:3).

But now the decisive point: Jesus does not have this glory of himself; it is given him by the Father. This takes up a movement that runs
throughout the whole of the Fourth Gospel: everything Jesus has and
gives to the disciples comes from the Father. Jesus is in God, and God
is in him. But he is also in those who believe in him, and they are in
him. So the disciples are also in God because they are in Jesus. And
when they see his glory in its full brilliance they see the Father, just
as they have previously encountered the Father in Jesus, though only
veiled and through faith (John 14:9).

In any case, the ultimate beholding of Jesus' glory and in it the
glory of the Father is more than "seeing." It is, as it already was in
the disciples' lives, a complete "existing within" the love of the Father:

> . . . so that the love with which you have loved me may be in
> them, and I in them. (John 17:26)

With this the New Testament theology of participation achieves its
ultimate depth. To say it once more: in the event of resurrection the
pre-human creation will participate in the glory of the liberated and
healed human world, the saints will rejoice together in their bliss,
they all have a share in the glory of the risen Jesus, and Jesus in the

glory of the Father. And so all creation will be brought within the life of the triune God. Here, in this incomprehensible movement of incorporation of the whole universe in the love of God (cp. Eph 4:1), we may also locate all pre-human and still-undeveloped human life that never had a chance to become a person. That life, too, has a share in the glory that is to come.

To repeat, in conclusion: the statement that nothing can rise that did not exist in the history of the life in question, and for that very reason the history of every person, every day and every hour of a human person has such power for eternity—that remains true, but it must be augmented. If human existence already means participation, here in this history—namely, participation in the lives of others and above all in what others make possible for us through their representation—then eternal life is most certainly and most deeply participation: the gift of being together in the communion of saints and, above all, absolutely unearned participation in the life of the triune God.

This concludes the major part of this book, and I have no intention even to attempt to describe what Sacred Scripture hints at when it speaks of the unending progress "from glory to glory."[11] But I have to add one last note. If I have spoken in this book primarily of death as an encounter *with God*, I did so in a sense for convenience. The present chapter has already shown how much of a simplification it was. Now I have to correct my abbreviated language. In God we will meet not only God but the risen and rising Jesus. Everything, without exception, that I have said about the final encounter of the human with God is spoken of in the New Testament, in the same way, as encounter with Jesus. Our death is the great, final encounter with him; *he* will appear before us as the Crucified: indeed, the Crucified in power and glory. *He* will judge the world; *he* will separate good from evil; *he* will bestow eternal life; *he* will transform our mortal bodies into the form of his glorified body. The New Testament says all that about Jesus the Christ.

So is there a "parallel" existence of God and Jesus in the end-time events? No! If we want to be precise we have to say: we will encounter

God *in* Jesus the Christ. God will illuminate us in him. In his face we will behold the face of God. In the encounter with him we will experience God's judgment. In him God will bestow divine mercy on us. In him we will be drawn into the life of the triune God.

If we inquire beyond the bald statements of the New Testament and the tradition about why this is so, the answer can only be: because it was already that way in history. God has spoken at many times and in many ways to our ancestors, but God's final, definitive, and unsurpassable Word was spoken in Jesus Christ (Heb 1:1-2). In him God has become ultimate openness and ultimate presence in this world. In him God has spoken the whole of God's self and been bound definitively to the world. In him God's loving "yes" to the world and humanity has been finally and forever revealed. Those who from then on want to know who God is must look to Jesus. Whoever saw him, saw the Father. Whoever encountered him, encountered God's own self (John 14:6-11).

But if Jesus is the place where God's self-communication is definitively bestowed on our history, and if earthly history does not simply go on in that other world but instead finds its enduring finality there, a finality into which everything is absorbed that was ever important in earthly history—then Jesus Christ will also be, after the end of all history, the proper place of our encounter with God. He will then be forever what he has already been here on earth: the one in whom life is given to us; the one in whom God speaks to us the eternal word of divine love.

I will stop here because we have come to one of the most beautiful and profound mysteries of Christian faith: God has accepted us humans so completely, God loves the world so much, that we will encounter God for all eternity in no other way than as the Incarnate One, and so we will forever and ever find God's own self in a human heart.

PART FIVE

What We Can Do

1

Genuine Care for Our Dead

There are many examples showing that animals can grieve. The British biologist Ian Edmond and his team observed elephants who stood for a long time near a female that had died of a snakebite. Eventually they had to go in search of food, but the next day they returned and again remained standing by the dead animal. This process was repeated over several days; the great distance the group had to travel each time seemed to make no difference.[1]

It would be wrong to see this as a formal ritual of mourning. It would be just as wrong to deny that the returning animals felt anything like loss, sorrow, and solidarity. In the long process of humanization there must, from the beginning, have been sorrow over the dead, even with growing realization of what death meant. The more human the humans became, and the more they perceived the profundity of their separation from the dead, the more elementary and at the same time the more human must grieving have become.

Psychologists are right to counsel us not to repress grief for our beloved dead. It must be expressed in rituals, it must be communicated, and we have to leave time for it. In the ancient Near East there were extreme rituals of mourning, and they still exist there today. Probably they are more human and healing than the custom of swallowing one's suffering and not showing it to outsiders.

The death of a beloved person is affliction and loss. Suddenly there is an empty place that quickly becomes a dreadful desolation. And swiftly comes the painful question of whether one has done right by the dead. Long-forgotten scenes arise in which one has wounded the person, done her or him injustice.

But gratitude also grows: often gratitude that sees the deceased with new eyes and finds things that had remained hidden before. Perspectives change and the life of the dead person rearranges itself. But above all, one begins to have a deep solidarity with the deceased. We want to do everything possible to honor their memory, make them present in many symbolic ways, and forge a new bond with them.

All that is common throughout the world, in all cultures, and it is profoundly human. It is also normal for Christians—but there are differences. Christians cannot grieve in the same way as those "who have no hope" (1 Thess 4:13). Nor can they practice a cult of the ancestors with long genealogies, small home altars, offerings, and above all they cannot see ancestors as having a kind of divine function in the lives of descendants.

Nevertheless, the solidarity that ties every healthy person who is not utterly desolate to his or her dead exists for Christians also, but here it has an immeasurably deeper dimension and is based on utter freedom. The "fear of the dead" that played such an immense role in many ancient cultures has been overcome by Jewish-Christian faith.

In the previous chapter I spoke of the "togetherness" and "mutual aid" that Paul repeatedly urges on his congregations. They are to "love one another with mutual affection" (Rom 12:10), "have the same care for one another" (1 Cor 12:25), and "bear one another's burdens" (Gal 6:2). But above all, when other communities are in need of help they are to share with them in solidarity and "supply the needs of the saints," that is, their fellow Christians (2 Cor 9:12).

I concluded from this that if such solidarity is already essential for Christian communities *in this world* it is most certainly essential also for the perfected communities in heaven. Now let me go a step further: that solidarity must not only exist within the congregations on earth and adorn the community in heaven; it applies also to Christians who have died, who are in that "transition," that "between" of which I have spoken (see part 4, chap. 7), confronted with the returning Christ, namely, the fire of his judgment that becomes a flaming and purifying fire because it is pure love. In other words: that solidarity must be maintained with all those we used to call "the poor souls in purgatory." Nowadays we don't like to call them "poor" souls because they are not only suffering but are already on the way to becoming infinitely rich in their encounter with Christ and the assurance of his love. And we no longer simply call them "souls" without any further thought, because they contain their whole histories and thus are also bodies, since the sum of a life's story cannot exist without a body. (See part 4, chap. 11.) Finally, we know that their "transition" from death to eternal life can in no way be understood in earthly categories of time. It is a real "interim" but it can no longer be measured in days or years or millennia.

Thus Christian solidarity is in place not only within the pilgrim church on earth and not only in the perfected church in heaven; it must also be true of the church that is "in transition," that is being purified and cleansed before the face of Christ.[2]

We must go even a step further than that. The solidarity of Christian communities extends constantly beyond the limits of particular community or congregational structures. Christians help (we hope!) not only their sisters and brothers in faith but all those who are in need of help. Christian sisterly and brotherly love must constantly expand its boundaries within the world. For that very reason our solidarity with the deceased must not be only with our sisters and brothers in faith but with all the dead. Everyone, after all, comes before the face of Christ, whether baptized or unbaptized, those who believe in Christ and those who are far from him, seekers and non-seekers alike. (See part 4, chap. 5.)

But enough of these more or less abstract reflections! Let us finally get down to the concrete and ask what Christian solidarity with the dead, with those "in transition," might look like. Then, of course, our relationship to our own dead comes first to the fore, our deceased relatives and friends, those close to us and above all those we have loved. How can our care for these dead find concrete expression?

Leaving aside things like burial, tending graves, dealing with inheritance, and so on, what about "real" care for our dead? They are not much interested in how their funerals are carried out and their graves decorated; this is about their happiness and their need, about what they have left behind in the world—the good and the bad seeds they sowed in their lives.

What is the good seed? Above all it is the faith modeled for us by our parents, relatives, and friends. If we are untrue to that faith it must surely bring them a burning stab of pain. On the other hand, in their encounter with Christ they will behold with a clarity never perceptible before what the reign of God is and what history is all about. If they know that those they have left behind are putting their lives on the line for the Gospel and for the expansion of God's cause it must be one of the profound joys that comes over them in the "moment" of purification. When we ourselves act out of concern for the reign of God we have the right relationship to our dead. Then they are near us; then we have never lost them. A woman who had experienced the sudden death of her mother said to me:

> I often talk with my dead mother. I thank her for the good things I received from her. I tell her about all she did for me. Above all I thank her for the faith she modeled for me in her quiet and matter-of-fact way. I ask her to help me remain in that faith. Then I tell her how things are with me, talk about everything that worries me and what makes me glad. I think of her very often. Sometimes I implore her to help me when I don't know how to go on.

Should we lay the prayers of this woman to her mother on the carefully calibrated golden scale of dogmatic theology and discuss whether it is permissible for a Christian to pray to her dead? That kind of carping would be out of bounds, so long as those left behind are aware that ultimately all help comes from God and that their appeals to the dead are also an expression of a deep sense of communion.

We are on much safer ground, of course, in praying to God *for* the dead, a practice with a very long tradition, traceable as far back as 2 Maccabees (second century BCE).[3] The early Christians also prayed for their dead,[4] and even today prayer for the dead has an established place in the eucharistic canons of Catholic churches. For example, the second Eucharistic Prayer in the Roman Missal reads:

Remember also our brothers and sisters
who have fallen asleep in the hope of the resurrection,
and all who have died in your mercy:
welcome them into the light of your face.

Similarly, the Episcopal Church in the United States prays in Eucharistic Prayer D:

Remember all who have died in the peace of Christ, and those whose faith is known to you alone; bring them into the place of eternal joy and light.

The form of the Eucharistic Prayer itself is that of pure thanksgiving to God, the Father. But where it contains petitions they have a *gathering* function. This fundamental action of the church is intended to bring all together: those near and far, the living and the dead, angels and humans, saints known and unknown, so that, whenever this great official praise is brought before God, the whole church, earthly and heavenly, is gathered together. The irreplaceable center is the Crucified and Risen One. Just here, in the Eucharistic Prayer, is the proper place for the church to pray for its dead.[5]

Here the church prays to God to receive all deceased "brothers and sisters," that is, all deceased Christians, into God's glory, but beyond that not only all Christians but all people who "have died in your mercy."[6] These petitions are instructive. They point, as the overall course of the Eucharistic Prayer shows, to Jesus' sacrifice of his life, his suffering and resurrection. Here is the source of all the mercy and forgiveness God gives. The prayer for the dead, and above all the making-present of Christ's sacrifice of his life, are the center and summit of care for our dead.

But consider again what the deceased have left behind them: not only the good seeds they sowed, but also the evils they may have brought into the world. In his book on eschatology Joseph Ratzinger, as we have seen, rightly poses the problem:

We can ask whether a human being can be said to have reached his fulfillment and destiny so long as others suffer on account of him, so long as the guilt whose source he is persists on earth and brings pain to other people.[7]

What does he mean by "guilt whose source he is persists on earth"? Simply that every sin has "consequences."[8] Even when a guilty act has been forgiven, its results remain in the world. A rape, even if it is regretted and even if the rapist has been forgiven, is not simply rubbed out. It can have traumatic consequences for both victim and perpetrator that shadow their whole lives. To take another example: adultery, even if repented of, even if the spouses have forgiven one another, has destroyed trust, and that cannot be cheaply restored. A third example: the abyss of evil brought about by Adolf Hitler and his subalterns was not removed from the world by his death. It has its imitators even today and, begetting evil after evil, can go on giving birth to more evils *ad infinitum.*[9] It is that kind of process the church has in mind when it distinguishes between "sin" and the "consequences of sin."

Hence care for the dead means above all limiting or even eliminating the consequences of what they have done wrong because those consequences beset the dead and make the process of their purification more difficult, since it is also part of that purification that they are made free from all the negatives they have left behind in the world. They need not be the consequences of serious crimes. They can be things left unfinished, narrowness, lovelessness, unresolved issues within the family, subtle egoism, fear, resentment, hard-heartedness, perhaps even silent lack of faith. A great many attitudes can be passed on and are in the process of hardening themselves within others.

But how can such spreading consequences of sin be eliminated? First of all by our refusal to enter into the narrowness or even evil ourselves, by doing good in place of evil, being faithful where there is no faith, loving instead of hating. The interruption is accomplished by forgiveness, atonement, works of love, and our own repentance. This last is more important than all the flowers we lay on the graves of our dead.

But everyone who has experienced the forces of evil and the power that can be exercised by bad example also knows how difficult, and often even impossible, such an "interruption" of its progress can be. And that brings us back to prayer for the dead, whose genuine place is in the Eucharistic Prayer. Only in Jesus' surrender of his life could and can the river of evil in the world be stemmed, and therefore everything we can do for the dead has its true place in that life-surrender.

Ultimately we can only rightly care for our dead by bringing our prayers and petitions to God in light of the crucified Jesus. And we can do this only in the community of the church, in the communion of those who work together, by the grace of Christ, to restore the world and to resist evil and its consequences.

It may be that at this point one or another reader will ask about the "indulgences" that have caused such deep division within the church. Why does this book say nothing about them precisely here, where they belong? But I have not been saying nothing. Everything I have just said was a paraphrase, a different way of describing what that word "indulgences" meant, in spite of all the horrible ways it was misused: *acting against the "consequences" of sin, by the grace of Christ, in the communion of the church.* Today we can no longer in good conscience use the word "indulgence." It has created too much mischief. But what it meant is correct, and even unavoidable.

2

Christian Dying

The Kaiserdom in Frankfurt contains the famous "Dormition of Mary" altar by an unknown Frankfurt artist, completed in the year 1434. Mary, the mother of Jesus, has died and lies on a bed under a costly coverlet, her head resting on a high pillow. Around her are gathered the twelve apostles, sorrowing and weeping. Peter kneels by the bed and holds Mary's hand. The figures are vividly rendered, their garments falling in wonderfully soft folds, each face with a different character. Above it all, but still within the baldachino that surrounds the scene, a small flat relief depicts how Mary's soul, in the form of a child, is borne aloft by angels. The risen Christ bends down to it and receives it lovingly.

That is how medieval people hoped to die: surrounded by the believing community, accompanied by prayers, led into Paradise by angels, received by Christ. And they wanted to be buried in the "churchyard,"* that is, as close as possible to the house of God and the relics of the saints it contained—the Latin expression was *ad sanctos*, "near the saints."[1] At the resurrection one wanted to be as close as possible to the confessors and martyrs who could lead one by the hand.

---

* Cemeteries outside the church grounds were regarded as pagan.

240

When, not long afterward, Johannes Gutenberg invented printing with moveable type and made the way for the first media revolution and its creation of new forms of imagery, it became possible to disseminate handbills illustrated with copper engravings showing Christian dying and how one could prepare for a good death. In contrast, the beholder was often shown, in gruesome detail, what it would look like for a person who had led a licentious life.

To take one eloquent example of such fliers: Between 1644 and 1655 the Nuremberg publisher and bookseller Paulus Fürst produced a handbill entitled "Description of the penitent . . ." with Christian death as its theme.[2] The upper half shows a copper engraving with a wealth of motifs: the dying person lies in bed and speaks (in words printed on a ribbon) the words of Stephen in the book of Acts: "Lord Jesus, receive my spirit." Around his bed stand not only his family and friends but King David, who recites the "Miserere" psalm for him. There are also three allegorical figures designated as faith, hope, and love. The good thief is likewise present, inviting the dying person to say with him: "Lord, remember me when you come into your kingdom!"

But there is even more to be seen in the engraving: a kind of swimming crowd of images, including the tree of Paradise with the serpent, hell, the devil holding out his account ledger to the dying person, showing him the whole sum of his sins in order to cause him to despair; then there are the instruments of Christ's suffering and the scales of justice, with Christ's sufferings on one side and the weight of the dying person's sins on the other (Christ's sufferings are heavier). Finally, there are a great many angels and, on the upper margin, the Risen One, from whose wounded side redemption flows down upon the dying person.

Still, that is only the upper half of the handbill. The lower half contains rhyming texts to be spoken by pious readers. There is a dramatic shifting among the sinner, King David, faith, hope, then the sinner again, then the thief, patience, love, Christ, and at the end the sinner once again, now prepared to depart this world, comforted by Christ.

Countless such fliers and devotional pictures were published in the following century, in Germany and elsewhere. We should also mention the many large-scale catechetical paintings of the late sixteenth to early nineteenth centuries, "all of them important testimony to the earlier pedagogical art of communicating ongoing religious instruction to the faithful."[3] Then there are the many reverse paintings on glass that one could purchase at pilgrimage sites. These contain pictorial motifs admonishing to a Christian life, with texts such as this one, printed under a picture of the Holy Family:

> Jesus, Mary, and Joseph, I give you my heart and my soul. Jesus, Mary, and Joseph, be with me in my fear of death. Jesus, Mary, and Joseph, let my soul live and die with you in peace.[4]

Here the Holy Family is not only presented as a model; St. Joseph was also regarded as the patron of a good death because it was supposed that he had died in Jesus' arms. We could go on listing other items, such as the so-called "Brotherhoods." In 1648 Vincenzo Carafa, then the Superior General of the Society of Jesus, founded a "brotherhood of the good death." It quickly spread throughout Europe and countless Roman Catholics joined it. "Its purpose was the achievement of a blessed death. In order to prepare for that hour the members promised to live an intensive Christian life, with frequent (not only annual) confession and communion and regular devotions, together with mutual aid. Above all they were to see to it that no one need die without the Last Sacraments."[5]

In traveling through Bavaria one will constantly come across villages with, at the center, often on a small hill, the former parish church, usually a cheerful baroque building, surrounded by the churchyard with many lovingly tended graves. Once when I was spending some restful time in such a churchyard and looking at the gravestones I noticed that almost all the stones bore not only the name, profession or calling, birth and death dates of the person, but also the note "died after receiving the Last Sacraments." That moved me deeply, and since then I have often visited such churchyards.

I was also moved when, many years ago (I was ten), a believing relative showed me the two small, black-inlaid crosses for the dying that hung over her bed and that of her husband. "They are there," she said, "so that when we are dying we may hold them in our hands. We will also hold them in our coffins, and now they are meant to remind us of our deaths every day, especially when we go to sleep at night." They were good people, that old couple. They laughed a lot. And never, during the years I lived with them because of the bombing raids in Frankfurt, did I hear them speak ill of others or fight between themselves. Today it is clear to me that they both owed that civilized behavior to their faith, as they did their comfortable relationship with Christian death. There is no other way I can explain the purity and serenity of their lives.

Why am I saying all this? Past centuries were certainly no better than our own, but there is still much we can learn from them—for example, from their many efforts at the *ars moriendi*, the art of dying. Certainly times have changed. Today many die in large hospitals and clinics, often in intensive care, surrounded by the medical apparatus that is indispensable in such places and by the equally unavoidable traffic of the variety of people without whom a modern hospital cannot do its job. There is little of the silence, the quiet needed for a good preparation for death.

But there is also something else, something much more serious. It is evident in the mentality that now underlies many "living wills" and that, in turn, is created by them. Giovanni Maio, Professor of Bioethics and Director of the Institute for Ethics and History of Medicine at the University of Freiburg, quotes in one of his publications from a brochure produced by the federal Ministry of Justice that is intended as an introductory guide for living wills. It contains the following suggestion for how to shape a model for such decisions:

> The idea of being no longer mentally capable and becoming dependent on others for help is unbearable for me. I have seen how my friend was changed by dementia. I don't want to live that way. It is very important to me to be able to converse with my friends and family. When I become so confused that I no longer know who I am, where I am, and do not recognize my family and friends, I don't want it to be very long before I die.[6]

Professor Maio rightly comments on the fact that "becoming dependent on others for help" is seen as "a completely normal reason for a mandate to stop treatment." We ought to consider how it is "that people today are more and more inclined to give the fact of being dependent on others as an adequate reason in itself for a complete rejection of such a life." He continues: "As long as living wills that

reject a life that can only be lived with the support of third parties"
are recommended, there will be an increasing "tendency to disdain
all handicapped lives, a tendency to eliminate lives that are fragile."
Behind it all is a point of view "according to which only the independent, self-sufficient person can live a valuable and meaningful life."[7]

Giovanni Maio is right to question this image of the human as the
independent, self-sufficient, autarchic person. The human being is
always dependent on others, from generation to death. As children
we needed our parents to feed us, raise us, wipe our noses, and tie
our shoes—until we could finally do those things for ourselves. Then
we needed teachers who very patiently taught us to write and do
arithmetic. And so it went on. Even as adults we are constantly dependent on the knowledge and help of others. When I drive my car
over a high bridge I trust in the competence of the structural engineers
who built the bridge and the technicians who assess it year after year.
Every person, every society lives with the aid of an infinite number
of representatives. Most certainly the church lives on the basis of the
faith of its saints, and first and primarily from the path Jesus trod.

When we grow old we need the care of others more than ever,
conversation with relatives and friends, often even the awareness of
those around us when our own awareness becomes weaker and
weaker. In short: we need help, we need helpers, we need representatives who can do things we ourselves cannot. To think we have to
do everything for ourselves, have everything in hand, control everything, and be autarchic in all things is to absolutely miss the meaning
of human life. We need others' solidarity and readiness to help
throughout our whole lives, and most certainly in old age. Death is
then the positively culminating point when we must let go of everything and hand ourselves over completely.

Unless someone is overcome by a sudden death, that handing-over
of everything can be very concrete and pass through many phases.
Consider someone who suddenly, within a few seconds, loses the
power to speak. Those around him call the emergency squad; he is
taken to the hospital and brought into intensive care, is treated, then
later is transferred to a rehabilitation center, but has suffered permanent damage from the stroke and is ultimately placed in a nursing
home for care.

That person's life has been fundamentally changed within the briefest of moments. He has to give up his usual surroundings, can no longer read books, is confused by other media, no longer is given his usual diet, no longer sees many familiar faces, can no longer go for walks, is suddenly in quite different life-circumstances that he simply has to accept. He even has to let other people take over the arrangement of his papers and the many things he had accumulated over his long life. He has to abandon roles he had come to love and surrender almost all the opportunities he used to enjoy. He has to let go. His life becomes more and more limited, and the limitations close in on him more and more.

But is that all new to him? With such intense force, yes. And yet it is not completely new. During his school years he suffered a severe illness that kept him out of school for half a year. He was happily married for thirty years, but then lost his wife in an automobile accident. He had to move for job reasons, and when he settled in his new apartment he discovered that someone was starting to build a high-rise next door. The following years were beset with annoying racket. Still worse: he was anxious about the lives of his children. They took a direction entirely different from what he had hoped for—especially in their faith lives.

So even here, in the midst of one's "normal" and "orderly" life, there are hurts, disappointments, separations, losses, good-byes, fears, experiences of death. There is also the "little death" that can come to all of us throughout our lives.

For Christians who have decided not to live only for themselves but still more for others—for God, for the Gospel, for parish work—other disappointments await: disappointments in the church in its concrete form, troubles in the parish, the inability to really reach others, suffering in companionship with the crises of Christianity. Here, too, there is suffering alongside happiness and joy.

In the Old Testament these shifting or interwoven experiences of happiness and suffering are enunciated especially in the Psalms, with unbelievable power—and they are again and again laid in God's hands. In the New Testament there is no author who is so eloquent as Paul in putting into words his joy in his congregations and at the same time expressing the sufferings that come to him as an apostle.

This is clearest in his letters to the congregation in Corinth; here he opens his heart. He speaks of his defeats and disappointments, his fears and tribulations, his daily dying and rising.

Above all, Paul connects it all to Christ. His whole life, his work, his efforts, and his devotion are suffering-with, dying-with, and rising-with Christ:

> We are hunted from every side, but not cornered; perplexed, but not driven to despair; persecuted, but not forsaken; struck down, but not destroyed. Wherever we go, we always carry in our body Christ's mortal suffering, so that the life of Jesus [that is, his resurrection] may also be made visible in our bodies. (2 Cor 4:8-10)

The apostle's life is completely immersed in the death and resurrection of Jesus Christ. But what Paul feels compelled to say here because of the attacks of his opponents is not only about the specific life of this apostle. It applies to the life of every Christian. Paul expresses that with the utmost clarity in his letter to the Christian community in Rome:

> Do you not know that all of us who have been baptized into Christ Jesus were baptized into his death? Therefore we have been buried with him by baptism into death, so that, just as Christ was raised from the dead by the glory of the Father, so we too might walk in newness of life. For if we have been united with him in a death like his, we will certainly be united with him in a resurrection like his. (Rom 6:3-5)

That is the fundamental statement of Christian life. We do not live our own lives; we live with and in Christ—and so all our farewells, all our separations, all our losses and fears acquire an ultimate meaning. Nothing in life is then in vain. Everything is living with Christ and thus cooperation with him in the building up of his body, the church.

From this point of view, then, the death of a Christian also acquires its profundity. Christian death, like that of Jesus, involves being helpless, powerless, abandoned, handed over.[8] And yet in that very way one has finally come to life and gained one's whole life. How lovely to be able to die as a Christian in that way, and how lovely when one is allowed to accompany a Christian who is living and dying thus! There are two different worlds, widely separated: to die swiftly, painlessly, without care, easily, at best without any thought of what comes after, or to die in Christ, full of hope and ultimate trust.

3

When Does Eternity Begin?

The chapter title seems to make no sense. Eternity, in the strict sense, has no beginning. God alone is eternal, and to speak of a beginning for God would be insane. In the catechism from which I learned the essentials of faith when I was a child God's eternity was explained this way:

> Why do we say God is eternal?
>
> We say God is eternal because God has always existed and always will exist. God has no beginning or end.

Of course, that definition was designed for children: it explained the existence of God in terms of linear time, an endlessly long line with no beginning or end. Normally we imagine eternity just that way: no beginning, no end, without interruption, endlessly on and on . . .

I must admit that I often tried to imagine my own eternity that way: my life with God goes on forever, without limit; there is no end point; an endless future of bliss opens out before me, and it goes on and on and on—forever. I used almost to get dizzy at the thought of being "without end." The whole thing was unsettling; it aroused fear and was beautiful at the same time, fearfully beautiful. At some point I read the great Teresa of Avila's autobiography, and how as a child she used to repeat the words "For ever—ever—ever" over and over again with her little brother.[1]

On the whole we can certainly recognize how hard it is to think of God or of things beyond this world. Our spatial and temporal ideas continually creep in. Certainly God does not exist in time—not even in the sense that God's time has neither beginning nor end. But because we humans can only think in temporal categories we cannot imagine it in any other way Can we at least *think* of it differently? Boethius, a philosopher of late antiquity (ca. 480–525), offered the insightful definition:

> *Aeternitas est interminabilis vitae tota simul et perfecta possessio.*
> Eternity is the whole, simultaneous, perfect possession of
>   limitless life.[2]

What is the genius of this definition? It is that here the concept of eternity is considered completely independently of time. Eternity is the complete and limitless fullness of life: pure being.[3]

Certainly that does not yet encompass what is Christian in the concept of eternity, for God is not only the limitless fullness of life but also the ruler of time. God is not removed from time but has power over it. God created the world, and with it, time. And God holds all time in hand, in order to be able to give God's very self, in Jesus, into time and history.

In contrast, we can only speak of eternity for humans in a derived and conditioned sense, because human eternity comes from history or, more precisely, from the flow of the time lived on earth, the countless "moments" of the life that will be drawn into one's "eternity." (See part 4, chap. 10.) Human eternity is the harvest of time lived and endured. That is something completely different from God's eternity.

It is also something different insofar as human persons do not bring forth their "eternity" *out of themselves*, but receive it as a gift, *as participation* in the fullness of divine life. (See part 4, chap. 12.) That, in turn, is so shockingly beautiful that we can only stammer when we speak of it. At this point we have to ask ourselves, falteringly: Can that really be true? But Sacred Scripture[4] and Christian tradition[5] say exactly that: eternal life is a sharing in the life of God.

But when does that sharing begin? When does eternal life start? When does *our* "eternity" begin, now that we know what that means? In this book I have tried to establish that it begins "in" death. "In" death all earthly time ends: its flow, its before and after, its no-longer and its not-yet. "In" death we already arrive at the end of all history. "In" death we arrive at resurrection and judgment, the end and consummation of the world.

But by locating the end-time events "in" death we by no means do justice to the broad arc of suspense that is Christian eschatology. The New Testament contains a tension between what theologians call "already" and "not yet." Christian eschatology is in tension between the "already" of the salvation that has come and the "not yet" of completed salvation, and that "already" is happening, unceasingly, in this history.

"Already" is entirely in the foreground of Jesus' preaching. As we have seen (in part 3, chap. 1), the reign of God "comes" in this world, and not at just any time. It comes *now*, for Jesus "announces" the reign of God, "proclaims" it. Jesus' disciples are told literally to "shout out" the coming of God's reign in the squares and streets of Israel. But what is announced and proclaimed is not something that lies in an indefinite future. It is about to happen immediately. As we have seen, Jesus goes even further. He can say that the reign of God is already present:

> If it is by the finger of God that I cast out the demons, then the kingdom of God has come to you. (Luke 11:20)

The question, of course, is: Did the early church maintain Jesus' radicality of the "already"? Did it cling to the tension between the "already" and the "not yet" in such a way that the "today" was not lost?

We can clearly see what Paul thought. (Cp. part 5, chap. 2.) His theology thrives on the tension between what is already present and the salvation yet to come. In baptism, Christians are drawn into the fate of Christ: they die with Christ, are buried with him, and live thereafter within the force field of his resurrection (Rom 6:1-14). In faith and baptism Jews and Gentiles become persons "in Christ."

That is, they live in a new communion that is no longer shaped by the powers in society that make people unfree, but by the new world of God that is freedom and hope:

> So if anyone is in Christ, there is a new creation: everything old has passed away; see, everything has become new! (2 Cor 5:17)

The Holy Spirit is given in baptism, and the Spirit is a "guarantee," a "first installment" on the glory to come (2 Cor 1:22; 5:5). The "last things" for the human have thus already begun in the existence of the baptized. But Paul is careful about what he writes. In Romans 6:4 he does not say that "as Christ was raised from the dead by the glory of the Father, so we have already been raised [in baptism] from the dead." Instead, he writes that "we have been buried with him by baptism into death, so that

> . . . just as Christ was raised from the dead by the glory of the Father, so we should live in newness of life."

It was only Paul's disciples who wrote in a radical indicative what Paul preferred to state as a challenge ("so we too might [or: should]"):

> But God, who is rich in mercy, out of the great love with which he loved us even when we were dead through our trespasses, made us alive together with Christ. By grace you have been saved. God has raised us up with him and set us in the heavenly places in Christ Jesus. (Eph 2:4-6)

Of course, the author of Ephesians knew that Christians still had their physical death ahead of them, that they could fall back into sin, that they were not yet definitively in the state of perfection and were not yet risen from the dead. And yet they have already left the power sphere of sin and death behind them. To that extent they are "already" raised with Christ.

Let us test another passage, one in the Gospel of John, the latest gospel in the New Testament, written in the 90s of the first century. According to John 5:24-25, Jesus says:

> Very truly, I tell you, anyone who hears my word and believes him who sent me has eternal life, and does not come under judg-

ment, but has [already] passed from death to life. Very truly, I
tell you, the hour is coming, and is now here, when the dead will
hear the voice of the Son of God, and those who hear will live.

This text simply revolutionizes the usual Christian teaching about
the end time.[6] Because what would the ordinary eschatology that had
already established itself in the primitive church at the time when
the Fourth Gospel was edited, and that would continue to dominate,
say to this? It would say: one day the final hour will come, the Last
Day, the day of Christ's return, the day of the Lord's *parousia*. Then
the voice of God, or of the Son of Man, will sound; it will awaken the
dead and they will come forth from their graves. Then the Son of
Man will judge each according to his or her works.

That is how people envisioned the course of things only decades
after Easter. But John 5:24-25 consistently sets that sequence of the
future end-time events in the present:

1. It does not speak of the *parousia* of the Son of Man at the end
   of the world. His *parousia*, that is, his appearance, coincides
   with his "sending" into the world.
2. The last "hour," which properly must come only with his
   return at the end of time, is already present.
3. The "voice" that is to call the dead from their tombs on the
   Last Day is already sounding: it is the word of Jesus that awak-
   ens the spiritually dead to life.
4. Those who believe Jesus' word of proclamation, now pro-
   nounced, have thereby already "passed over" into eternal life.
5. But Jesus' word of proclamation brings division as well. Those
   who do not believe his word have already brought "judgment" upon themselves. The present hour demands human
   decision and determines one's whole existence.

We can see right away that this present eschatology that says the
hour of the eschatological awakening of the dead is already present
is constructed with the word-inventory of future eschatology. It uses
the same expressions and transfers them consistently to the present.
Jesus' discourses in the Gospel of John as a whole formulate this
present eschatology.[7]

If we ask how the Evangelist came to this radical present eschatology, the answer can only be that with it the author was developing

the preaching of the historical Jesus. The Fourth Evangelist had a profound understanding of what Jesus' words and his deeds of power meant. The Evangelist did nothing but interpret Jesus' appearance as what it really was: *the* eschatological event that determines death and life, judgment and resurrection.

In the New Testament—as the texts of Paul, the Pauline school, and the Gospel of John have shown—Jesus' radical present eschatology was retained. Today, now, at this moment everything is already happening (2 Cor 6:2). Now the decision is being made, and therefore the judgment is happening now (John 5:24), as is, in daily dying with Christ, the resurrection to eternal life (Eph 2:4-6).

But how is something like that possible? How can it be? Where is such a present eschatology being realized? What is its location? Romans 6:1-14; 2 Corinthians 5:17; Ephesians 2:4-5 point the way. There the "now already" has its basis in baptism. In baptism Christians have died with Christ and been raised to the communion of saints. The real "location" of present eschatology is in the sacraments. Every baptism immerses someone in the fate of Christ and the communion of believers. Every reception of the sacrament of reconciliation means placing oneself even now before the Last Judgment, and in that judgment, through the mercy of God, being set free. Every reception of the Eucharist is participation in Jesus' Last Supper, and the bread that is there broken and eaten is a participation in his death, the breaking of his life, his self-surrender. At the same time the eucharistic meal is also the beginning of the eternal wedding feast with God. At their eucharistic feasts the early Christians shouted *marana tha* ("Our Lord, come!") and so anticipated the *parousia*.[8] The Lord's *parousia* is happening already when the Risen One is present, in worship.

Fundamentally the whole church is the sacramental presence of eschatological reality in the world. Everything a baptized person does—with or against Christ—happens in this eschatological realm. So Georg Bätzing can write:

> What a Christian expects after death is not a completely different life but the perfection of what she or he is now already doing and experiencing in life with and for others out of faith in Jesus Christ. It is the perfection of being Christ's disciple and being made like him.[9]

Thus eternal life is not only the absolute Other, the radically New, that is, the revealed encounter with God in Jesus Christ; at the same time it is the completion of what we have lived here in the power of the sacraments. In the chapter on the relativity of time (part 4, chap. 10) it became clear that in death our whole earthly existence will be brought into and "updated into" eternal life. What is gathered then is the harvest of the many hours of our lives.

If in this way our whole existence is brought before God in death, then already before that every earthly hour was an encounter with Christ, with God. That is precisely what is meant by the sacramentality of Christian life, founded in baptism, nourished by the Eucharist, and renewed in the sacrament of reconciliation.

If that is so, then every moment of our lives takes on an enormous weight. After all: what is not lived here will not exist there.* What has been lacking in love here cannot be magically produced there. The repentance and reconciliation that did not happen here cannot be gathered up as repentance and reconciliation there. The thanksgiving, praise, and adoration of God that did not happen here cannot appear there as thanksgiving, praise, and adoration. What did not happen in this history cannot be raised, cannot be brought into eternity with God. Gisbert Greshake is correct when he writes:

> What remained undone in time, the opportunities and possibilities that were passed up, missed, avoided will remain missed and absent in the new world. What is built in time is built forever; what is left undone will remain undone.[10]

But doesn't that make Christian existence (and that of all others)** unbearably hard? Doesn't it make life a constant burden? In light of such consequences, don't I have to ask myself continually, at every moment: What does this hour, this situation mean for my eternity?

---

*Of course, this statement must be combined with what was said in part 4, chap. 12 about our freely bestowed sharing in the fullness of divine life.

**I have been speaking about the sacramental existence of Christians, but what has been said here is true in some way of all people, because all human beings, whether they are aware of it or not, live in relationship to what has come into the world with Christ. Theology speaks, in this connection, of the *votum ecclesiae*.

No, I don't have to ask that. It would be senseless and even perverse to be thinking constantly of the "results" for one's own eternity. We do not need to live within the prisons of our own selves. The presence of eternal life only becomes a burden if I let it lock me inside my own self and try to store up what is owed to me for my service. Then it would be about *my* works and not the works of *God*. Then it would not be about hope for all but only about hope for myself.

And that is what the coming of the reign of God is *not* about. The reign of God means being free for others, not "insisting on one's own way" (cp. 1 Cor 13:5) but giving oneself for the sake of the reign of God. Only those who lose their lives will gain them, Jesus says (Luke 17:33). Precisely when we forget ourselves, when we engage on behalf of others, when we struggle for a more just society—and above all, when we are intent on building up Christian communities and helping the church, we build ourselves a share in eternity. For eternal life is not unworldly; it is a world elevated, healed, and transformed for God—and everything that is done now for a just world living in peace is done for eternity and endures forever.

So: When does eternity begin? Today, now, here! "The reign of God is among you!" Jesus says (cp. Luke 17:21), and "See, now is the acceptable time; see, now is the day of salvation," says Paul (2 Cor 6:2).

Here we have the solution to an ancient problem that troubled even the early church. We could put it this way: Closeness to the world, or separation from the world? Engagement for the world or turning away from it? May a Christian be worldly? May one love the world, or must one flee from the world? Many Christians, beginning with the anchorites who withdrew to the desert in the third century and continuing to modern Christians who long for a different society, were and are driven by this question.

After all, it is really a grandiose but only apparent problem, because it is precisely when Christians are at home in the world, tasting its joys in gratitude, caring for it as a creation entrusted to us and giving ourselves to it in order to gain it for the reign of God—only then are we loving God.

In the Our Father, the prayer Jesus taught his disciples and that contains everything essential, there is not a single petition asking God to remove us from this evil world. Instead, in the very first petition it speaks of the honor, the dignity of God that we ask may bloom in this world: God's good name is to be hallowed. Nor does the Our Father beg: "bring us to heaven!" but "thy kingdom come!"— and of course that means "may your kingdom, your reign, come in this world, here, on this earth!" Then we pray for the things we need so that we can live in the force field of the reign of God: bread for the coming day, constant forgiveness, rescue from the temptation to surrender our faith. The Our Father is about the honor of God, and the honor of God is the success of God's plan for history.

The reign of God comes in this world to change and heal it. It sets in motion a history whose outcome we cannot foresee. Those who live for the reign of God certainly know their own powerlessness and daily dying, but they also know that the reign of God, with its non-violence, is stronger than all the powers and forces that exist.

Hence living in Christian hope in no way means being resigned to the way things are in the world because we look for a very different world beyond this one; it means opening the world to God so that the reign of God may come. Being oriented to eternal life in no way means despising the world, but rather the highest degree of commitment to the world, because it is within this world and nowhere else that the world to come can be built. We could also say that it is precisely because all history is directed to the coming world that it has its own proper value, its own proper dignity, an infinite importance, and it demands of us our whole lives.

At the end of this book I have to be even more radical and inflammatory than ever. It is good to regard everything we do from the point of view of eternal life. It cannot be wrong always to have the end in view and never to lose sight of the purpose of life. And yet at some point the question arises: If we do that, are we really doing full justice to people and things? Must we really always consider everything *sub specie aeternitatis*,[11] really see everything constantly "in light of eternity"?

Is not a rose simply a rose, something we can take delight in simply because it is a rose? Is a young woman not simply charming because she is a young woman? When I look at the shining face of a child, should I be thinking of eternity? And must I not help another human being in need—simply because she or he is in need? And am I not to work for change simply because conditions are intolerable?

It should be clear where I am going with this. Certainly it is necessary to consider everything in terms of its goal. It is indispensable to regard the world in light of the resurrection. This book has done that. And yet God's creation is still something in its own right: it lies before our eyes and wants to be looked at. It is what it is, itself, and it must not be constantly asked about where it is going. It is precisely in its purposelessness that it glows before us and smiles at us.

If, besides all our theology, all our concern for others and ourselves, we do not grow into this self-forgetful acceptance and simply surrender ourselves to people and things, if we cannot be happy as children, we are not doing justice either to God or to God's creation. Then, for example, we remain incapable of the highest form of prayer that exists: adoration.

For what does it mean to adore God? Why is it so elementary, so beautiful, and ultimately also so beneficial for human beings? In adoration we ask nothing more of God. When I *lament* before God it is usually my own suffering that is the starting point. Even when I *petition* God, the occasion is often my own problem. I need something from God. And even when I *thank* God, unfortunately I am usually thankful for something *I* have received. But when I *adore*, I let go of myself and look only to God.

Lament, petition, and thanksgiving are good and right, but something happens in adoration that reaches still deeper because it is completely without purpose, forgets the self, its needs, and its joys and simply—adores. In adoration we look only to God, leave everything else behind, and praise God in pure wonder at the truth that God alone is the Holy One, the Mighty One, the Glorious. Everything drops away, and it is only about *God's* glory. That we are able to do such a thing at all, that we can forget ourselves and our "high importance," is a miracle, only possible because God gives the divine Spirit into our hearts and entices us to praise God.

In the miracle of adoration we are already with God, entirely with God, and the boundary between time and eternity is removed. It is true that we cannot now comprehend that adoring God will be endless bliss. We always want to be doing something. We want to criticize, intervene, change, improve, shape. And rightly so! That is our duty. But in death, when we come to God, that all ceases. Then our existence will be pure astonishment, pure looking, pure praise, pure adoration—an unimaginable and unnameable happiness.

That is why there is also a form of adoration that uses no words. In it I hold out my own life to God, in silence, and with it the whole world, knowing God as Creator, as Lord, as the one to whom belong all honor and praise. Adoration is the oblation of one's own life to God. Adoration is surrender. Adoration means entrusting oneself entirely to God.

As we dwell in that adoration, eternity begins—an eternity that does not withdraw from the world but opens to it utterly.

Acknowledgments

My brother Norbert, of St. Georgen in Frankfurt, has read this book, as he has my previous ones, and given me valuable suggestions. I am grateful to him for that, and I rejoice every day that we are so deeply united not only as brothers but in all that concerns theology and the church.

I am also grateful to my good friend Professor Dr. Marius Reiser of Mainz, with whom I have discussed a whole series of New Testament texts that are treated in this book. It is always a pleasure to profit from his profound knowledge of Greek.

I send greetings, too, to Dr. Yeong Deok Lee in Switzerland. He has not only translated two of my books into Korean but has helped me to a better understanding of Buddhism, even though I am far from truly comprehending it.

Sincere thanks also to Professor Dr. Norbert Krüger of Odense in Denmark. We came to one another's attention by accident, and he has helped me a very great deal by reading through the manuscript. The same thanks are due to Antje Bitterlich of Munich, who has improved my style, my orthography, and all my biblical references and has constantly encouraged me by her joy in theology.

Hans Pachner of the Katholische Integrierte Gemeinde has helped me, as often before, in gathering materials. Professor Dr. Michael Drieschner reviewed the sections of the book on natural science. The book could never have been possible without the theological passion and lively faith of my brothers and sisters in the Integrierte Gemeinde.

Last but not least: I do not know how to offer the thanks she deserves to my former doctoral student in Tübingen, the Rev. Dr. Linda Maloney, for her sensitive translation of this book into English. She not only had to translate my own text, but to seek out or provide new versions of a parade of ancient inscriptions, classical citations, and poems. She has mastered this difficult and arduous task with finesse.

I am equally indebted, once again, to Hans Christoffersen, academic publisher at Liturgical Press, who has again encouraged and accompanied this English edition from the beginning and in the most generous fashion.

Gerhard Lohfink

Works Consulted

Alt, Peter-André. *Ästhetik des Bösen*. Munich: Beck, 2010.

Assmann, Jan. "Death and Initiation in the Funerary Religion of Ancient Egypt." In *Religion and Philosophy in Ancient Egypt*, edited by W. K. Simpson, 135–39. Yale Egyptological Studies 3. New Haven: Yale University Press, 1989.

————. *Der Tod als Thema der Kulturtheorie. Todesbilder und Totenriten im Alten Ägypten*. edition suhrkamp 2157. Frankfurt: Surkamp, 2000.

————. *Ma'at. Gerechtigkeit und Unsterblichkeit im Alten Ägypten*. Munich: Beck, 1990.

————. *Tod und Jenseits im Alten Ägypten*. 2nd ed. Munich: Beck, 2010. English: *Death and Salvation in Ancient Egypt*. Translated by David Lorton. Ithaca: Cornell University Press, 2005.

Balthasar, Hans Urs von. "Eschatologie." In *Fragen der Theologie heute*, edited by Johannes Feiner, Josef Trütsch, and Franz Böckle, 403–21. Einsiedeln: Benziger, 1957.

————. "Umrisse der Eschatologie." In *Verbum Caro*. Skizzen zur Theologie I. Einsiedeln: Johannes Verlag, 1960. English: "Some Points of Eschatology." In *Explorations in Theology I: The Word Made Flesh*, 255–77. Translated by A. V. Littledale with Alexander Dru. San Francisco: Ignatius Press, 1989.

————. "Eschatologie im Umriss." In *Pneuma und Institution*. Skizzen zur Theologie IV. Einsiedeln: Johannes Verlag, 1974. English: "Eschatology in Outline." In *Explorations in Theology IV: Spirit and Institution*, 432–68. Translated by Edward T. Oakes. San Francisco: Ignatius Press, 1995.

————. "Gericht." *Internationale katholische Zeitschrift* 9 (1980): 227–35.

Barbiero, Gianni. "Das Rätsel von Psalm 49." Supplements to *Vetus Testamentum* 133 (2010): 41–56.

Barth, Christoph. *Die Errettung vom Tode in den individuellen Klage- und Dankliedern des Alten Testamentes.* Zollikon: Evangelischer Verlag, 1947.

Bätzing, Georg. *Kirche im Werden. Ekklesiologische Aspekte des Läuterungsgedankens.* Trierer Theologische Studien 56. Trier: Paulinus Verlag, 1996.

Berger, Klaus. *Die Auferstehung des Propheten und die Erhöhung des Menschensohnes. Traditionsgeschichtliche Untersuchungen zur Deutung des Geschickes Jesu in frühchristlichen Texten.* Studien zur Umwelt des Neuen Testaments 13. Göttingen: Vandenhoeck & Ruprecht, 1976.

Berlejung, Angelika, and Bernd Janowski, eds. *Tod und Jenseits im alten Israel und in seiner Umwelt. Theologische, religionsgeschichtliche, archäologische und ikonographische Aspekte.* Forschungen zum Alten Testament 64. Tübingen: Mohr Siebeck, 2009.

Betz, Otto. *Die Eschatologie in der Glaubensunterweisung.* Würzburg: Echter Verlag, 1965.

Beutler, Johannes. "Die Stunde Jesu im Johannesevangelium." *Bibel und Kirche* 52 (1997): 25–27.

Bieberstein, Klaus. "Jenseits der Todesschwelle. Die Entstehung der Auferstehungshoffnungen in der alttestamentlich-frühjüdischen Literatur." In Berlejung and Janowski, eds., *Tod und Jenseits im alten Israel und in seiner Umwelt* (2009), 423–46.

Boros, Ladislaus. *Mysterium mortis. Der Mensch in der letzten Entscheidung.* 4th ed. Olten and Freiburg: Walter Verlag, 1964. English: *The Mystery of Death.* Translated by Gregory Bainbridge. New York: Herder & Herder, 1965.

Brandt, Wilhelm. *Das Schicksal der Seele nach dem Tode. Nach mandäischen und parsischen Vorstellungen.* Libelli 152. Darmstadt: Wissenschaftliche Buchgesellschaft, 1967.

Brückner, Wolfgang. *Die Sprache christlicher Bilder.* Kulturgeschichtliche Spaziergänge im Germanischen Nationalmuseum 12. Nuremberg: Verlag des Germanischen Nationalmuseums, 2010.

———. "Katechetische Bilder vom guten Tod in nachmittelalterlicher Zeit aus Süddeutschland. Vom Wissen um Bildtraditionen." In *Gesammelte Schriften* XIV, Supplements 2, 385–412. Würzburg: Bayerische Blätter für Volkskunde, 2010.

Brunner, Emil. *Das Ewige als Zukunft und Gegenwart.* Siebenstern-Taschenbuch 32. Munich: Siebenstern, 1965. English: *Eternal Hope.* Translated by Harold Knight. Philadelphia: Westminster Press, 1954.

Buber, Martin. *Ich und Du*. 15th ed. Gütersloh: Gütersloher Verlagshaus, 2010. English: *I and Thou*. Translated by Walter Kaufmann. New York: Scribners, 1970.

Catechism of the Catholic Church. 2nd ed. Washington, DC: USCC, 2000.

Christe, Wilhelm. "'Unsterblichkeit der Seele'. Versuch einer evangelisch-theologischen Rehabilitierung." *Neue Zeitschrift für Systematische Theologie und Religionsphilosophie* 54 (2012): 262–84.

Czopf, Tamás. *Neues Volk Gottes? Zur Geschichte und Problematik eines Begriffs*. Münchener theologische Studien II: Systematische Abteilung, 78. St. Ottilien: Eos Verlag, 2016.

Feiner, Johannes, and Lukas Vischer, eds. *Neues Glaubensbuch. Der gemeinsame christliche Glaube*. 14th ed. Freiburg: Herder, 1978.

Fischer, Alexander Achilles. *Tod und Jenseits im Alten Orient und im Alten Testament*. Neukirchen-Vluyn: Neukirchener Verlag, 2005.

Fleischhack, Erich. *Fegfeuer. Die christlichen Vorstellungen vom Geschick der Verstorbenen geschichtlich dargestellt*. Tübingen: Katzmann Verlag, 1969.

Frühauf, Martin, and Ludwig Bertsch, eds. *Humanes Heilen, inhumanes Sterben?* Sankt Georgener Hochschulschriften 2. Frankfurt: Josef Knecht, 1999.

Fuchs, Ottmar. *Das jüngste Gericht. Hoffnung auf Gerechtigkeit*. 2nd ed. Regensburg: Pustet, 2009.

Fuchs, Thomas, Andreas Kruse, and Grit Schwarzkopf, eds. *Menschenbild und Menschenwürde am Ende des Lebens*. Schriften des Marsilius-Kollegs 2. Heidelberg: Universitätsverlag Winter, 2010.

Gehring, Petra. *Theorien des Todes zur Einführung*. Hamburg: Junius Verlag, 2010.

Georgi, Dieter. "Die Visionen vom himmlischen Jerusalem in Apk 21 und 22." In *Kirche. FS für Günther Bornkamm zum 75. Geburtstag*, edited by Dieter Lührmann and Georg Strecker, 351–72. Tübingen: J. C. B. Mohr, 1980.

German Bishops' Conference. "Menschenwürdig sterben und christlich sterben" (20 November 1978). "Schwerstkranken und Sterbenden beistehen" (20 February 1991). Bonn: Secretariate of the German Bishops' Conference, 1978; 1991.

Gese, Hartmut. *Zur biblischen Theologie. Alttestamentliche Vorträge*. Beiträge zur Evangelische Theologie 78. Munich: Kaiser, 1977. English: *Essays on Biblical Theology*. Translated by Keith Crim. Minneapolis: Augsburg, 1981.

Görres, Ida Friederike. *Der Geopferte. Ein anderer Blick auf John Henry Newman*. Edited by Hanna-Barbara Gerl-Falkovitz. Vallendar-Schönstatt: Patris Verlag, 2004.

Greshake, Gisbert. "Auferstehung der Toten. Auferstehung des Fleisches." In *Lexikon für Theologie und Kirche* 1, 1191–1206. Sonderausgabe. 3rd ed. Freiburg: Herder, 2006.

———. *Auferstehung der Toten. Ein Beitrag zur gegenwärtigen theologischen Diskussion über die Zukunft der Geschichte.* Koinonia 10. Essen: Ludgerus-Verlag, 1969.

———. "Auferstehung im Tod. Ein 'parteiischer' Rückblick auf eine theologische Diskussion." *Theologie und Philosophie* 73 (1998): 538–57.

———. "Bemerkungen zur Endentscheidungshypothese." In Greshake and Lohfink, *Naherwartung, Auferstehung, Unsterblichkeit* (1986), 121–30.

———. "Das Verhältnis 'Unsterblichkeit der Seele' und 'Auferstehung des Leibes' in problemgeschichtlicher Sicht." In Greshake and Lohfink, *Naherwartung, Auferstehung, Unsterblichkeit* (1986), 82–120.

———. *Erlöst in einer unerlösten Welt?* topos taschenbücher 170. Mainz: Matthias Grünewald, 1987.

———. *Geschenkte Freiheit. Einführung in die Gnadenlehre.* Freiburg: Herder, 1977.

———. *Maria–Ecclesia. Perspektiven einer marianisch grundierten Theologie und Kirchenpraxis.* Regensburg: Pustet, 2014.

———. *Stärker als der Tod. Zukunft, Tod, Auferstehung, Himmel, Hölle, Fegfeuer.* topos taschenbücher 50. 5th ed. Mainz: Matthias Grünewald, 1980.

———. "Tod und Auferstehung." In *Enzyklopädische Bibliothek*, edited by Franz Böckle, et al., volume 5, 63–180. Freiburg: Herder, 1980.

———. *Tod: und dann? Ende, Reinkarnation, Auferstehung. Der Streit der Hoffnungen.* Herderbücherei 1504. Freiburg: Herder, 1988.

———, and Jacob Kremer. *Resurrectio mortuorum. Zum theologischen Verständnis der leiblichen Auferstehung.* Darmstadt: Wissenschaftliche Buchgesellschaft, 1986.

———, and Gerhard Lohfink. *Naherwartung, Auferstehung, Unsterblichkeit. Untersuchungen zur christlichen Eschatologie.* Quaestiones Disputatae 71. 5th ed. Freiburg: Herder, 1986.

Grom, Bernhard. "Der 'gute Tod'—früher und heute." *Jesuiten. Informationen der Deutschen Provinz der Jesuiten* 66, no. 1 (2015): 2.

Gronemeyer, Reimer. "Auf dem Weg zur Selbstverwaltung des Sterbens?" In Fuchs, Kruse, and Schwarzkopf, eds., *Menschenbild und Menschenwürde* (2010), 267–79.

Guardini, Romano. *Die letzten Dinge. Die christliche Lehre vom Tode, der Läuterung nach dem Tode, Auferstehung, Gericht und Ewigkeit.* Würzburg: Werkbund-Verlag, 1949. English: *The Last Things: Concerning Death,*

Purification after Death, Resurrection, Judgment, and Eternity. Notre Dame, IN: University of Notre Dame Press, 1954.

Hengel, Martin. "Ist der Osterglaube noch zu retten?" *Theologische Quartalschrift* 153 (1973): 252–69.

Janowski, Bernd. "Jhwh und die Toten. Zur Geschichte des Todes im Alten Israel." In Berlejung and Janowski, eds., *Tod und Jenseits im alten Israel und in seiner Umwelt* (2009), 447–77.

Kaiser, Otto. *Der eine Gott Israels und die Mächte der Welt: Der Weg Gottes im Alten Testament vom Herrn seines Volkes zum Herrn der ganzen Welt*. Forschungen zur Religion und Literatur des Alten und Neuen Testaments 249. Göttingen: Vandenhoeck & Ruprecht, 2013.

Kamlah, Jens. "Grab und Begräbnis in Israel / Juda. Materielle Befunde, Jenseitsvorstellungen und die Frage des Totenkultes." In Berlejung and Janowski, eds., *Tod und Jenseits im alten Israel und in seiner Umwelt* (2009), 257–97.

Kasper, Walter. *Barmherzigkeit. Grundbegriff des Evangeliums, Schlüssel christlichen Lebens*. Freiburg: Herder, 2012. English: *Mercy: The Essence of the Gospel and the Key to Christian Life*. Translated by William Madges. New York and Mahwah, NJ: Paulist Press, 2014.

———, and George Augustin, eds. *Hoffnung auf das ewige Leben. Kraft zum Handeln heute*. Theologie im Dialog 15. Freiburg: Herder, 2015.

Katholischer Katechismus der Bistümer Deutschlands. Freiburg: Herder, 1955.

Katholischer Katechismus für das Bistum Limburg. Limburg: Bistum Limburg, 1936.

Kehl, Medard. *Eschatologie*. 2nd ed. Würzburg: Echter Verlag, 1988.

———. *Und was kommt nach dem Ende? Von Weltuntergang und Vollendung, Wiedergeburt und Auferstehung*. topos taschenbücher 571. 2nd ed. Kevelaer: Topos plus, 2008.

Kellermann, Ulrich. *Auferstanden in den Himmel. 2 Makk 7 und die Auferstehung der Märtyrer*. Stuttgarter Bibelstudien 95. Stuttgart: Katholisches Bibelwerk, 1979.

Kelly, J. N. D. *Early Christian Creeds*. 3rd ed. New York: Continuum, 2006.

Kessler, Hans. *Was kommt nach dem Tod? Über Nahtoderfahrungen, Seele, Wiedergeburt, Auferstehung und ewiges Leben*. 2nd ed. Kevelaer: Butzon & Bercker, 2014.

Kinnebrock, Werner. *Was macht die Zeit, wenn sie vergeht? Wie die Wissenschaft die Zeit erklärt*. Munich: Beck, 2012.

Köster, Barbara. *Der missverstandene Koran. Warum der Islam neu begründet werden muss*. 2nd ed. Berlin and Tübingen: Hans Schiler, 2015.

Krüger, Annette. "Auf dem Weg 'zu den Vätern'. Zur Tradition der alttestamentlichen Sterbenotizen." In Berlejung and Janowski, eds., *Tod und Jenseits im alten Israel und in seiner Umwelt* (2009), 137–50.

Küng, Hans. *Ewiges Leben?* 2nd ed. Munich and Zürich: Piper, 1982. English: *Eternal Life? Life after Death as a Medical, Philosophical, and Theological Problem.* Garden City, NY: Doubleday, 1984.

Lang, Bernhard. "Der Himmel. Zur Kulturgeschichte des ewigen Lebens." *Zeitwende* 62 (1991): 209–20.

———. "Himmel oder Paradies? Zwei Grundformen der christlichen Jenseitserwartung." *Religionsunterricht an höheren Schulen* 36 (1993): 343–54.

———, and Colleen McDannell. *Der Himmel. Eine Kulturgeschichte des ewigen Lebens.* Frankfurt: Insel, 1996. English: *Heaven: A History.* 2nd ed. New Haven: Yale University Press, 2001.

Lee, Yeong Deok. *Transzendenz, Erleuchtung und Erlösung.* Theos 118. Hamburg: Verlag Dr. Kovač, 2014.

Lehmann, Karl. "Was bleibt vom Fegfeuer?" *Internationale Katholische Zeitschrift* 9 (1980): 236–43.

Lepp, Ignace. *Der Tod und seine Geheimnisse.* Würzburg: Arena, 1967.

Lohfink, Gerhard. *Das Vaterunser neu ausgelegt.* 2nd ed. Stuttgart: Katholisches Bibelwerk, 2013.

———. "Das Zeitproblem und die Vollendung der Welt." In Greshake and Lohfink, *Naherwartung, Auferstehung, Unsterblichkeit* (1986), 131–55.

———. "Der Ablauf der Osterereignisse und die Anfänge der Urgemeinde." In *Studien zum Neuen Testament,* 149–67. Stuttgarter biblische Aufsatzbände 5. Stuttgart: Katholisches Bibelwerk, 1989.

———. *Die Himmelfahrt Jesu. Untersuchungen zu den Himmelfahrts- und Erhöhungstexten bei Lukas.* Studien zum Alten und Neuen Testament 26. Munich: Kösel, 1971.

———. *Gegen die Verharmlosung Jesu. Reden über Jesus und die Kirche.* Freiburg: Herder, 2013. English: *No Irrelevant Jesus: On Jesus and the Church Today.* Translated by Linda M. Maloney. Collegeville, MN: Liturgical Press, 2014.

———. *Im Ringen um die Vernunft. Reden über Israel, die Kirche und die Europäische Aufklärung.* Freiburg: Herder, 2016.

———. "Jesus und die Kirche." in *Handbuch der Fundamentaltheologie,* edited by Walter Kern, Hermann Josef Pottmeyer, and Max Seckler, volume 3, 27–64. Section "Kirche." Uni-Taschenbücher 8172. 2nd ed. Tübingen and Basel: Francke, 2000.

———. *Jesus von Nazaret. Was er wollte. Wer er war.* 4th ed. Freiburg: Herder, 2014. English: *Jesus of Nazareth: What He Wanted; Who He Was.*

Translated by Linda M. Maloney from the 1st ed. Collegeville, MN: Liturgical Press, 2012.

―――. "Senfkorn und Weltenbaum (Mk 4,30-32 Parr). Zum Verhältnis von Natur und Gesellschaft bei Jesus." In ". . . *Bäume braucht man doch.*" *Das Symbol des Baumes zwischen Hoffnung und Zerstörung,* edited by Harald Schweizer, 109–26. Sigmaringen: Jahn Thorbecke Verlag, 1986.

―――. "Zur Möglichkeit christlicher Naherwartung." In Greshake and Lohfink, *Naherwartung, Auferstehung, Unsterblichkeit* (1986), 38–81.

―――, and Ludwig Weimer. *Maria: nicht ohne Israel. Eine neue Sicht der Lehre von der Unbefleckten Empfängnis.* 2nd ed. Freiburg: Herder, 2012.

Lohfink, Norbert. "'Ich komme nicht in Zornesglut' (Hos 11,9). Skizze einer synchronen Leseanweisung für das Hoseabuch." In *Ce Dieu qui vient. Mélanges offerts à Bernhard Renaud,* 163–90. Lectio Divina 159. Paris: Cerf, 1995.

―――. *Im Schatten deiner Flügel. Große Bibeltexte neu erschlossen.* Freiburg: Herder, 1999. English: *In the Shadow of Your Wings: New Readings of Great Texts from the Bible.* Translated by Linda M. Maloney. Collegeville, MN: Liturgical Press, 2003.

―――. *Kohelet.* Die Neue Echter Bibel. Würzburg: Echter Verlag, 1980.

Lüke, Ulrich. "Auferstehung am Jüngsten Tag als Auferstehung im Tod." *Stimmen der Zeit* 123 (1998): 45–54.

―――. "Auferstehung: Im Tod? Am Jüngsten Tag?" in *Auferstehung der Toten. Ein Hoffnungsentwurf im Blick heutiger Wissenschaften,* edited by Hans Kessler, 234–51. Darmstadt: Wissenschaftliche Buchgesellschaft, 2004.

―――. *Das Säugetier von Gottes Gnaden. Evolution, Bewusstsein, Freiheit.* Freiburg: Herder, 2016.

Lux, Rüdiger. "Moses Schwanengesang. Gott und die Gewalt im Alten Testament." *Freiburger Rundbrief* 17 (2010): 102–11.

Maier, Michael P. "Festbankett oder Henkersmahlzeit? Die zwei Gesichter von Jes 25,6-8." *Vetus Testamentum* 64 (2014): 445–64.

―――. *Völkerwallfahrt im Jesajabuch.* Beiträge zur *Zeitschrift für die alttestamentliche Wissenschaft* 474. Berlin and Boston: de Gruyter, 2016.

Maio, Giovanni. *Eine neue Kultur des Sterbens. Patientenverfügung und aktive Sterbehilfe.* Kirche und Gesellschaft 373. Cologne: J. P. Bachem, 2010. English: *Essays in Medical Ethics: Plea for a Medicine of Prudence.* Electronic book. New York: Thieme Medical Publishers, 2007.

Merklein, Helmut. "Die Auferweckung Jesu und die Anfänge der Christologie." *Zeitschrift für die neutestamentliche Wissenschaft* 72 (1981): 1–26.

Metz, Johannes Baptist. "*Caro cardo salutis.* Zum christlichen Verständnis des Leibes." *Hochland* 55 (1962/63): 97–107.

Moltmann-Wendel, Elisabeth, and Jürgen Moltmann. "Mit allen Sinnen glauben. Überlegungen zur Auferstehung des Fleisches." *Stimmen der Zeit* 130 (2005): 723–35.

Müller, Gerhard Ludwig. *Katholische Dogmatik. Für Studium und Praxis der Theologie.* 9th ed. Freiburg: Herder, 2012.

Mussner, Franz. "Implikate der Parusie des Herrn." In *Weltgericht und Weltvollendung. Zukunftsbilder im Neuen Testament,* edited by Hans-Josef Klauck, 225–31. Quaestiones Disputatae 150. Freiburg: Herder, 1994.

Nachtwei, Gerhard, ed. *Hoffnung auf Vollendung. Zur Eschatologie von Joseph Ratzinger.* Ratzinger-Studien 8. Regensburg: Pustet, 2015.

Nocke, Franz-Josef. *Eschatologie.* Leitfaden Theologie 6. Düsseldorf: Patmos, 1982.

———. "Eschatologie zwischen Glaubensüberlieferung und neuer Erfahrung. Vier Beispiele." *Katholische Blätter* 105 (1980): 109–21.

———. *Liebe, Tod und Auferstehung. Über die Mitte des Glaubens.* Munich: Kösel, 1978.

Nötscher, Friedrich. *Altorientalischer und alttestamentlicher Auferstehungsglaube.* New revised ed. with an introduction by Josef Scharbert. Darmstadt: Wissenschaftliche Buchgesellschaft, 1970.

Nützel, Johannes M. "Zum Schicksal der eschatologischen Propheten." *Biblische Zeitschrift* 20 (1976): 59–94.

Peek, Werner. *Griechische Grabgedichte.* Greek and German. Schriften und Quellen der Alten Welt 7. Berlin: Akademie-Verlag, 1960.

Plato. *Phaedo.* Translated by Benjamin Jowett. Jersey City, NJ: Start Publishing LLC, 2012.

Pope Francis. *God's Name Is Mercy. A Conversation with Andrea Tornielli.* Translated by Oonagh Stransky. New York: Random House, 2016.

Rahner, Johanna. *Einführung in die christliche Eschatologie.* 2nd ed. Freiburg: Herder, 2016.

Rahner, Karl. "The Human Question of Meaning in Face of the Absolute Mystery." In *Theological Investigations* 18, *God and Revelation,* 89–104. Translated by Edward Quinn. New York: Crossroad, 1983.

———. *Foundations of Christian Faith: An Introduction to the Idea of Christianity.* Translated by William V. Dych. New York: Seabury, 1978.

———. *On the Theology of Death.* Translated by C. H. Henkey. New York: Seabury, 1973.

Ratzinger, Joseph. *Auferstehung und ewiges Leben. Beiträge zur Eschatologie und zur Theologie der Hoffnung.* Gesammelte Schriften 10. Freiburg: Herder, 2012.

———. *Introduction to Christianity.* Translated by J. R. Foster. San Francisco: Ignatius Press, 2004.

———. "Ewigkeit. II. Theologisch." *Lexikon für Theologie und Kirche.* 2nd ed. Volume 3, 1268–70. Freiburg: Herder, 1959.

———. *Eschatologie. Tod und ewiges Leben.* New ed. Regensburg: Pustet, 2012. English: *Eschatology: Death and Eternal Life.* Translated by Michael Waldstein. 2nd ed. Washington, DC: Catholic University of America Press, 2007.

———. "Hölle." In *Lexikon für Theologie und Kirche.* 2nd ed. Volume 5, 446–49. Freiburg: Herder, 1960.

Reiser, Marius. *Die Gerichtspredigt Jesu. Eine Untersuchung zur eschatologischen Verkündigung Jesu und ihrem frühjüdischen Hintergrund.* Neutestamentliche Abhandlungen, new series 23. Münster: Aschendorff, 1990. English: *Jesus and Judgment.* Translated by Linda M. Maloney. Minneapolis: Fortress Press, 1997.

———. *Die letzten Dinge im Licht des Neuen Testaments. Bilder und Wirklichkeit.* Heimbach: Patrimonium-Verlag, 2013.

———. *Sprache und literarische Formen des Neuen Testaments. Eine Einführung.* Uni-Taschenbücher 2197. Paderborn: Schöningh, 2001.

Remenyi, Matthias. *Auferstehung denken. Anwege, Grenzen und Modelle personaleschatologischer Theoriebildung.* Freiburg: Herder, 2016.

———. "Hoffnung, Tod und Auferstehung." *Zeitschrift für katholische Theologie* 129 (2007): 75–96.

Römische Grabinschriften. Gesammelt und ins Deutsche übertragen von Hieronymus Geist. Munich: Heimeran, 1969.

Sattler, Dorothea. "Gottes Gericht und die geläuterte Selbsterkenntnis des Menschen. Versuch einer Verhältnisbestimmung in ökumenischer Perspektive." in *Gemeinsame Hoffnung über den Tod hinaus. Eschatologie im ökumenischen Gespräch,* edited by Uwe Swarat and Thomas Söding, 109–30. Quaestiones disputatae 257. Freiburg: Herder, 2013.

Scherer, Georg. *Das Problem des Todes in der Philosophie.* Grundzüge 35. Darmstadt: Wissenschaftliche Buchgesellschaft, 1979.

———. "Zukunft und Eschaton. Philosophische Aspekte." In *Eschatologie und geschichtliche Zukunft,* edited by Georg Scherer, Ferdinand Kerstiens, and Franz Joseph Schierse, et al., 11–65. Thesen und Argumente 5. Essen-Werden: Fredebeul & Koenen, 1972.

Schnackenburg, Rudolf. *Das Johannesevangelium*. I. Teil. Herders Theologischer Kommentar IV 1. Freiburg: Herder, 1965. English: *The Gospel According to John*. Translated by Kevin Smyth. London: Burns & Oates; New York: Herder & Herder, 1968.

Schnocks, Johannes. *Rettung und Neuschöpfung. Studien zur alttestamentlichen Grundlegung einer gesamtbiblischen Theologie der Auferstehung.* Bonner Biblische Beiträge 158. Göttingen: Vandenhoeck & Ruprecht unipress, 2009.

Schulze, Markus. "Ist die Hölle menschenmöglich? Zum Wandel der Theologie der negativen Endgültigkeit in den letzten fünfzig Jahren." In Kasper and Augustin, eds., *Hoffnung auf das ewige Leben* (2015), 167–203.

Schwienhorst-Schönberger, Ludger. *Das Hohelied der Liebe.* Freiburg: Herder, 2015.

———. "Martyrium der Gewaltlosigkeit. Gibt es ein 'Makkabäer-Syndrom'?" In *Religion, Martyrium und Gewalt*, edited by Jan-Heiner Tück, 148–89. Freiburg: Herder, 2015.

———. "Recht und Gewalt im Alten Testament." In *Macht, Gewalt, Krieg im Alten Testament. Gesellschaftliche Problematik und das Problem ihrer Repräsentation*, edited by Irmtraud Fischer, 318–51. Quaestiones Disputatae 254. Freiburg: Herder, 2013.

Scoralick, Ruth. *Gottes Güte und Gottes Zorn. Die Gottesprädikationen in Ex 34,6f und ihre intertextuellen Beziehungen zum Zwölfprophetenbuch.* Herders biblische Studien 33. Freiburg: Herder, 2002.

Sörries, Reiner. *Ruhe sanft. Kulturgeschichte des Friedhofs.* Kevelaer: Butzon & Bercker, 2009.

Stemberger, Günter. "Auferstehung I/2. Judentum." *Theologische Realenzyklopädie* 4, 443–50.

———. "Das Problem der Auferstehung im Alten Testament." In *Studien zum rabbinischen Judentum*, 19–45. Stuttgarter biblische Aufsatzbände 10. Stuttgart: Katholisches Bibelwerk, 1990.

———. "Zur Auferstehungslehre in der rabbinischen Literatur." In *Studien zum rabbinischen Judentum* (1990), 47–88.

Stettler, Hanna. *Heiligung bei Paulus. Ein Beitrag aus biblisch-theologischer Sicht.* Wissenschaftliche Untersuchungen zum Neuen Testament, second series 368. Tübingen: Mohr-Siebeck, 2014.

Stubenrauch, Bertram. *Was kommt danach? Himmel, Hölle, Nirwana oder gar nichts.* Munich: Pattloch, 2007.

Stuhlmacher, Peter. *Biblische Theologie des Neuen Testaments.* Volume 2: *Von der Paulusschule bis zur Johannesoffenbarung. Der Kanon und seine Auslegung.* 2nd ed. Göttingen: Vandenhoeck & Ruprecht, 2012.

———. "Kritischer müssten mir die Historisch-Kritischen sein!" *Theologischer Quartalschrift* 153 (1973): 244–51.

Swarat, Uwe. "Jenseits des Todes: Unsterblichkeit der Seele oder Auferstehung des Leibes?" In Swarat and Söding, eds., *Gemeinsame Hoffnung: über den Tod hinaus* (2013): 13–35.

Thausing, Gertrud. *Der Auferstehungsgedanke in ägyptischen religiösen Texten.* Sammlung orientalischer Arbeiten 16. Leipzig: Harrassowitz, 1943.

Vechtel, Klaus. *Eschatologie und Freiheit. Zur Frage der postmortalen Vollendung in der Theologie Karl Rahners und Hans Urs von Balthasars.* Innsbrucker theologische Studien 89. Innsbruck and Vienna: Tyrolia, 2014.

Vorgrimler, Herbert. *Der Tod im Denken und Leben des Christen.* Düsseldorf: Patmos, 1978.

———. *Hoffnung auf Vollendung. Aufriss der Eschatologie.* Quaestiones Disputatae 90. Freiburg: Herder, 1980.

Weissmahr, Béla. "Kann Gott die Auferstehung Jesu durch innerweltliche Kräfte bewirkt haben?" *Zeitschrift katholischer Theologie* 100 (1978): 441–69.

Wenz, Gunther. "Evangelische Gedanken zum Fegfeuer." *Münchener theologische Zeitschrift* 67 (2016): 2–34.

Notes

PART ONE

Chapter 1: The Question of Questions—pages 3–9

[1] Jan Assmann, "Death and Initiation in the Funerary Religion of Ancient Egypt," in *Religion and Philosophy in Ancient Egypt*, ed. W. K. Simpson, Yale Egyptological Studies 3 (New Haven: Yale University Press, 1989), 135–59: "[T]he Egyptian 'Book of the Dead' [was] a late canonized corpus of spells which first appeared on papyrus-scrolls . . . in the tomb equipment of deceased persons at the beginning [of the] 16ᵗʰ century B.C. (New Kingdom). Quite a few of these spells can be found centuries earlier . . . on Middle Kingdom coffins" (p. 136). See esp. Assmann, *Death and Salvation in Ancient Egypt* (Ithaca: Cornell University Press, 2005), esp. 249, 297. For the judgment of the dead see pp. 73–86.

[2] Scholars speak of "negative confessions."

[3] E. Wallis Budge, *The Book of the Dead: The Papyrus of Ani in the British Museum* (London: British Museum, 1895), chap. 125, p. 346.

[4] Plato, *Phaedo* 63 (114d), trans. Benjamin Jowett (Jersey City, NJ: Start Publishing LLC, 2012), 164.

Chapter 2: Between Skepticism and Belief in the Soul—pages 10–18

[1] Hieronymus Geist, with Gerhard Pfohl, *Römische Grabinschriften* (Berlin: de Gruyter, 2014), no. 575. Original text: *Fabius Zoilus sibi et Consuadulliae Primillae, maritae karissimae. Vivus ut haberemus feci.*

[2] Werner Peek, *Greek Verse Inscriptions: Epigrams on Funerary Stele and Monuments = Griechische Vers-Inschriften: Grab-Epigramme* (Chicago: Ares, 1988), no. 320.

[3] Andrzej Wypustek, *Images of Eternal Beauty in Funerary Verse Inscriptions of the Hellenistic Period* (Leiden: Brill, 2013), 42. From Peek, *GV*, no. 1031.

[4] Wypustek, *Images of Eternal Beauty*, 50. Translation by A. Chaniotis from Peek, *GV*, 1097.

[5] Thomas H. Carpenter and Christopher A. Faraone, *Masks of Dionysus* (Ithaca: Cornell University Press, 1993), 293.

[6] Translation LMM.

[7] *CIL* 6, 26003. Translation LMM. Original text: *Nihil sumus et fuimus mortales. Respice, lector: In nihil ab nihilo quam cito recidimus.*

[8] *CIL* 5, 1813. Translation in Paul Zanker and Björn C. Ewald, *Living with Myths: The Imagery of Roman Sarcophagi* (Oxford and New York: Oxford University Press, 2012), 108. Original text: *Non fueram, non sum, nescio, non ad me pertinet.*

[9] See Ludwig Friedländer, *Roman Life and Manners under the Early Empire*, 4 vols., trans. J. H. Freese (London: Routledge, 1907), 3:284.

[10] *CIL* 6, 30112. See "The Petrified Muse: Latin Poetry and the Limits of Roman Medicine," https://thepetrifiedmuse.blog/2015/06/02/latin-poetry-and-the-limits-of-roman-medicine. The original is a hexameter: *Quid tibi nunc prodest stricte vixisse tot annis?*

[11] Later called "Gegen Verführung" ("Against Deception") and printed at the end of Brecht's *Hauspostille* (1927). Brecht also published it separately as "Luzifers Nachtlied."

[12] Bertolt Brecht, *Manual of Piety (Die Hauspostille)*, trans. Eric Bentley (New York: Grove Press, 1994), 232.

[13] Marie Luise Kaschnitz, "I am not brave," from *Kein Zauberspruch. Gedichte* (Frankfurt: Insel, 1972), trans. Eavan Boland, at http://voiceseducation.org/content/marie-luise-kaschnitz-german.

[14] From Kurt Marti, *Leichenreden* (Frankfurt: Luchterhand, 1969), trans. Thorwald Lorenzen in his *Toward a Culture of Freedom: Reflections on the Ten Commandments Today* (Eugene, OR: Cascade Books, 2008), 109.

Chapter 3: Survival in Our Descendants?—pages 19–26

[1] See Hartmut Gese, *Essays on Biblical Theology* (Minneapolis: Augsburg, 1981), chap. 2, "Death in the Old Testament."

[2] Translations of biblical passages, unless otherwise noted, follow the author's.

[3] The real author was Joseph Christian Freiherr von Zedlitz, in his tragedy *Der Stern von Sevilla [The Star of Seville]* (1830). See "Trauersprüche-Universität Bielefeld," at www.uni-bielefeld.de/lili/personen/useelbach/STUD/trauersprüche.html.

[4] The author of the original of this saying is Michelangelo Buonarroti. Sometimes his full text is quoted in obituaries:

Too early fallen asleep here, I'm alive,
though fate says dead. I've moved; my lodging's new.
I'm living in your thoughts. You miss me too.
While love lives on in lovers, I survive.
Here I'm thought dead. Alive, I comforted

the world by being there. A thousand souls
played in my heart a thousand loving roles.
Now I'm but one soul less. That means I'm dead?

Translation from John Frederick Nims, *The Complete Poems of Michelangelo* (Chicago and London: University of Chicago Press, 1998), pp. 111, 109, nos. 194, 190.

[5] The quotation is often attributed to Augustine or Victor Hugo. See www .uni-bielefeld.de/lili/personen/useelbach/STUD/trauersprüche.htm.

[6] Often attributed to Rainer Maria Rilke or Antoine de Saint-Exupéry. See ibid.

[7] Obituary for Gerard Mortier, *Frankfurter Allgemeine Zeitung*, 15 March 2014, p. 17. Translation LMM.

[8] Lee Child, *The Enemy* (New York: Random House Dell, 2015), 349.

[9] "Conversation between d'Alembert and Diderot" (1769), from *Diderot, Interpreter of Nature*, trans. Jean Stewart and Jonathan Kemp (International Publishers: 1943), at https://www.marxists.org/reference/archive/diderot/1769/conversation.htm. See also Arthur M. Wilson, *Diderot* (New York: Oxford University Press, 1972).

[10] Woody Allen, quoted by Niko Kolodny in his introduction to Samuel Scheffler, *Death and the Afterlife* (Oxford: Oxford University Press, 2013), 3.

Chapter 4: Continual Reincarnation?—pages 27–36

[1] Thomas Ryan, "25 percent of US Christians believe in reincarnation. What's wrong with this picture?" *America* (21 Oct. 2015), at www.americamagazine.org.

[2] For a discussion of the doctrine of reincarnation see Medard Kehl, *Eschatologie*, 2nd ed. (Wurzburg: Echter Verlag, 1988), 71–76; Gisbert Greshake, *Tod—und dann? Ende, Reinkarnation, Auferstehung. Der Streit der Hoffnungen*, Herderbücherei 1504 (Freiburg: Herder, 1988), 53–90; Hans Kessler, *Was kommt nach dem Tod? Über Nahtoderfahrungen, Seele, Wiedergeburt, Auferstehung und ewiges Leben*, 2nd ed. (Kevelaer: Butzon & Bercker, 2014), 98–120.

[3] For more detail see Yeong Deok Lee, *Transzendenz, Erleuchtung und Erlösung* (Hamburg: Kovac, 2014), 77–137.

[4] Ibid., 29–76.

[5] Greshake, *Tod—und dann?*, 55.

Chapter 5: Dissolution into the Universe?—pages 37–47

[1] The fragment was attributed to Goethe during his own lifetime. See his remark to Chancellor von Müller: "I do not exactly remember having written these reflections, but they very well agree with the ideas which had at that time become developed in my mind." However, the fragment is not by Goethe; it is by Georg Christoph Tobler, whom Goethe had met in Switzerland in the Lavater circle. For this quotation and the translation, by T. H. Huxley, see "Goethe: Aphorisms on Nature," in *Nature* 1 (4 Nov. 1869), available at http://www.nature.com /nature/about/first/aphorisms.html.

² Now usually called "Ode to Nature" and correctly attributed to Tobler.

³ Recent translations call it *The World as Will and Representation*.

⁴ All quotations from Arthur Schopenhauer, *The World as Will and Representation*, trans. E. F. J. Payne, 2 vols. (New York: Dover Publications, 1958).

⁵ For what follows see Thomas Mann, *Buddenbrooks: The Decline of a Family*, trans. John E. Woods (New York: Random House Vintage, 1994), Part X, chap. 5, 631–36.

⁶ Edward Mackinnon, *Heartland Germany* (Beeston, Nottingham: Shoestring Press, 2014). The Jandl poem can also be found at http://edwardmackinnon .com/jandl.html.

⁷ See the instructive book by Reiner Sörries, *Ruhe sanft. Kulturgeschichte des Friedhofs* (Kevelaer: Butzon & Bercker, 2009).

⁸ Lorenz Marti, *Eine Hand voll Sternenstaub. Was das Universum über das Glück des Daseins erzählt* (Freiburg: Kreuz Verlag, 2012), 197, 200.

⁹ Thich Nhat Hanh, *No Death, No Fear: Comforting Wisdom for Life* (New York: Riverhead, 2002), 171.

¹⁰ Martin Buber, *I and Thou*, trans. Walter Kaufmann (New York: Scribners, 1970), 28.

¹¹ Jean Paul, "Speech of the Dead Christ," excerpt, at http://50watts.com /Jean-Paul-Speech-of-the-Dead-Christ.

¹² Ibid.

Chapter 6: The Longing for Extinction—pages 48–56

¹ Epicurus, *Letter to Menoeceus*, no. 124–26. Available at http://www.epicurus .net/en/menoeceus.html.

² See the description of Pavel Nikolayevich Rusanov in Alexander Solzhenitsyn, *Cancer Ward* (London: Bodley Head, 1968), part 1.

³ Simon Beckett, *The Chemistry of Death* (New York: Bantam Dell, 2006), 1.

⁴ See, e.g., Jeff Malpas and Robert C. Solomon, eds., *Death and Philosophy* (London and New York: Routledge, 1998); Ben Bradley, Fred Feldman, and Jens Johansson, eds., *The Oxford Handbook of Philosophy of Death* (Oxford: Oxford University Press, 2013).

⁵ See, e.g., Lars Sandman, *A Good Death: On the Value of Death and Dying* (Maidenhead: Open University Press, 2005), for an ethical treatment. Elisabeth Kübler-Ross, *On Death and Dying* (New York: Scribner, 1969), retains its popularity; also very well received is Michael Vocino and Alfred G. Killilea, *Befriending Death: 100 Essayists on Living and Dying* (Bloomington, IN: iUniverse, 2012), with perspectives from both believers and atheists, and those in between.

⁶ See, e.g., Sheldon Solomon, Jeff Greenberg, and Tom Pyszczynski, *The Worm at the Core: On the Role of Death in Life* (New York: Random House, 2015), esp. chap. 1, "Managing the Terror of Death."

⁷ Michael de Ridder, *"Wie wollen wir sterben?" Ein ärztliches Plädoyer für eine neue Sterbekultur in Zeiten der Hochleistungsmedizin* ["How do we want to die?"

A doctor's plea for a new culture of dying in a time of high-performance medicine"] (Munich: Deutsche Verlagsanstalt, 2010).

[8] See Reimer Gronemeyer, "Auf dem Weg zur Selbstverwaltung des Sterbens" [On the Way to Self-Administration of Death], in *Menschenbild und Menschenwürde am Ende des Lebens* [Image and Dignity of Humanity at the End of Life], ed. Thomas Fuchs, et al. (Heidelberg: Universitätsverlag Winter, 2011), 267–79. Cp. Johanna Hefel, "Will You Be With Me to the End? Personal Experiences of Cancer and Death," in *Narrating Social Work Through Autoethnography*, ed. Stanley L. Witkin (New York: Columbia University Press, 2014), 197–230.

[9] Oliver Tolmein, "Chronik eines angekündigten Todes," *Frankfurter Allgemeine Zeitung*, 17 September 2010, p. 33.

[10] Schopenhauer, *The World as Will and Representation*, vol. 2, 469.

[11] German text in *German Poetry from the Beginnings to 1750*, ed. Ingrid Walsøe-Engel, The German Library (New York: Continuum, 1992), 260. Translation LMM.

[12] Ibid.

[13] Reinhold Schneider, *Winter in Wien. Aus meinen Notizbüchern 1957/58*, 6th ed. (Freiburg: Herder, 1961), 98–99.

[14] Friedrich Nietzsche, *Ecce Homo*, trans. Anthony M. Ludovici (Mineola, NY: Dover, 2004), 28–29, from the chapter "Why I Am so Clever."

[15] See Karlhans Abel, "Poseidonios und Senecas Trostschrift an Marcia (dial. 6,24,5ff.)," *Rheinisches Museum* 107 (1964): 221–60, esp. 258.

[16] Seneca, "Of Consolation: to Marcia," trans. Aubrey Stewart, from *L. Annaeus Seneca, Minor Dialogs Together with the Dialog "On Clemency,"* Bohn's Classical Library Edition (London: George Bell and Sons, 1900), XXV, available at https://en.wikisource.org/wiki/Of_Consolation:_To_Marcia.

PART TWO

Chapter 1: Faith Seeking Understanding—pages 59–63

[1] Friedrich Nietzsche, *Thus Spake Zarathustra: A Book for All and None*, trans. Thomas Common (North Charleston, SC: Pantianos Classics, 2016), 251.

[2] Augustine, *Confessions*, trans. Henry Chadwick, Oxford World's Classics (Oxford: Oxford University Press, 2009), 3.

Chapter 2: Radical Worldliness—pages 64–68

[1] Christoph Barth, *Die Errettung vom Tode in den individuellen Klage- und Dankliedern des Alten Testaments* (Zollikon: Evangelischer Verlag, 1947), 165.

[2] See, e.g., Gen 25:8, 17; 35:29; 49:23, 33; Num 20:24, 26; 27:13; 31:2; Deut 32:50. "People" is literally "fathers"; all the references are to male individuals.

[3] See Annette Krüger, "Auf dem Weg 'zu den Vätern.' Zur Tradition der alttestamentlichen Sterbenotizen," in Angelika Berlejung and Bernd Janowski, eds.,

Tod und Jenseits im alten Israel und in seiner Umwelt. Theologische, religionsgeschicht-liche, archäologische und ikonographische Aspekte, FAT 64 (Tübingen: Mohr Siebeck, 2009), 137–50, at 137–44.

[4] For Qoheleth's worldview see esp. Norbert Lohfink, *Kohelet*, NEB (Würzburg: Echter Verlag, 1980).

[5] According to Bernd Janowski, Qoheleth is already aware of sayings in Israel about salvation that extends beyond death, but he remains skeptical about them. The goal of the text here cited was not to devalue the world but to insist on the present time as God's gift. Bernd Janowski, "Jhwh und die Toten: Zur Geschichte des Todes im Alten Israel," in Berlejung and Janowski, eds., *Tod und Jenseits* (2009), 447–77, at 470.

Chapter 3: Dissociation from Faith in the Hereafter—pages 69–74

[1] See Jan Assmann, *Der Tod als Thema der Kulturtheorie: Todesbilder und Totenriten in alten Ägypten* (Frankfurt: Suhrkamp, 2015), "Death [in ancient Egypt] was the quintessence of the holy, the primal form of the divine. It is the origin and goal of all living things. . . . In the Bible, as in Judaism, the holy and death moved as far apart as possible. Nothing is more foreign to the holy than death; nothing pollutes and desecrates more powerfully than a corpse."

[2] Cp. Matthias Remenyi, *Auferstehung denken: anwege, grenzen und modelle per-sonaleschatologische Theoriebildung* (Freiburg, et al.: Herder, 2016), 174–75, 183.

[3] For example, the difficult text of Ezek 43:7-9 may presuppose a royal ances-tral cult.

[4] See Jens Kamlah, "Grab und Begräbnis in Israel/Juda. Materielle Befunde, Jenseitsvorstellungen und die Frage des Totenkultes," in Berlejung and Janowski, *Tod und Jenseits* (2009), 257–97, at 290–92. In English see Stephen L. Cook, "Funerary Practices and Afterlife Expectations in Ancient Israel," *Religion Compass* 1, no. 6 (2007): 660–83, available at https://www.academia.edu/694584 /Funerary_Practices_and_Afterlife_Expectations_in_Ancient_Israel.

[5] For quick reference on the Baal myth see Wolfgang Herrmann, "Baal," *Dic-tionary of Deities and Demons in the Bible* (Grand Rapids: Eerdmans, 1999), 132–39; Alexander A. Fischer, *Tod und Jenseits im Alten Orient und im Alten Testament. Eine Reise durch antike Vorstellungs- und Textwelten* (Leipzig: Evangelische Verlagsan-stalt, 2014), 96–105.

[6] See Otto Kaiser, *Der eine Gott Israels und die Mächte der Welt: der Weg Gottes im Alten Testament vom Herrn seines Volkes zum Herrn der ganzen Welt* (Göttingen: Vandenhoeck & Ruprecht, 2013), 22–24.

[7] Assmann, *Death and Salvation*, 17.

[8] See R. Tournay, "En marge d'une traduction des Psaumes (Ps 10,2-8; 29,3 et 9; 18,36; 58,10, 16; 22)," *RB* 63 (1956): 161–81; 496–512, at 502n2.

Chapter 4: Security in God—pages 75–80

[1] I am following the exegesis by Gianni Barbiero, "Das Rätsel von Ps. 49," *Congress Volume Llubljana 2007* (Leiden and Boston: Brill, 2010), 41–56. Other interpreters attribute the internal tensions in the Psalm to different literary layers.

[2] See Janowski, "Jʜwʜ und die Toten," 465–66. Janowski speaks of the "expansion of Jʜwʜ's competence" to include the underworld (449–50). On this see also Gönke Eberhardt, *JHWH und die Unterwelt. Spuren einer Kompetenzausweitung JHWHs im Alten Testament*, FAT 2nd ser. 23 (Tübingen: Mohr Siebeck, 2007).

[3] Translation and interpretation based on Norbert Lohfink, *In the Shadow of Your Wings: New Readings of Great Texts from the Bible*, trans. Linda M. Maloney (Collegeville, MN: Liturgical Press, 2003), 99.

Chapter 5: Faith in Resurrection Begins to Sprout—pages 81–86

[1] See James H. Charlesworth, et al., *Resurrection: The Origin and Future of a Biblical Doctrine* (New York and London: T & T Clark, 2006); Stephen L. Cook, "Apocalyptic Writings," in *The Cambridge Companion to the Old Testament*, ed. Stephen B. Chapman and Marvin W. Sweeney (Cambridge and New York: Cambridge University Press, 2016), 331–48: "Indeed, Israel was apparently comfortable with resurrection already by the time of the Babylonian exile, long before the notion's supposedly surprise appearance in Daniel 12:1-3" (p. 337). Similarly Günter Stemberger, "Das Problem der Auferstehung im Alten Testament," *Kairos* 14 (1972): 273–90; also in his *Studien zum rabbinischen Judentum*, SBAB 10 (Stuttgart: Katholisches Bibelwerk, 1990), 47–88, at 45. See also the nuanced presentation by Klaus Bieberstein, "Jenseits der Todesschwelle. Die Entstehung der Auferstehungshoffnungen in der alttestamentlich-frühjüdischen Literatur," in Berlejung and Janowski, eds., *Tod und Jenseits*, 423–46, esp. 424–48; also Johannes Schnocks, *Rettung und Neuschöpfung. Studien zur alttestamentlichen Grundlegung einer gesamtbiblischen Theologie der Auferstehung*, BBB 158 (Göttingen: Vandenhoeck & Ruprecht, 2009).

[2] Isaiah 25:6-7, contrary to the usual Christian interpretation, does not portray an eschatological banquet for the nations but the destruction of everything opposed to God, in a fatal feast. Verses 6-7 are thus a prophecy of evil things, as has been shown, with convincing arguments, by M. P. Maier, "Festbankett oder Henkersmahlzeit? Die zwei Gesichter von Jes 25,6-8," *VT* 64 (2014): 445–64. See also his *Völkerwallfahrt im Jesajabuch*, BZAW 474 (Berlin and Boston: de Gruyter, 2016), 221–40.

[3] See ibid., 229–30.

[4] For this and what follows see Ludger Schwienhorst-Schönberger, "Martyrium der Gewaltlosigkeit. Gibt es ein 'Makkabäer-Syndrom'?" in *Religion, Martyrium und Gewalt*, ed. Jan-Heiner Tück (Freiburg: Herder, 2015), 148–89.

[5] On this passage see now esp. Schnocks, *Rettung und Neuschöpfung*, 161–243.

[6] Günter Stemberger, "Auferstehung I/2. Judentum," *TRE* 4:443–50, at 444, emphasizes that the imagery in Ezekiel 37 could only have been possible "if certain ideas about an overcoming of the grave [were] already given."

⁷ Thus Schnocks, *Rettung und Neuschöpfung*, 161, 241.

⁸ Ps.-Philo, *Liber Antiquitatum Biblicarum* 3.10. For the interpretation of this text see Marius Reiser, *Die letzten Dinge im Licht des Neuen Testaments. Bilder und Wirklichkeit* (Heimbach: Patrimonium, 2013), 28–30.

⁹ *The Biblical Antiquities of Philo*, trans. M. R. James (London: SPCK, 1917), available at http://ccat.sas.upenn.edu/rak/publics/pseudepig/LAB.html #trans.

Chapter 6: Israel's Enduring Discovery—pages 87–93

¹ Heinrich Heine, *Germany, A Winter Tale*, historic bilingual ed., trans. Edgar Alfred Bowring (New York: Mondial, 2007), 3–4.

² Dietrich Bonhoeffer, *Letters and Papers from Prison*, Bonhoeffer's Works, Readers Edition, ed. John W. DeGruchy (Minneapolis: Fortress Press, 2015), 192.

³ In recent decades the interpretation of the Song of Songs has shifted. While its verses were regarded for a long time as purely secular love songs, now many Old Testament scholars see an allegorical meaning in them. In that case they would speak of the love between Yʜwʜ and Yʜwʜ's people—either from the beginning or through the incorporation of the Song into the canon of the Old Testament. See now esp. Ludger Schwienhorst-Schönberger, *Das Hohelied der Liebe* (Freiburg: Herder, 2015), 11–25.

PART THREE

Chapter 1: Jesus' Preaching—pages 97–103

¹ See Gerhard Lohfink, *Das Vaterunser neu ausgelegt* (Stuttgart: Katholisches Bibelwerk, 2015), 51–59.

² For a more extensive treatment of this subject see Marius Reiser, *Jesus and Judgment*, trans. Linda M. Maloney (Minneapolis: Fortress Press, 1997).

³ See Matt 10:7, 27; 24:14; Mark 3:14; 6:12; 13:10; Luke 9:2; 12:3; 24:47.

⁴ See Gerhard Lohfink, *Jesus of Nazareth*, trans. Linda M. Maloney (Collegeville, MN: Liturgical Press, 2012), 326–28.

⁵ For "stocking" or "stalking" of seed see ibid., 106–8.

⁶ For this kind of similitude see ibid., 116–20.

Chapter 2: Jesus' Deeds of Power—pages 104–7

¹ See esp. Mark 1:40-45 and Luke 17:11-19; cp. Matt 10:8; 11:5.

² See Matt 9:32-34; 12:22-23; Mark 1:21-28; 3:22, 27; 5:1-20; 7:24-30; 9:14-29; Luke 10:17-20.

³ For more details on Jesus' expulsions of demons see Lohfink, *Jesus of Nazareth*, 143–45.

Chapter 3: Jesus' Powerlessness—pages 108–12

[1] See *Sura* 4.157-158: "and [they] said, 'We have killed the Messiah, Jesus, son of Mary, the Messenger of God.' (They did not kill him, nor did they crucify him, though it was made to appear like that to them; those that disagreed about him are full of doubt, with no knowledge to follow, only supposition; they certainly did not kill him—No! God raised him up to Himself. God has the power to decide." (*The Qur'an.* A New Translation by M. A. S. Abdel Haleem, Oxford World's Classics [Oxford: Oxford University Press, 2004], 65. All references to the Qur'an are taken from this edition, unless otherwise noted.)

[2] See Moses Maimonides, *Mishnah Torah,* Melachim and Milchamot, XI, 1-4. I am grateful to Professor Michael P. Maier, Rome, for this reference.

[3] See Matt 10:9-10; Luke 9:3.

Chapter 4: Jesus' Resurrection—pages 113–18

[1] Martin Hengel, "Ist der Osterglaube noch zu retten?" *Theologische Quartalschrift* 153 (1973): 252–69.

[2] For what follows see, at greater length, Gerhard Lohfink, *Jesus of Nazareth,* 288–307; idem, "Der Ablauf der Ostereignisse und die Anfänge der Urgemeinde," in idem, *Studien zum Neuen Testament,* SBAB 5 (Stuttgart: Katholisches Bibelwerk, 1989), 149–67.

[3] See, e.g., 2 Cor 12:1-7.

[4] On this see the relevant work of Béla Weissmahr, esp. "Kann Gott die Auferstehung Jesu durch innerweltliche Kräfte bewirkt haben?" *Zeitschrift für katholische Theologie* 100 (1978): 441–69, at 441–43.

[5] Ibid., 451: "The more intensively God works in the world, the more intensively does the creature capable of its own activity also work." Toward the end of his enlightening essay Weissmahr, speaking of the interpenetration of divine and human action in the Easter experiences, rightly points to the basic principle of Christology formulated at Chalcedon: "unconfused and inseparable" (469).

[6] This is the oldest kerygmatic formula for Jesus' resurrection, widely attested in the New Testament. See Acts 3:15; 4:10; 13:30, 34; 17:31; Rom 4:24; 8:11; 10:9; Gal 1:1; Eph 1:20; Col 2:12; 1 Thess 1:10; 1 Pet 1:21; cp. Heb 13:20. The formula is directly connected with "Jesus" only in Rom 8:11; cp. 10:9, but most of these passages presuppose Jesus. Additional titles of honor may be added to the simple "Jesus."

[7] It is true that the book of Wisdom speaks of the "souls of the righteous" (3:1) and even their "immortality" (3:4) in chapters 3–5. But even if Jesus' disciples knew that book (as, for example, Paul did), it speaks of the righteous "going from us" (3:2) in less precise, almost vague terms that would be rather inappropriate for interpreting Jesus' fate. Moreover, we need not suppose that Wisdom speaks of disembodied souls in the Platonic sense. See to the contrary, and rightly, Fischer, *Tod und Jenseits* (see chap. 2, n. 3 above), 232. If we want to look for a more precise concept we might most appropriately think of being "taken up" (Wis 4:10-11; cp. 2:18).

[8] There seems to be a contradiction between v. 9, in which fish is already on the grill, and v. 10, where Jesus says: "Bring some of the fish that you have just caught." The conflict probably results from combining a story of a large catch of fish with an Easter narrative.

[9] Lucian of Samosata, *A True Story*, trans. A. M. Harmon, LCL (London: Heinemann; New York: Macmillan, 1913), Book II, p. 315. Available at http://www .sacred-texts.com/cla/luc/true/tru02.htm.

Chapter 5: The Firstborn from the Dead—pages 119–23

[1] We owe a great deal to Klaus Berger for his having persistently introduced the question of the genuine category of the Easter experience in exegetical discussions. See his *Die Auferstehung des Propheten und die Erhöhung des Menschensohnes. Traditionsgeschichtliche Untersuchungen zur Deutung des Geschicks Jesu in frühchristlichen Texten*, SUNT 13 (Göttingen: Vandenhoeck & Ruprecht, 1976). Even though there are many aspects of his conclusions with which I cannot agree, since the publication of his monograph exegetes can no longer avoid the question.

[2] For a fuller presentation of the idea of "being taken up," with numerous textual witnesses from Greco-Roman and Judeo-Christian religions, see Gerhard Lohfink, *Die Himmelfahrt Jesu: Untersuchungen zu den Himmelfahrts- und Erhöhungstexten bei Lukas*, SANT 26 (Munich: Kösel, 1971).

[3] See Lohfink, *Die Himmelfahrt Jesu*, 74–79.

[4] In 1 Cor 15:4 "from the dead" is missing, but it is presumed. Cp. Matt 17:9; 28:7; Luke 24:46; John 2:22; 20:9; 21:14; Acts 3:15; 4:10; 10:41; 13:30, 34; 17:3, 31; Rom 4:24; 6:4, 9; 8:11; 10:9; 1 Cor 15:12, 20; Gal 1:1; Eph 1:20; Col 2:12; 1 Thess 1:10; 2 Tim 2:8; 1 Pet 1:3, 21.

[5] Ulrich Kellermann's study, *Auferstanden in den Himmel: 2 Makkabäer 7 und die Auferstehung der Märtyrer*, SBS 95 (Stuttgart: Katholisches Bibelwerk, 1979) was important for its reconstruction of this idea. But an investigation of the sources Kellermann adduces for martyrs' immediate resurrection in heaven shows that by no means all are conclusive. Some are Christian texts that may have been influenced by the idea of Jesus' resurrection. Some can be interpreted differently. For example, I find not a single instance in 2 Macc 7 that goes to prove Kellermann's thesis. Certainly that text speaks of the resurrection of the dead! But where, precisely, does it say anything about an *immediate* reception of the martyrs in heaven?

Klaus Berger's extensive work, *Die Auferstehung des Propheten* (see n. 1 above), appeared three years before Kellermann's work. Here again it must be said that the texts he brings into play for the idea of the "resurrection of an *individual* independently of the general resurrection" are not truly probative. Some are very late and already colored by Christian ideas (that is, they know of Jesus' resurrection and the corresponding terminology); some do not really speak of resurrection. I cannot undertake an extended critique here, but I will make four points: (1) Mark 6:14-16 uses Christian terminology, but in popular thinking an idea of rapture may have played a significant role, and (2) the two "witnesses" in Rev 11:3-14 (Berger's most important instance) are taken up to heaven. In this case it is necessary that God bring them to life beforehand because as dead persons they cannot be taken up. Their vivification is described with reference to Ezek 37:5, 10. We cannot conclude from this to a *resurrection* of individual prophets. Ultimately, the narrative is rooted in the idea of "rapture." Also, (3) I will not exclude the possibility that the idea of an immediate resurrection—or, perhaps better, rapture—of martyrs existed. But how old was the idea and how widely was it known? Finally, (4) whatever we may assume or not assume here, what is absolutely conclusive is that Klaus Berger has to play down the clear connection in the New Testament between the resurrection of Jesus and the general resurrection of the dead. But in doing so he does not do justice to Matt 27:52-53; Acts 3:15; 26:23; Rom 8:29; 1 Cor 15:20, 23; Col 1:18; and Rev 1:5.

Rudolf Pesch took up Berger's theses in a guest lecture in Tübingen, published in a thematic number of the *Theologische Quartalschrift* (1973) together with critical comments by Tübingen professors. Among these see esp. Martin Hengel, "Ist der Osterglaube noch zu retten?" and Peter Stuhlmacher, "Kritischer müssten mir die Historisch-Kritischen sein!" See also Johannes M. Nützel, "Zum Schicksal der eschatologischen Propheten," *BZ* 20 (1976): 59–94; Eduard Schweizer's article in *TLZ* 103 (1978): 874–78; Helmut Merklein, "Die Auferweckung Jesu und die Anfänge der Christologie," *ZNW* 72 (1981): 1–26, at 2–3.

[6] See, e.g., Acts 2:33; 5:31; Rom 1:3-4; 8:34; Phil 2:6-11; Col 3:1; Heb 1:3; 12:2; 1 Pet 3:22.

[7] Romans 1:4—a statement about exaltation and part of an early credal formula—is incomprehensible without the statement of resurrection, which is immediately added: "by resurrection from the dead." Philippians 2:9, also one of the oldest exaltation statements, is combined with pre-existence theology and thus clearly secondary in relation to the still older formula of resurrection.

[8] Thus Herbert Vorgrimler, *Der Tod im Denken und Leben des Christen* (Düsseldorf: Patmos, 1978), 60, 108. In his sketch of eschatology, *Hoffnung auf Vollendung. Aufriss der Eschatologie*, QD 90 (Freiburg: Herder, 1980), Vorgrimler seeks consistently to keep the motif of the collective resurrection of the dead separate from the oldest statements about the Easter event. He writes: "God exalted Jesus from death as Messiah, whose coming was immediately expected" (p. 46). But the exaltation statement is not at the beginning; rather, at the beginning is the statement "God raised Jesus from the dead," with all its implications. Here Vorgrimler is relying far too much on Berger's reconstructions in *Die Auferstehung des Propheten*.

[9] What I am saying here is verified by the real history immediately after Easter. To take only one example: the group of the Twelve was completed by the selection of Matthias very soon after Easter (Acts 1:15-26). Later, for example after the execution of James, son of Zebedee (Acts 12:1-2), the number was not filled up. The reason for this is that immediately after Jesus' resurrection the young church was convinced that the general resurrection of the dead was about to happen and, at the judgment that would immediately follow, the Twelve would be seated with the Son of Man to judge the twelve tribes of Israel (Matt 19:28). That was why an immediate replacement was necessary. For the post-Easter events see Lohfink, *Jesus of Nazareth*, 288–307.

Chapter 6: New Creation—pages 124–28

[1] *1 En.* 45:4-5; 72:1; 91:16-17; *Jub.* 1:29; 4:26; 5:12; 19:25; *2 Bar.* 31:5–32:6; 44:12; 57:2; *4 Ezra* 7:75.

[2] For modern translations of these works see James H. Charlesworth, ed., *The Old Testament Pseudepigrapha*, 2 vols. (Peabody, MA: Hendrickson, 1983).

PART FOUR

[1] See Medard Kehl, *Eschatologie*, 29–31; Remenyi, *Auferstehung denken*, 39–40.

Chapter 1: The Ultimate Encounter with God—pages 133–43

[1] For the incomprehensibility and inexplicable nature of God see Karl Rahner, "The Human Question of Meaning in Face of the Absolute Mystery," *Theological Investigations* 18, *God and Revelation*, trans. Edward Quinn (New York: Crossroad, 1983), 89–104.

[2] Hans Urs von Balthasar, "Some Points of Eschatology," in *Explorations in Theology I: The Word Made Flesh* (San Francisco: Ignatius Press, 1989), 255–77, at 260–61. See also Thomas Aquinas, *De rationibus fidei* 9: "God is our ultimate goal [*ultimum finem*]."

[3] The Introit is based on Ps 139 in the Vulgate, vv. 18, 5-6, 1-2. The Hebrew text speaks not of resurrection but of sitting and standing, and in the Psalm *adhuc* does not mean "still" in the sense of "from now on" but "constantly."

[4] Augustine, *Ennarationes in psalmos*, on Ps 30[31] (*PL* 36:252: *Abscondes eos in abscondito vultus tui. Qualis est locus iste? Non dixit, Abscondes eos in coelo tuo: non dixit, Abscondes eos in paradiso: non dixit, Abscondes eos in sinu Abrahae [. . .] Qui nos tuetur in loco vitae huius, ipse post istam vitam sit locus noster.*)

[5] See Christoph Barth, *Die Errettung vom Tode*, 150.

[6] See also 1 John 3:2 and Rev 22:4.

[7] Haleem: "triumph."

[8] See *Suras* 3,198; 4,57; 4,122; 5,12; 5,85; 5,119; 7,43; 9,21-22; 9,89; 9,100; 10,9; 13,35; 14,23; 15,45-48; 16,31-32; 18,31; 22,14; 22,23; 22,56; 25,10; 25,15-16; 29,58; 30,15; 32,19; 36,55-58; 37,41-49; 38,49-52; 39,20; 39,73-75; 41,30-32; 43,70-73; 44,51-57; 47,12; 47,15; 48,5; 48,17; 50,34-35; 51,15-16; 52,17-24; 55,46-78; 56,12-40; 56,88-89; 57,12; 57,20-21; 58,22; 61,12; 64,9; 65,11; 66,8; 68,34; 69,21-24; 74,39-40; 76,5-6; 76,11-22; 77,41-44; 78,31-35; 83,22-28; 88,8-16; 98,8.

[9] There is now a Western exegesis of the Qur'an that puts it on the dissecting table and views it through the lens of historical criticism. It asserts that the sense of the consonantal text of the Qur'an was altered in many places through vocalization. The "houris," for example (44,54; 52,20), were originally white grapes. The hermeneutics of this critical exegesis of the Qur'an, as propagated, for example, in Barbara Köster's book, *Der missverstandene Koran: warum der Islam neu begründet werden muss* (Berlin: Schiler, 2010), is extremely naïve. The basis for an adequate exegesis of the Qur'an cannot be some kind of historically reconstructed early layers of the book; as with the Christian canon it must be exclusively *the*

version of the Qur'an that is regarded as Islam's sacred book and is read today in official Islam.

[10] See *Suras* 5,119; 9,72: "God has promised . . . —greatest of all—God's good pleasure"; 58,22; 98,8.

[11] *Sura* 75,22-23 may be another exception: "On that day there will be radiant faces, looking towards their Lord." But that, too, is something of an aside. The vision of God is nowhere visible as a subject in itself, above all not in the descriptions of Paradise.

[12] *Sura* 7,44 is not a real exception, since it is not explicit praise of God.

[13] The starting points for the discussion are *Suras* 7,143 and 75,22-23.

[14] Colleen McDannell and Bernhard Lang, *Heaven: A History*, 2nd ed. (New Haven: Yale University Press, 2001).

[15] Cp. ibid., 265.

[16] Thus "heaven romances" were among the best-read works of popular literature in the nineteenth century.

[17] *b.Berakhot* 34b, accessed at http://halakhah.com/berakoth/berakoth_34 .html, 27 February 2017.

[18] See Simcha Paull Raphael, *Jewish Views of the Afterlife*, 2nd ed. (Lanham, MD, et al.: Rowman & Littlefield, 2009), 123. For this section see also Günter Stemberger, "Zur Auferstehungslehre in der rabbinischen Literatur," in *Studien zum rabbinischen Judentum*, SBAB 10 (Stuttgart: Katholisches Bibelwerk, 1990), 47–88, at 86–87.

[19] "Pascal's Memorial." Slightly altered from the translation by Elizabeth T. Knuth, available at http://www.users.csbsju.edu/~eknuth/pascal.html.

[20] Latin *vacabimus*, from *vacare*: be free, be at leisure.

[21] This sentence comes almost at the end of Augustine's great work, *De civitate Dei*, trans. Marcus Dods, *Nicene and Post-Nicene Fathers*, 1st ser. 2, ed. Philip Schaff (Buffalo, NY: Christian Literature Publishing Co., 1887). Revised and edited for New Advent by Kevin Knight; http://www.newadvent.org/fathers/1201.htm. The Latin reads: *Ibi vacabimus et videbimus, videbimus et amabimus, amabimus et laudabimus.*

Chapter 2: Death as Judgment—pages 144–53

[1] See the Wikipedia article, "International Criminal Court," as modified on 22 February 2017. As of this date four signatory states—the United States, Sudan, Israel, and Russia—have withdrawn their signatures and declared themselves no longer subject to the court's jurisdiction.

[2] Massimo Tosco, *Alzo zero: provocazioni quotidiane per vincere l'isolamento in questo mondo tutto da rifare* (Turin: Gribaudi, 1968).

[3] The facets of what I am describing here are what the church means by the too easily misunderstood term "original sin." See Gerhard Lohfink and Ludwig Weimer, *Maria: Nicht ohne Israel. Eine Neue Sicht der Lehre von der unbefleckten Empfängnis* (Freiburg, et al.: Herder, 2013).

4 Friedrich Schiller, end of the next-to-last verse of his poem "Resignation." (The standard English translation of the line is "The world's long story is the world's own doom.") The poem denies that there is a world judgment and heavenly reward after death; anyone who hopes for reward and punishment in the afterlife will be bitterly disappointed. Earthly history is the world's judgment, and it offers only two possible rewards: enjoyment or belief.

5 Emil Brunner, *Eternal Hope*, trans. Harold Knight (Philadelphia: Westminster Press, 1954), 174.

6 See esp. Jan Assmann, *Ma'at. Gerechtigkeit und Unsterblichkeit im Alten Ägypten* (Munich: Beck, 1990), 122–59.

7 See Medard Kehl, *Und was kommt nach dem Ende? Von Weltuntergang und Vollendung, Wiedergeburt und Auferstehung*, topos taschenbücher 571, 2nd ed. (Kevelaer: Topos plus, 2008).

8 It is true that a systematic idea governed in Israel for a long time: while God is the sole judge, and is also the Merciful One, there is a system of justice in the world according to which evil has consequences for the perpetrator. Old Testament scholars call this system a "fateful, power-laden sphere" (Klaus Koch) or "cause and effect." In this system whoever is in trouble must have done something bad—in person, or the deed might have been done by an ancestor. But this system of thought was increasingly disputed, especially by Qoheleth, the book of Job, and then Jesus (cp. Matt 5:45; John 9:1-3). For Koch's idea of the power-sphere see Robert L. Hubbard, "Is the 'Tatsphäre' always a Sphere?" *JETS* 25 (1982): 257–62.

9 The first clear evidence is the *Letter of Barnabas*, which is dated between 90 and 120 CE; see esp. *Barn.* 4,7; 5,7, 14,4, 5.

10 Medard Kehl, *Und was kommt nach dem Ende?*, 155. Cp. also Joseph Ratzinger, *Eschatology: Death and Eternal Life*, trans. Michael Waldstein, 2nd ed. (Washington, DC: Catholic University of America Press, 2007), esp. chap. 7; Herbert Vorgrimler, *Der Tod im Denken und Leben des Christen* (Düsseldorf: Patmos, 1978), 91; Hans Urs von Balthasar, "Gericht," *IkZ* 9 (1980), 231–33; Franz-Josef Nocke, *Eschatologie*, Leitfaden Theologie 6 (Düsseldorf: Patmos, 1982), 127–28; Ottmar Fuchs, *Das jüngste Gericht. Hoffnung auf Gerechtigkeit*, 2nd ed. (Regensburg: Pustet, 2009), 121; Johanna Rahner, *Einführung in die christliche Eschatologie*, 2nd ed. (Freiburg: Herder, 2016), 227–28; Klaus Vechtel, *Eschatologie und Freiheit. Zur Frage der postmortalen Vollendung in der Theologie Karl Rahners und Hans Urs von Balthasars*, ITS 89 (Innsbruck and Vienna: Tyrolia, 2014), 207–11.

11 This aspect of judgment is treated especially by Karl Barth, *Church Dogmatics* IV/2, and Dorothea Sattler, "Gottes Gericht und die geläuterte Selbsterkenntnis des Menschen. Versuch einer Verhältnisbestimmung in ökumenischer Perspektive," in *Gemeinsame Hoffnung über den Tod hinaus. Eschatologie im ökumenischen Gespräch*, ed. Uwe Swarat and Thomas Söding, QD 257 (Freiburg: Herder, 2013), 109–30, at 122.

Chapter 3: Judgment as Mercy—pages 154–59

[1] A fundamental treatment of this theme is Marius Reiser, *Jesus and Judgment* (see part 3, chap. 1, n. 3 above).

[2] Authors include Pope Francis, *God's Name Is Mercy: A Conversation with Andrea Tornielli*, trans. Oonagh Stransky (New York: Random House, 2016), and Walter Kasper, *Mercy: The Essence of the Gospel and the Key to Christian Life*, trans. William Madges (New York and Mahwah, NJ: Paulist Press, 2014).

[3] See Gisbert Greshake, *Maria—Ecclesia. Perspektiven einer marianisch grundierten Theologie und Kirchenpraxis* (Regensburg: Pustet, 2014); also Gerhard Lohfink and Ludwig Weimer, *Maria* (see part 4, chap. 2, n. 3 above), 285–86.

[4] See Kasper, *Mercy*, 79.

[5] For the scenario played out in Exodus 32 in the phrase "new people," see Tamás Czopf, *Neues Volk Gottes? Zur Geschichte und Problematik eines Begriffs*, MTS II, 78 (St. Ottilien: Eos, 2016).

[6] I cannot go into the multiple problems of interpretation of Exod 34:6-7. There are three primary questions: (1) who is speaking in v. 6, God or Moses? (2) how is the double Yhwh Yhwh to be understood syntactically? and (3) what should we make of the sequence of generations in 34:7? For all this see Ruth Scoralick, *Gottes Güte und Gottes Zorn: die Gottesprädikationen in Exodus 34,6f und ihre intertextuellen Beziehungen zum Zwölfprophetenbuch*, HBS 33 (Freiburg and New York: Herder, 2002).

[7] See ibid.

[8] Norbert Lohfink, "Ich komme nicht in Zornesglut (Hos 11,0). Skizze einer synchronen Leseanweisung für das Hoseabuch," in *Ce Dieu qui vient. Mélanges offerts à Bernhard Renaud*, LD 159 (Paris: Cerf, 1995), 163–90, at 188. I am following this essay for the translation and interpretation of this text from Hosea.

[9] See Reiser, *Jesus and Judgment*.

[10] Norbert Lohfink, *In the Shadow of Your Wings*, 72.

Chapter 4: Purification in Death—pages 160–65

[1] The Reformers for the most part rejected "purgatory," for various reasons: first and primarily because of the abuses in the contemporary use of indulgences, then because of the apparent lack of Scriptural witnesses, then on the basis of the doctrine of justification, but also because of the naïve notions of time in the theology of that era and the popular piety associated with the doctrine of purgatory. The issue is more nuanced in Orthodoxy, which accepts petitions on behalf of the dead but rejects the vindictive and punishing aspects of the Western doctrine of purgatory. What was decisive for Orthodox reticence was always the suspicion that the Western doctrine of purgatory was connected with Origen's teaching on *apokatastasis* (universal salvation in the form of restoration to the original). For the different doctrinal developments between Latin and Eastern church theologies see Ilaria Ramelli, *The Christian Doctrine of Apokatastasis*, VCSupp. 120 (Leiden: Brill, 2013). It should also be said that as late as 1519

Martin Luther had not only *not* rejected but even advocated strongly for the doctrine of purgatory. His rejection came later and was directed primarily against the abuse of indulgences. On this see Owen Chadwick, *The Early Reformation on the Continent* (Oxford: Oxford University Press, 2001), esp. chap. 4, "Death," pp. 69–81.

[2] From the title of a book by Gisbert Greshake, *Geschenkte Freiheit: Einführung in die Gnadenlehre* (Freiburg: Herder, 1992).

[3] *John Henry Newman: A Portrait in Letters*, ed. Roderick Strange (Oxford: Oxford University Press, 2015), 33.

[4] The biblical basis for the fire metaphor in this context is especially 1 Cor 3:12-15. The text speaks of God's judgment, in which the deeds of those who work in God's service are revealed. The final judgment will show the value of their work. If it is useless, it will burn away, but the person in question will be saved "as through fire." That is not yet *purgatorium* in the developed sense of later Catholic dogmatics, but in substance it has a great deal to do with it, because here also the fire of judgment burns away everything that is false, useless, and resistant to God.

[5] Refer here to the corresponding passages in Romano Guardini, *The Last Things: Concerning Death, Purification after Death, Resurrection, Judgment, and Eternity* (Notre Dame, IN: University of Notre Dame Press, 1954), chap. 2; Karl Rahner, *Foundations of Christian Faith: An Introduction to the Idea of Christianity*, trans. William V. Dych (New York: Seabury, 1978), chap. 9, "Eschatology"; Joseph Ratzinger, *Eschatology*, 218–32; Nocke, *Eschatologie*, 128–29, 132–33; Karl Lehmann, "Was bleibt vom Fegfeuer?" *IkZ* 9 (1980): 236–43, at 241–42; Bertram Stubenrauch, *Was kommt danach? Himmel, Hölle, Nirwana oder gar nichts?* (Munich: Pattloch, 2007), 238–39; Medard Kehl, *Und was kommt nach dem Ende?* 161–62; Marius Reiser, *Die letzten Dinge*, 207 (with reference to John Henry Newman's *The Dream of Gerontius*); Klaus Vechtel, *Eschatologie und Freiheit*, 116–28, 216–20.

[6] Lehmann "Was bleibt vom Fegfeuer?" 239.

[7] *Katholischer Katechismus für das Bistum Limburg* (Limburg: Bistum Limburg, 1936); *Katholischer Katechismus für die Bistümer Deutschlands* (Freiburg: Herder, 1955). Or see Erich Fleischhack, *Fegfeuer. Die christlichen Vorstellungen vom Geschick der Verstorbenen geschichtlich dargestellt* (Tübingen: Katzmann, 1969), 8: "Every sin means not only forgiveness but also a punishment." The theological term was *reatus poenae*. Its precise meaning was the consequences of sin still in the person after the sin (*reatus culpae*) was forgiven. That, at least, was how Karl Rahner interpreted it. Cp. Vechtel, *Eschatologie und Freiheit*, 116–17.

[8] Unfortunately, the easily misunderstood concept of "punishment for sin" still stalks the church's teaching. However, the *Catechism of the Catholic Church* explains the concept correctly: punishment for sin "must not be conceived of as a kind of vengeance inflicted by God from without, but as following from the very nature of sin," *Catechism of the Catholic Church* (1993, §1472. Available at http://www.vatican.va/archive/eng0015/_index.htm).

[9] Ibid., §§1030–32.

[10] Ladislaus Boros, *The Mystery of Death*, trans. Gregory Bainbridge (New York: Herder & Herder, 1965).

[11] See Georg Bätzing, *Kirche im Werden: ekklesiologische Aspekte des Läuterungsgedankens*, TTS 56 (Trier: Paulinus Verlag, 1996), 21.

[12] See now the fundamental work of Hanna Stettler, *Heiligung bei Paulus: Ein Beitrag aus biblisch-theologischer Sicht*, WUNT, 2nd ser. 368 (Tübingen: Mohr Siebeck, 2014). Stettler rightly distinguishes, within the New Testament concept of sanctification, between passive and active aspects, the indicative and the imperative. See esp. 42–44, 638–40.

[13] Boros, *The Mystery of Death*, 86–99.

[14] Ibid., 97.

[15] Cp. ibid., 88.

[16] Ibid., 104.

[17] On this see also Gisbert Greshake, "Bemerkungen zur Endentscheidungshypothese," in Gisbert Greshake and Gerhard Lohfink, *Naherwartung, Auferstehung, Unsterblichkeit. Untersuchungen zur christlichen Eschatologie*, QD 71, 5th ed. (Freiburg: Herder, 1986), 121–30, at 129; Bätzing, *Kirche im Werden*, 103–7.

[18] Under these conditions the doctrine of purgatory might also be acceptable to Protestant theology. See Gunther Wenz, "Evangelische Gedanken zum Fegfeuer," *MTZ* 67 (2016): 2–34, at 27: "When someone encounters Jesus Christ eschatologically, with unconditioned responsiveness, that person's eyes are opened not only with regard to all the good that had been given in her or his earthly lifetime, and in which she or he had been able to cooperate, but that person will also be painfully aware of how often she or he failed and fell short of the necessary works of love. We can think of this process of coming to awareness as a process of purification."

[19] The purpose of the monograph by Bätzing, *Kirche im Werden*, is to describe that dimension.

Chapter 5: And What about Hell?—pages 166–71

[1] See Markus Schulze, "Ist die Hölle menschenmöglich? Zum Wandel der Theologie der negativen Endgültigkeit in den letzten fünfzig Jahren," in *Hoffnung auf das ewige Leben. Kraft zum Handeln heute*, ed. Walter Kasper and George Augustin, Theologie im Dialog 15 (Freiburg: Herder, 2015), 167–203, at 171: "Among the principal contemporary systematic theologians the word 'punishment' to describe what makes hell to be hell has been dropped."

[2] See, e.g., Pss 28:4; 31:24; 58:11; 69:28; 91:8; 94:1-2.

[3] For what follows cp. Rüdiger Lux, "Moses Schwanengesang. Gott und die Gewalt im Alten Testament," *Freiburger Rundbrief* 7 (2010): 102–11.

[4] Erich Zenger, in Frank-Lothar Hossfeld and Erich Zenger, *Psalms 2: A Commentary on Psalms 51–100*, trans. Linda M. Maloney, Hermeneia (Minneapolis: Fortress Press, 2005), 306–7.

[5] So Ludger Schwienhorst-Schönberger, "Recht und Gewalt im Alten Testament," in *Macht, Gewalt, Krieg im Alten Testament. Gesellschaftliche Problematik und das Problem ihrer Repräsentation*, ed. Irmtraud Fischer, QD 254 (Freiburg: Herder, 2013), 318–51, at 349.

⁶ See, e.g., Nocke, *Eschatologie*, 140–41; Kehl, *Und was kommt*, 182–87; Vechtel, *Eschatologie und Freiheit*, 247–55.

⁷ For this interpretation of Matt 25:31-46 see Gerhard Lohfink, *Im Ringen um die Vernunft. Reden über Israel, die Kirche und die Europäische Aufklärung* (Freiburg: Herder, 2016).

⁸ See Joseph Ratzinger, "Hölle," *LTK*² 5 (Freiburg: Herder, 1960), 446–49.

⁹ Thus correctly Gisbert Greshake, *Stärker als der Tod. Zukunft, Tod, Auferstehung, Himmel, Hölle, Fegfeuer*, topos taschenbücher 50, 5th ed. (Mainz: Matthias Grünewald, 1980), 81.

¹⁰ Ratzinger, *Eschatology*, 219.

¹¹ See Romano Guardini, *The Last Things*, 80–84. Of course, Guardini does not speak of a "fundamental decision" but an "attitude" (in the published English translation a "longing"). The concept of the fundamental decision or "fundamental option" (*optio fundamentalis*) has long been established in theological ethics, among other branches of theology, through the work of Jacques Maritain, Karl Rahner, Johann Baptist Metz, Heribert Mühlen, Josef Spindelböck, and others. It marks an immense step forward in theology: a person's moral character is not constituted by individual actions but by an attitude or disposition of one's whole existence that lies much deeper.

¹² Karl Rahner speaks of the "real possibility" of "absolute rejection" of the "last goal" of the human being, and simultaneously of the "concealed nature" of this fundamental decision, in *Foundations*, 100–102.

¹³ See, for example, the book *Ästhetik des Bösen* by the literary scholar Peter-André Alt (Munich: Beck, 2010), esp. 482–511. [LMM: In English see Philip Tallon, *The Poetics of Evil: Toward an Aesthetic Theodicy* (Oxford and New York: Oxford University Press, 2012), and Barry L. Whitney, *Theodicy: An Annotated Bibliography on the Problem of Evil, 1960–1991* (Charlottesville, VA: Philosophy Documentation Center, 1998)].

Chapter 6: The Whole Person—pages 172–77

¹ Either in the form "resurrection of the dead" (cp., e.g., Matt 22:31; Acts 17:32; 23:6; 24:21; 26:23; Rom 1:4; 1 Cor 15:12, 13, 21, 42; Heb 6:2) or "resurrection from the dead" (cp. Luke 20:35; Acts 4:2; 1 Pet 1:3).

² J. N. D. Kelly, *Early Christian Creeds* (London and New York: Continuum, 2006), 296.

³ See the texts of the various creeds in ibid., *passim*.

⁴ Cp. *1 Clem*. 26,3; *2 Clem*. 9,1; Irenaeus, *Adv. haer*. I, 22,1.

⁵ In 1970 the working group on liturgical texts of the churches in German-speaking regions adopted an ecumenical translation that, in place of "resurrection of the flesh" now speaks in the Apostles' Creed also (probably coordinating with the Great Confession) of the "resurrection of the dead." Apparently this is meant to make it easier for believers to understand. The decision is questionable, and more recently the Congregation for the Doctrine of the Faith in Rome has called

for the restoration of the literal translation. In the United States, both *The Roman Missal* and the Episcopal Church's *Book of Common Prayer* use "resurrection of the body." See now Brian Schmisek, *Resurrection of the Flesh or Resurrection from the Dead? Implications for Theology* (Collegeville, MN: Liturgical Press, 2013).

[6] Origen, *Contra Celsum* V, 14 [altered], available at http://www.newadvent .org/fathers/04165.htm.

[7] See Kelly, *Early Christian Creeds*, 163–65. Such gnosticizing tendencies were being combatted even in the New Testament, especially in the Pastorals (1 Tim 1:4; 6:20; 2 Tim 2:16-18; Titus 3:9-11), in Acts (20:27, 29), and in 1 John (1:1; 2:4, 18-27; 4:1-3).

[8] This is a frequent idea in Homer and other ancient authors; cp., e.g., the appearances of the goddess Athena in Homer, *Odyssey* II, 267-69, 382-85; VI, 13-24; VII, 19-21; VIII, 7-10; XVI, 155-63; XX, 30-32.

[9] For the phenomenon of possession from a psychosomatic and theological point of view see Gerhard Lohfink, *Jesus of Nazareth*, 143–45.

[10] See Rudolf Schnackenburg, *The Gospel According to John*, trans. Kevin Smyth (London: Burns & Oates; New York: Herder & Herder, 1968), I, 267–68.

[11] It is remarkable that the expression "resurrection of the flesh" came to be used, despite 1 Cor 15:50 ("flesh and blood cannot inherit the kingdom of God"). Could Job 19:26, in its LXX and Vulgate versions, have played a role? In itself the Hebrew text of Job says exactly the opposite: "when this skin will have fallen into shreds, divested of my flesh, I shall see God." (See Aron Pinker, "A New Interpretation of Job 19:26," *Journal of Hebrew Scriptures* 15 [2015]: 1–23, at 5.) The LXX reads: "[may he] raise up my skin, which endures these things." The Vulgate says: "In my flesh shall I see God" (*in carne mea videbo deum*). *1 Clem.* 26,3 reads: "Job says: Thou shalt raise up this flesh of mine, which has suffered all these things" (ANF). Of course, Acts 2:26 should also be brought into play: "My body will rest in hope" (= Ps 15:9 LXX) and the corresponding interpretation of Jesus' resurrection in Peter's speech.

[12] See, e.g., *1 Clem.* 26,3; *Barn.* 5,6; *2 Clem.* 9; 14,5; Irenaeus, *Adv. haer.* I, 22, 1; V, 2, 2; Tatian, *Address to the Greeks*, 6.

[13] Tertullian, "On the Resurrection of the Flesh," 8,2. Or: "Salvation hinges on the flesh." The sentence puns on *caro* (flesh) and *cardo* (pivot, hinge).

[14] Gen 2:24; Matt 19:5; Mark 10:8; 1 Cor 6:16.

[15] Yevgeny Yevtushenko, "People." Available at https://www.poemhunter .com/poem/people-32. The poem begins with the line, "No people are uninteresting."

[16] See Georg Scherer, "Zukunft und Eschaton. Philosophische Aspekte," in idem, Ferdinand Kerstiens, Franz Joseph Schierse, et al., *Eschatologie und geschichtliche Zukunft*, Thesen und Argumente 5 (Essen-Werden: Fredebeul & Koenen, 1972), 11–65, at 64–65.

Chapter 7: The Whole History of the World—pages 178–83

[1] Hans Urs von Balthasar, "Eschatology in Outline," in *Explorations in Theology IV: Spirit and Institution*, trans. Edward T. Oakes (San Francisco: Ignatius Press, 1995), 423–68, at 445: "everyone's actions are interwoven with everyone else's."

[2] "People, Nation, Leader."

[3] See in detail Gerhard Lohfink, *Jesus of Nazareth*, 304–7.

[4] Joseph Ratzinger, *Eschatology*, 187.

[5] Ibid., 190.

[6] Ibid.

[7] Ratzinger certainly challenges the concept of earthly time in regard to the *eschata*, especially the event of purification, with reference to Augustine. For his position see Gerhard Lohfink, "Das Zeitproblem und die Vollendung der Welt," in Greshake and Lohfink, *Naherwartung*, 131–55, at 151. Ratzinger writes: "The transforming 'moment' of this encounter [the reference is to the event of purification] cannot be quantified by the measurements of earthly time. It is, indeed, not eternal but a transition, and yet trying to qualify it as of 'short' or 'long' duration on the basis of temporal measurements derived from physics would be naïve and unproductive. The 'temporal measure' of this encounter lies in the unsoundable depths of existence, in a passing-over where we are burned ere we are transformed. To measure such an 'existential time' in terms of the time of this world would be to ignore the specificity of the human spirit in its simultaneous relationship with, and differentiation from, the world" (*Eschatology*, 230). Ratzinger thus certainly distinguishes between "earthly time" and the "time" after death, which can only be understood analogously. This insight must be taken seriously, but obviously it must be true not only of the process of purification but, in principle, of any statement about existence beyond death. If we take that seriously, any kind of parallelization between "time" beyond death and "earthly time" is out of the question. Strictly speaking, we thus arrive at the idea of a "resurrection in death," because when "earthly time" and "existential time" cannot be "measured against" one another, at the moment when the human person leaves "earthly time" behind, the "resurrection of the dead" has "already" happened. See Ratzinger's objections to my position in *Eschatology*, 109–11, 182, and my response in Lohfink, "Das Zeitproblem," 148–51.

[8] See, e.g., Johannes Feiner and Lukas Vischer, eds., *Neues Glaubensbuch/Der gemeinsame christliche Glaube*, 14th ed. (Freiburg: Herder, 1978), 341–42; Franz-Josef Nocke, *Liebe, Tod und Auferstehung. Über die Mitte des Glaubens* (Munich: Kösel, 1978), 146–47; idem, "Eschatologie zwischen Glaubensüberlieferung und neuer Erfahrung. Vier Beispiele," *Katechetische Blätter* 105 (1980): 109–21, at 113–14; Ulrich Lüke, "Auferstehung—im Tod? Am Jüngsten Tag?" in *Auferstehung der Toten. Ein Hoffnungsentwurf im Blick heutiger Wissenschaften*, ed. Hans Kessler (Darmstadt: Wissenschaftliche Buchgesellschaft, 2004), 234–51; Elisabeth Moltmann-Wendel and Jürgen Moltmann, "Mit allen Sinnen glauben. Überlegungen zur Auferstehung des Fleisches," *StZ* 130 (2005): 723–35, at 728; Matthias Remenyi, *Auferstehung denken. Anwege, Grenzen und Modelle personaleschatologischer Theoriebildung* (Freiburg: Herder, 2016), 77, 290. See also the list in Gisbert

Greshake and Jacob Kremer, *Resurrectio mortuorum. Zum theologischen Verständnis der leiblichen Auferstehung* (Darmstadt: Wissenschaftliche Buchgesellschaft, 1986), 254 n. 270, and Greshake, "Auferstehung im Tod. Ein 'parteiischer' Rückblick auf eine theologische Diskussion," *TP* 73 (1998): 538–57, at 538 n. 4.

[9] Unfortunately, the difference between these two approaches is often ignored in the discussion of "resurrection in death." Gisbert Greshake approaches the question by way of the soul, while I myself have chosen the approach in terms of time. Greshake has quite rightly defended himself repeatedly against attempts simply to equate his approach with mine (though indeed the two have much in common). See esp. Greshake, "Auferstehung im Tod," 545–47.

Chapter 8: The Whole Creation—pages 184–93

[1] For the concept of apocalyptic see part 3, chap. 6 above.

[2] Cp. Isa 65:17; 66:22; *1 En.* 45:4-5; 72:1; 91:16-17; *Jub.* 1:29; 4:26; 5:12; 19:25; *Syr. Bar.* 31:5–32:6; 44:12; 57:2; *4 Ezra* 7:75.

[3] Joseph Ratzinger, *Introduction to Christianity*, trans. J. R. Foster (San Francisco: Ignatius Press, 2004), 320. For the relationship of the world and the human see ibid., 318–27.

[4] Cp., e.g., Isa 13:9-13; 24:18-23; Jer 4:23-28; 23:10; Ezek 32:6-8; Hos 2:14; 4:1-3; Amos 8:9. When God is named as the agent in these passages, that is an abbreviated form of expression. The real cause is human sin, which cannot remain unanswered.

[5] Hans Wildberger, *Jesaja 2*, BKAT X/2 (Neukirchen-Vluyn: Neukirchener Verlag, 1878), 921. See also J. J. M. Roberts, *First Isaiah*, Hermeneia (Minneapolis: Fortress Press, 2015), 310–18.

[6] When Paul speaks here of *ktisis* (creation) he means primarily the extra-human creation, because Rom 8:20 is about the curse of creation in Gen 3:17-18. Still, we should not draw the boundaries too definitively; non-Christian humanity may also be included. On the whole problem see the well-founded and considered position of Ernst Käsemann, *Commentary on Romans*, trans. Geoffrey W. Bromiley (Grand Rapids: Eerdmans, 1980), 230–36.

[7] Cp. 1 Cor 11:7; 15:49; 2 Cor 3:18; 4:4; Col 3:10, and see Hermann Kleinknecht, art. εἰκών, *TDNT* 2: 381–97, at 395.

[8] Exegetes take extreme pleasure in reconstructing hymns and songs, here and in other passages, but the effort inevitably fails. In Col 1:15-20 (and previously in 1:12-14) we find an elevated style that strings together long chains of relative clauses and prepositional phrases, but that is typical of solemn *prayer style*. The form is not that of a song to be sung by the congregation but of the solemn prayer recited by the presider at worship. Such prayers were freely formulated, but those who spoke them had to make use of established expressions and traditional formulae, more or less skillfully placed in sequence. For the whole subject see Marius Reiser, *Sprache und literarische Formen des Neuen Testaments. Eine Einführung*, UTB 2197 (Paderborn: Schöningh, 2001), 173–78. For this very reason I

have not presented the text in verse form, but as a paragraph—continuously, as it would have been prayed in worship.

⁹ For the history of interpretation of Col 1:15-20 see the overview in Peter Stuhlmacher, *Biblische Theologie des Neuen Testaments* 2, 4–14. Stuhlmacher rightly opposes any redaction of the text as given. In my opinion, however, this is not a community hymn but a freely composed prayer in elevated language. The presiders at the community's worship spoke in that prayer style, and the author of Colossians had a masterful control of the style.

¹⁰ Especially Prov 8:22-31.

¹¹ In his work *On the Theology of Death*, Karl Rahner tries to show that death itself leads to a deeper union between human and cosmos: "does the soul in death strictly transcend this world or does it rather, by virtue of the fact that it is no longer bound to an individual bodily structure, enter into a much closer, more intimate relationship to that ground of the unity of the universe which is hard to conceive yet is very real, and in which all things in the world are inter-related and communicate anteriorly to any mutual influence upon each other?" (p. 19).

¹² Following Elisabeth Moltmann-Wendell and Jürgen Moltmann, "Mit allen Sinnen glauben," 725.

¹³ Matthias Claudius, *Abendlied*, trans. Margarete Münsterberg, in *A Harvest of German Verse*, available at http://www.bartleby.com/177/27.html.

¹⁴ For the subject of "incorporation of creation" see esp. the reflections in Medard Kehl, *Eschatologie*, 240–44.

¹⁵ Béla Weissmahr, "Kann Gott die Auferstehung Jesu durch innerweltliche Kräfte bewirkt haben?" *ZKT* 100 (1978): 441–69, at 458.

¹⁶ Ratzinger, *Eschatology*, 192.

¹⁷ See Balthasar, "Some Points of Eschatology," *Explorations in Theology I*, 255–77, esp. 259–60.

Chapter 9: The City of Dreams—pages 194–202

¹ Cp. Isa 2:1-5; 18:7; 25:8; 66:22, and esp. chap. 60.

² Cp. Ezek 47:1-12, esp. v. 12.

³ See esp. Gen 2:10-14; Exod 6:7; Lev 26:11-12; Tob 13:17; Isa 24:23; 25:8; 43:19; 54:11-12; 60:1-11, 19; 61:10; 65:17; 66:22; Ezek 47:12; Zech 14:8.

⁴ For more detail see Gerhard Lohfink, "Jesus und die Kirche," in *Handbuch der Fundamentaltheologie*, 3. *Traktat Kirche*, ed. Walter Kern, Hermann Josef Pottmeyer, and Max Seckler, UTB 8172, 2nd ed. (Tübingen and Basel: Francke, 2000), 27–64.

⁵ For what follows see esp. Dieter Georgi, *Die Visionen vom himmlischen Jerusalem in Apk 21 und 22* (Tübingen: Mohr, 1980).

⁶ See Alan Ebenstein, *Introduction to Political Thinkers* (Boston: Wadsworth, 2002), 59–61.

⁷ Georgi, *Die Visionen*, 365.

[8] For the treasures of the nations in Isaiah 60 see Michael P. Maier, *Völkerwallfahrt im Jesajabuch*, BZAW 474 (Berlin and Boston: de Gruyter, 2016), 451–58. See also Leslie J. Hoppe, *The Holy City: Jerusalem in the Theology of the Old Testament* (Collegeville, MN: Liturgical Press, 2000), esp. "Pilgrimage to Zion," 32–33, 55.

[9] For the relationship between nature and society in Rev 21 and 22 see also Gerhard Lohfink, "Senfkorn und Weltenbaum (Mk 4,30-32 parr.). Zum Verhältnis von Natur und Gesellschaft bei Jesus," in Harald Schweizer, ed., ". . . Bäume braucht man doch." *Das Symbol des Baumes zwischen Hoffnung und Zerstörung* (Sigmaringen: Jahn Thorbecke, 1986), 109–26.

[10] See Georgi, *Die Visionen*, 354 n. 14.

[11] See Lohfink and Weimer, *Maria: nicht ohne Israel*, 231–37.

Chapter 10: On the Relativity of Time—pages 203–12

[1] Translation LMM. See G. W. F. Hegel, *Phenomenology of Spirit*, trans. A. V. Miller (Oxford: Oxford University Press, 1977), 35.

[2] "The image-quality of metaphors and the exactness of the concept are by no means mutually exclusive; rather, they augment each other." Matthias Remenyi, "Hoffnung, Tod und Auferstehung," *ZKT* 129 (2007): 75–96, at 88–89.

[3] This paragraph is based on a book by the mathematician Werner Kinnebrock, *Was macht die Zeit, wenn sie vergeht?* (Munich: Beck, 2014). For the wording, which I have not marked individually, see pp. 12, 20, 21, 22, 57, 79, 97, 122, 130, and 155 in that book. The contemporary classic in English is, of course, Stephen Hawking, *A Brief History of Time* (New York: Bantam, 1998).

[4] In 1974, in my essay "Zur Möglichkeit christlicher Naherwartung," I tried to think of the uniqueness of "time in the beyond" in terms of the medieval concept of the *aevum*. I will not retract anything of what I said then, even though some theologians were offended by it. They balked at the idea that medieval theology discussed that concept in connection with the doctrine of angels. I find nothing offensive in that. Because the angels do not live in "earthly" time, yet are created beings, they were an experimental field for medieval theologians, by means of which they were able to think out something that was important to them: What would a form of existence look like if it belonged neither to earthly continuous time nor to God's eternity? Obviously their starting point was human experience of time.

[5] Matthias Remenyi, *Auferstehung denken*, 521.

[6] The argument that Jesus only arose from the dead on the third day and therefore there must be a "time" dimension between death and resurrection in no way does justice to what the New Testament says. Jesus did not rise on the third day; his resurrection was *made manifest* on the third day—at least according to the tomb narratives in the gospels. That is something completely different. See Gerhard Lohfink, "Das Zeitproblem und die Vollendung der Welt," in Greshake and Lohfink, *Naherwartung, Auferstehung, Unsterblichkeit*, 131–55, at 139–41.

[7] Ladislaus Boros, "Der neue Himmel und die neue Erde," in *Christus vor uns*, ed. Franz Mussner, Theologische Brennpunkte 8/9 (Bergen-Enkheim: Kaffke, 1966), 19-27, at 21. Translation LMM. Also available as "The new heaven and the new earth," in Franz Mussner, et al., eds., *Readings in Christian Eschatology* (Derby, NY: Society of St. Paul, 19–).

[8] The most important of these was Karl Rahner, but they included also some twentieth-century Protestant theologians. On this see Gisbert Greshake, "Das Verhältnis 'Unsterblichkeit der Seele' und 'Auferstehung des Leibes' in problemgeschichtlicher Sicht," in Greshake and Lohfink, *Naherwartung, Auferstehung, Unsterblichkeit*, 82–120, at 113–20; Lohfink, "Zur Möglichkeit christlicher Naherwartung," ibid., 38–81, at 62–64. Emil Brunner had already written in 1953: "Here on earth there is a before and an after and intervals of time which embrace centuries or even millenniums. But on the other side, in the world of the resurrection, in eternity, there are no such divisions of time, of this time which is perishable. The date of death differs for each . . . for the day of death belongs to this world. Our day of resurrection is the same for all and yet is not separated from the day of death by intervals of centuries—for these time-intervals are here, not there in the presence of God, where 'a thousand years are as a day.'" (Emil Brunner, *Eternal Hope*, trans. Harold Knight [London: Lutterworth; Philadelphia: Westminster, 1954], 152). For an overview of newer ideas of "time" in eschatology up to 1965 see Otto Betz, *Die Eschatologie in der Glaubensunterweisung* (Würzburg: Echter Verlag, 1965).

[9] See the previous note. The first edition appeared in 1974. Gisbert Greshake and I addressed a number of objections to our position in the third edition (1978), and again in the fourth (1981) and fifth (1986) editions.

[10] As far as I can determine, the concept of the "perspective of those left behind" derives from Ulrich Lüke, "Auferstehung am Jüngsten Tag als Auferstehung im Tod," *StZ* 123 (1998): 45–54.

[11] Hans Urs von Balthasar, "Eschatology in Outline," *Explorations in Theology* IV, 458.

[12] Franz Mussner ("Implikate der Parusie des Herrn," in *Weltgericht und Weltvollendung. Zukunftsbilder im Neuen Testament*, ed. Hans-Josef Klauck, QD 150 [Freiburg: Herder, 1994], 225–31) argues as follows: those who restrict Christ's *parousia* to the encounter with him in death deny the "worldly orientedness" of the New Testament *parousia* kerygma, namely, its relationship to the history of the world and humans. Then Jesus' *parousia* would no longer possess any "public character." I hope that this present book has made it clear that Christ's *parousia* in death, because of the elimination of a false idea of time, is seen precisely as a *parousia in the presence of all humanity* (and thus of the world), and not only isolated individuals. I must object to Mussner's position in that it is precisely when the *parousia* is located at the end of a linear course of history that it loses its public character, because then billions of people have long since died and cannot experience the *parousia* as an event within history. They would experience it as those "already" dead—and then Mussner would also have arrived at the position I am presenting here.

[13] In this connection it is worth paying attention to the reticence and caution with which Joseph Ratzinger speaks of Christ's *parousia* in his *Eschatology* (201–4). He develops what he has to say about Christ's *parousia* out of the liturgy, and at the same time he avoids any formulation that might even give the impression that in speaking of the ultimate *parousia* he is describing a dateable event in the world of space and time.

Chapter 11: On the Endurance of the Soul—pages 213–18

[1] For an extensive treatment of this newer phase in Protestant eschatology in the twentieth century see Greshake, "Das Verhältnis," 98–113; idem and Jacob Kremer, *Resurrectio mortuorum*, 247–51. See also Christoph Schwöbel, art. "Auferstehung der Toten. Dogmatisch," *RGG*[4], 1 (Tübingen: 1998), 919–21, at 920: "For twentieth-century Protestant theology the confession of the resurrection of the dead 'is entirely contradictory' . . . to the idea of the soul's immortality. This corresponds to a concept of death as the death of the whole person, and not as a separation of the soul from the body, so that the resurrection must be understood as new creation, and not as the union of the soul with a new embodiment."

[2] See Wilhelm Christe, "'Unsterblichkeit der Seele.' Versuch einer evangelisch-theologischen Rehabilitierung," *NZST* 54 (2012): 262–84, and Uwe Swarat, "Jenseits des Todes: Unsterblichkeit der Seele oder Auferstehung des Leibes?" in *Gemeinsame Hoffnung, über den Tod hinaus. Eschatologie im ökumenischen Gespräch*, ed. idem and Thomas Söding, QD 257 (Freiburg: Herder, 2013), 13–35, as well as the information in Vechtel, *Eschatologie und Freiheit*, 95 n. 48.

[3] So also Greshake and Kremer, *Resurrectio mortuorum*, 269–70: "But if resurrection happens to the individual in its unique identity and is not the new creation of something else, there must be a principle binding the earthly and postmortal being, a principle that in Western tradition is called soul." See also against the whole-death thesis Remenyi, *Auferstehung denken*, 161–62.

[4] For a critique of the "mind" or "memory" of God in this connection see also Johanna Rahner, *Einführung*, 186–87.

[5] Gisbert Greshake has reflected most extensively and clearly on these connections. See esp. his *Auferstehung der Toten. Ein Beitrag zur gegenwärtigen theologischen Diskussion über die Zukunft der Geschichte*, Koinonia 10 (Essen: Ludgerus-Verlag, 1969), 384–93; idem, *Stärker als der Tod*, 63–72; idem, "Tod und Auferstehung," in *Enzyklopädische Bibliothek* 5, ed. Franz Böckle, et al. (Freiburg: Herder, 1980), 63–130, at 116–20; idem, "Das Verhältnis," 280–320; idem (with Jacob Kremer), *Resurrectio mortuorum*, 255–76; idem, "Auferstehung im Tod"; idem, "Auferstehung der Toten. Auferstehung des Fleisches," 1204–05.

[6] This is obviously still inadequately and superficially stated in this form, but nothing more is possible within the framework of this book. Let me refer to the publications by Gisbert Greshake listed in the previous note, and now to the penetrating presentation by Remenyi in his profound work *Auferstehung denken*.

[7] Ratzinger, *Introduction to Christianity*, 355: "'having a spiritual soul' means precisely being willed, known, and loved by God in a special way; it means being a creature called by God to an eternal dialogue and therefore capable for its own part of knowing God and of replying to him."

[8] *Luther's Works*, vol. 5: *Lectures on Genesis: Chapters 26–30*, ed. Jaroslav J. Pelikan, Hilton C. Oswald, and Helmut T. Lehmann (St. Louis: Concordia Publishing House, 1970), 76.

[9] *The Roman Missal*, 3rd ed. (Collegeville, MN: Liturgical Press, 2011), 649.

Chapter 12: On Participation—pages 219–30

[1] This was precisely the subject of my 1974 essay, "Zur Möglichkeit christlicher Naherwartung."

[2] For speaking in complementary eschatological models see Lohfink, "Das Zeitproblem," 151–55. Joseph Ratzinger also speaks, regarding eschatology, of series of concepts or images that must be mutually correcting (*Auferstehung und ewiges Leben. Beiträge zur Eschatologie und zur Theologie der Hoffnung*, Gesammelte Schriften 10 [Freiburg: Herder, 2012]).

[3] We can set aside the question of baptism altogether in the scenario under discussion. Of course, baptism is important, and when rightly understood it is even necessary for salvation—namely, in the sense in which Christ and the church are necessary for salvation. But that does not change the problem we are dealing with here. Even an infant baptized at the right time is not yet made a person by baptism, a person who can make free decisions. The baptized infant also lives by participation, and that is precisely what is under scrutiny here. Something similar can be said of the church's teaching about the creation of each individual human soul. "[It] does not mean an intervention of God in a continuing course of nature, but the disposition to self-transcendence, self-possession, and openness to the world that is part of the complexity of matter and that belongs to every human by nature and makes up its personality." (Gerhard Ludwig Müller, *Katholische Dogmatik. Für Studium und Praxis der Theologie*, 9th ed. [Freiburg: Herder, 2012], 120). The problem we are examining still remains: What about an embryo that, in principle, is a person, but whose personhood has not developed in any way?

[4] See the article by the South African paleoanthropologist J. Francis Thackeray, "Der Mensch ist schwer zu greifen," *FAZ*, 23 Nov. 2016, p. 2. For scientific detail see idem, M. C. Dean, A. D. Beynon, and G. A. Macho, "Histological reconstruction of dental development and age at death of a juvenile *Paranthropus robustus* specimen, SK 63, from Swartkrans, South Africa," *American Journal of Physical Anthropology* 91 (1992): 401–19.

[5] Cp. Ulrich Lüke, *Das Säugetier von Gottes Gnaden. Evolution, Bewusstsein, Freiheit*, 3rd ed. (Freiburg: Herder, 2016), 176–77.

[6] Ibid., 178–79.

⁷ Elizabeth Antkowiak, ed., *Die grosse Scheidung* (translation of C. S. Lewis, *The Great Divorce*, by Helmut Kühn; series Kriterien 47; Einsiedeln: Johannes Verlag, 1978). The quotation is from Antkowiak's "Introduction," p. 15.

⁸ For this see Reiner Sörries, *Ruhe sanft*, 34–35.

⁹ In addition to the texts listed here see also Rom 8:29; Eph 2:5-6; Phil 3:10-11; Col 3:1, 4.

¹⁰ [LMM: See Bonnie B. Thurston in eadem and Judith M. Ryan, *Philippians and Philemon*, Sacra Pagina 10 (Collegeville, MN: Liturgical Press, 2005), 134, 138].

¹¹ 2 Cor 3:18 NAB.

PART FIVE

Chapter 1: Genuine Care for Our Dead—pages 233–39

¹ See, e.g., http://www.dailymail.co.uk/news/article-2270977/Elephants -really-grieve-like-They-shed-tears-try-bury-dead--leading-wildlife-film-maker -reveals-animals-like-us.html.

² This ecclesial aspect of purification in death is examined thoroughly in Georg Bätzing, *Kirche im Werden*.

³ Cp. 2 Macc 12:42, 44.

⁴ Cp. Bätzing, *Kirche im Werden*, 18–20.

⁵ That is why the ECUSA, for example, in another of its Eucharistic Prayers, asks: "In the fullness of time, put all things in subjection under your Christ; and bring us to that heavenly country where, with [. . . and] all your saints, we may enter the everlasting heritage of your sons and daughters; through Jesus Christ our Lord, the firstborn of all creation, the head of the Church, and the author of our salvation." *The Book of Common Prayer Prayer and Administration of the Sacraments and Other Rites and Ceremonies of the Church, together with The Psalter or Psalms of David, According to the use of The Episcopal Church* (New York: Church Publishing, 1979), Eucharistic Prayer B.

⁶ The formula makes room for all who have not known Christ but have sought the truth and done what is good (see part 4, chap. 5 above). The church prays for them as well. (They are "those who have died in your mercy" in the *Roman Missal*, and "those whose faith is known to you alone" in the Episcopal Church's prayer.)

⁷ Ratzinger, *Eschatology*, 187.

⁸ What I will discuss here and in the next sections as "consequences" of sin was often treated in earlier stages of the church's traditions as "punishment for sin." For a correct understanding of the concept of "punishment for sin" see Gisbert Greshake, *Erlöst in einer unerlösten Welt?*, topos taschenbücher 50, 5th ed. (Mainz: Matthias Grünewald, 1980), 72–76.

⁹ Thus Friedrich Schiller, *Wallenstein. Die Piccolomini* V 1: "And there you have the curse of evil deeds, // That they continually create more evil." Friedrich Schiller, *Wallenstein and Mary Stuart*, ed. Walter Hinderer (New York: Continuum, 1991), 122.

Chapter 2: Christian Dying—pages 240–47

[1] For details see Sörries, *Ruhe sanft*, 33–36.

[2] The flier "Bussfertige Beschreibung [Description of the penitent . . .]" is illustrated in Wolfgang Brückner, *Die Sprache christlicher Bilder*, Kulturgeschichtliche Spaziergänge im Germanischen Nationalmuseum 12 (Nuremberg: Verlag des Germanischen Nationalmuseums, 2010), 182. I am grateful for being able to refer to Dr. Brückner's informative book at this point, and also for many pointers he gave me in person. The handbill is part of the vast collections of the German National Museum in Nuremberg.

[3] Wolfgang Brückner, "Katechetische Bilder vom guten Tod in nachmittelalterlicher Zeit aus Süddeutschland. Vom Wissen um Bildtraditionen," in idem, *Gesammelte Schriften* XIV, Supplement 2 (Würzburg: Bayerische Blätter für Volkskunde, 2010), 385–412, at 386.

[4] Brückner, *Die Sprache christlicher Bilder*, 204–5.

[5] Bernhard Grom, "Der 'gute Tod,' früher und heute," *Jesuiten. Informationen der Deutschen Provinz der Jesuiten* 66, no. 1 (2015): 2.

[6] Brochure of the Bundesjustizministeriums zur Patientenverfügung, 36, at http://www.bmjv.de/EN/Home/home_node.html.

[7] Giovanni Maio, *Eine neue Kultur des Sterbens. Patientenverfügung und aktive Sterbehilfe*, Kirche und Gesellschaft 373 (Cologne: J. P. Bachem, 2010). [English: *Essays in Medical Ethics: Plea for a Medicine of Prudence* (Electronic book; New York: Thieme Medical Publishers, 2007), chap. 7, "Living Wills: Are Forms Replacing Dialogue?"]. This translation LMM.

[8] On this see Greshake, "Auferstehung im Tod," 552.

Chapter 3: When Does Eternity Begin?—pages 248–58

[1] St. Teresa of Avila, *Autobiography*, ed. and trans. by E. Allison Peers, Dover Books on Western Philosophy (Mineola, NY: Dover Publications, 2010), 11.

[2] Anicius Manlius Severinus Boethius, *The Consolation of Philosophy*, trans. David R. Slavitt (Cambridge, MA: Harvard University Press, 2008), V, 6, 4, p. 168.

[3] Cp. Joseph Ratzinger, "Ewigkeit. II. Theologisch," *LTK*², vol. 3 (Freiburg: Herder, 1959), 1268–70, at 1269.

[4] See, e.g., the connections in John 17:5, 22, 24, 26.

[5] See, e.g., the closing prayer for the Twenty-Eighth Sunday of the year: ". . . as you feed us with [the sacrament of Christ's Body and Blood] so you may make us sharers of his divine nature." There are similar formulations in other closing prayers.

[6] Johannes Beutler, "Die Stunde Jesu im Johannesevangelium," *BK* 52 (1997): 25–27, gives a brief but precise overview of Johannine eschatology. However, Beutler, contrary to the next note, does not accept the idea of later additions to the text such as are otherwise emphasized in eschatology.

[7] The Johannine transformation of future eschatology was so radical that it immediately gave offense. John 5:28-29 was redacted, even before the editing of

the gospel, to expand the text in such a way that classic eschatology was added—not, in my opinion, to dispute the Evangelist's radical present eschatology but to remind the hearers that the text in no way eliminates the familiar future eschatology. If one looks more closely at vv. 24-30 one can see that the line of thought is interrupted: the authority of the Son to judge by his word of proclamation (v. 27) is extended and more clearly explained in v. 30; vv. 28-29 are a reworking of v. 25 back to a future sense. Verse 25 speaks of the present: note the word "now." But vv. 28-29 speak of the end of the world—whenever.

[8] *Maranatha*, attested as a community shout in 1 Cor 16:22 and *Didache* 10.6, can be read either as *marana tha* (Our Lord, come!) or *maran atha* (Our Lord has come). Because of Rev 22:20 ("Come, Lord Jesus!") *marana tha* is more likely. See the lovely interpretation by Joseph Ratzinger (*Jesus of Nazareth: Holy Week: From the Entrance into Jerusalem to the Resurrection*, part 2, trans. Philip J. Whitmore [San Francisco: Ignatius Press, 2011], Epilogue, 278–94).

[9] Georg Bätzing, *Kirche im Werden*, 93.

[10] Gisbert Greshake, *Auferstehung der Toten*, 394–95.

[11] The phrase *sub specie aeternitatis* is from Baruch Spinoza in his major philosophical work, *Ethica more geometrico demonstrata*, part 5, Propositions 29-36. See *Spinoza, Ethics*, trans. W. H. White, rev. A. H. Stirling, Wordsworth Classics of World Literature (Hertfordshire: Wordsworth, 2001), 246–51. The phrase is there translated "under the form of eternity."